*Religion and the Scientific Outlook*

# Religion and
# the Scientific Outlook

## T. R. MILES
M.A. (Oxon.)

*Department of Philosophy*
*University College of North Wales*
*Bangor*

*Ruskin House*
GEORGE ALLEN & UNWIN LTD
MUSEUM STREET LONDON

PRINTED IN GREAT BRITAIN
*in 10 on 12 pt. Plantin type*
BY JARROLD AND SONS LTD, NORWICH

# PREFACE

I have attempted, where possible, to make the arguments in this book intelligible to readers with no specialist philosophical training. References to books and articles of a more technical kind have been given in footnotes. I should like to take this opportunity of acknowledging my debt to all those whose work I have cited, and to any others whose ideas I may have unconsciously 'borrowed'.

I am particularly grateful to Professor A. G. N. Flew, Professor H. D. Lewis, and Professor C. W. K. Mundle, all of whom have read the book in typescript and have given me the benefit of their criticisms. They are not, of course, in any way committed to accepting the views which the book contains.

I should like to thank Miss E. Lewis and Miss S. Jones for typing both the original manuscript and a later revised draft.

Finally I should like to thank my wife for a large number of very valuable suggestions.

*Bangor* 1957

# CONTENTS

# PART ONE

# CHAPTER 1

---

# *Introduction*

This book is concerned with a single set of problems, those raised by the claims of religion in an age which has been largely dominated by the growth of science. An attempt is made to throw light on these problems by using the techniques of present-day philosophy.

Philosophy in the last forty years has undergone some striking changes; and since the position is still far from static, it is hard to give a really satisfactory account of what has been achieved.[1] In general, the legacy of recent thought seems to be a set of techniques, a methodology, a way of studying questions, rather than a cast-iron system of eternally irrefutable answers. The task of the professional philosopher, it seems, is not so much to express his personal views on religious or scientific questions as to focus attention on the questions themselves. One of his most important concerns, on this view, is to make people appreciate more fully what sort of question they are asking and what sort of method is appropriate for answering it. Without this preliminary clearing of the ground, it might be said, discussions are liable to give rise to misunderstanding and muddle, and the seeker after truth, like the young Omar, will inevitably 'come out by the same door as in he went'.

The approach of this book will be philosophical in this limited sense of the word. No attempt will be made to commend any one set of religious beliefs, nor to present any form of 'apology' for a particular brand of Christian orthodoxy. Personal convictions cannot, of course, be suppressed altogether, if only because the very choice of subjects to discuss is clearly dictated by what one considers important; but I have tried on the whole to avoid the sort of language that would be more appropriate in a sermon or a religious tract. The outcome of the

[1] For further discussion, see A. J. Ayer and others, *Revolution in Philosophy* (Macmillan, 1956).

13

argument will be to indicate in a general way the sorts of religious belief that can be regarded as compatible with modern scientific knowledge. My purpose is thus to rule out any religious language that is untenable rather than to make suggestions on what detailed religious beliefs ought to be adopted.

In accordance with this policy, there will be no exciting 'arguments for the existence of God', or would-be solutions to all the problems of the universe. The implicit claim of some popular writers on religious topics to 'know all the answers' seems to me an appalling one. As we shall see later in the book, the adoption of a religious belief is a matter for personal conviction rather than rational proof. Religious insights can still be very profound even when they cannot be supported by argument, and conversely the most skilful arguments often leave us unsatisfied.

The title of this book refers to 'the scientific outlook'. Such a phrase, of course, is far from precise; but the discussion in Parts I and II will bring out, I hope, the sorts of belief that go to make up such an outlook. In the case of the word 'religion', no attempt will be made to specify with any precision how it should be understood. There are certain sorts of language which everyone would unhesitatingly label 'religious', but it does not follow that what they have in common can be specified in a single formula. 'In the beginning God created the heaven and the earth',[1] 'What doth the Lord require of thee, but to do justly, and to love mercy, and to walk humbly with thy God?'[2] and 'Greater is he that is in you than he that is in the world'[3] are all examples of religious language, but it is unnecessary for present purposes to look for something which they all have in common.

To clear up verbal confusion it should be added that the very label 'religion' tends to give rise to misunderstanding and heated argument. The same applies to other labels that will be used in the course of this book, such as 'logical positivism' and 'behaviourism'. People regard themselves as free within limits to legislate as to how these labels should be understood; but if they dislike a label, they tend to offer a definition which makes the label an easy target for refutation. This tendency is particularly apparent in the case of the word 'religion'. It is always possible to concentrate on the many foolish things that have been said in the name of 'religion' and then to decide that one is 'against it'. If we do so, however, we may find that the things which we are attacking are things which no self-styled 'religious' person would wish to defend.

[1] Genesis i. 1.     [2] Micah vi. 8.     [3] 1 John iv. 4.

The argument is thus at cross-purposes simply because the two parties have failed to agree on how the word 'religion' should be understood. To avoid misunderstanding of this sort I shall attempt on all occasions to specify what particular religious claims are being discussed.

Although present-day philosophy does not attempt to be a substitute for religion, or to offer solutions for all problems of the universe, it is still an exacting inquiry, involving a discussion of a variety of complex technical questions. This book is not intended for those professional philosophers who are interested in technical problems for their own sake. They will find little that is new in either method or conclusions. I am concerned rather to use philosophical techniques for contributing to the problems of the layman. The layman, as here conceived, is impatient with much philosophical argument. Lengthy discussions on whether we *really know*, for instance, that Queen Anne is dead leave him cold. 'Let us pass on,' he might say, 'from these trivial speculations to problems that are really worth while.' The questions which I assume him to have in mind are ones such as these—'Has science disproved the existence of God?' 'Is there a conflict between science and religion?' and 'Is it reasonable for a person living in the twentieth century to accept some form of Christian orthodoxy?' People have put forward, in the name of 'science', allegedly world-shattering systems such as materialism, behaviourism, and determinism—'Nothing exists except matter', 'There is no such thing as mind', 'All our apparent choices are really determined'—while others, in the name of 'religion', have urged that such systems are not the whole truth. The layman, if he is fair-minded, will be puzzled by such conflicting views and will have little idea of how to resolve them.

Can present-day philosophical techniques be of help in this controversy? This book is an attempt to vindicate the claim that they can. I am not suggesting that they can lead people to profound religious truths or provide a full and adequate 'way of life'. Present-day techniques are not attempting to do anything of the kind. All that I am claiming is that these techniques can be used to throw light on the layman's questions about science and religion. They enable us to see more clearly what the issues are, what methods are appropriate for answering particular questions, and what degrees of certainty are possible in different cases. For example, the assertion 'Nothing exists except matter' cries out for philosophical treatment. It is not nearly as straightforward as it might appear; and, before we can determine its truth or falsity, we must try to understand what, if anything, it means. Behaviourism and determinism require similar critical study. More important still, there is the puzzling and challenging set of beliefs known as logical positivism.

Those who use present-day techniques have all, to a greater or lesser extent, been affected by the logical positivist whirlwind which, originating in Vienna in the 1920's and later spreading to England and America, shook the philosophical world to its foundations. Logical positivism in its early stages owed much to Bertrand Russell and the late Ludwig Wittgenstein, although neither of these thinkers gave it unqualified support. The importance of logical positivism for our present inquiry is twofold. In the first place, present-day techniques are themselves a development of logical positivism, purified of its grotesqueness and shorn of excrescences; or at least we may regard the positivistic caterpillar as the chrysalis from which the beauties of the present-day philosophical butterfly sprang. In the second place, logical positivism, like materialism, behaviourism, and determinism, took its inspiration from the advancement of science, and its original tenets were in conflict with the claims of religion. Logical positivism was never a static system, and it is not easy to pin-point a set of beliefs and say 'That is what logical positivism is'. But in general—to anticipate the further discussion in the next chapter—it involves the belief that the only meaningful assertions, apart from those of mathematics and logic, are those which can be verified or falsified by observational means. Thus 'There is a piano in the sitting-room' would be meaningful on this criterion, but not any assertion about God, or 'the Absolute'. The latter type of assertion is usually said to be 'metaphysical'; and it was one of the chief tenets of logical positivism that such metaphysical language was meaningless. This is clearly a championing of the cause of science against that of religion; and the claim that some would-be expressions of religious belief are meaningless is a very subtle form of attack.

Extremist versions of logical positivism are now agreed to be untenable. I shall insist, however, that the basic logical positivist viewpoint still requires to be taken seriously. To understand the general arguments is indispensable for anyone interested in the philosophy of religion, and to turn a blind eye to them is intellectually dishonest. The arguments, if correctly formulated, cannot deprive us of anything in religion that is worth keeping; but they force us, whether we like it or not, to reconsider the appropriateness of some of the things which we say about God.

## Introduction

Indeed one of the main purposes of this book is to suggest that some of our more unreflective ways of talking about God require to be abandoned.

In Part I, I shall discuss such of the logical positivist views as appear to be relevant to religious belief. I shall then indicate how logical positivist thinking develops, as a result of modification, into the techniques of present-day philosophy, and I shall indicate how far, in my opinion, the attack on metaphysics has failed and how far it has succeeded. In Part II, I shall examine in the light of these techniques the allegedly 'scientific' standpoints of materialism, behaviourism, and determinism. I shall also consider the relevance to religion of the findings of psychical research, and shall examine whether the development of psycho-analysis can be regarded as a threat to religious belief. In Part III, I shall discuss various sorts of religious language, with a view to assessing how far such language can still legitimately command our attention and respect.

# CHAPTER 2

## *Logical positivism*
## *The verification principle*

In this chapter I propose to present the logical positivist claims in their
most extreme form. I am not suggesting that any philosopher ever made
such claims unreservedly; but some account of these extreme versions
is essential for the main argument of this book. Reservations and
qualifications will be added later.

At the outset a word of warning is necessary. The words 'logical
positivism' have become something of a battle-cry, and discussion of
the merits and demerits of logical positivism tends to become rather
heated. People tend to be 'for' it or 'against' it with more passion than
understanding. The reason for this is quite simple. Logical positivism
is commonly thought of as the ally of science and the bitter enemy of
religion. It appears at first sight to be the creed of the tough-minded
scientist who is impatient of any inquiry not proceeding by scientific
method, and those who take religion seriously are immediately disposed
to regard it as outrageous. Philosophical progress is very difficult in this
atmosphere. The man who argues to himself: 'I like de-bunking religious
prigs, and here is a good weapon for doing so' is liable to produce rather
shallow arguments; and conversely the man who says 'Logical positivism
is wicked—I don't know what it is, but whatever it is I am going to
attack it' usually finds that at best he is able only to demolish views
which are not worth holding. The early logical positivist beliefs were
wrong, certainly; but they were wrong in an interesting way. To
appreciate the strength and weakness of these beliefs, we ourselves
need to become logical positivists, and to examine the whole movement
sympathetically from within, rather than attack it viciously from without
along with those who cannot or will not understand it.

18

## Logical positivism. *The verification principle*

The main tenet of logical positivism was usually expressed by saying that *metaphysics is impossible*, or that *metaphysical statements are meaningless*. The chief weapon of attack was the so-called 'verification principle'.

The following formulation of the verification principle was given by A. J. Ayer.[1] 'We say that a sentence is factually significant to a given person', he writes, 'if, and only if, he knows how to verify the proposition which it purports to express—that is, if he knows what observations would lead him, under certain conditions, to accept the proposition as being true or reject it as being false'. Ayer illustrates his point by referring to a passage from F. H. Bradley in his *Appearance and Reality*. Bradley writes of 'the Absolute' that 'it enters into, but is itself incapable of, evolution and progress'.[2] To apply the verification principle here is to ask, 'How do I verify this assertion?', or perhaps better, 'What observations should I have to make to tell if it is true or false?' We have only to ask this question, it would be said, to realize that Bradley cannot here be giving us straightforward factual information. As Ayer puts the matter, 'One cannot conceive of an observation which would enable one to determine whether the Absolute did, or did not, enter into evolution and progress'.[3] The suggestion is that Bradley's assertion is in some way a humbug. It purports to refer to some state of affairs, yet does not carry any indication of what state of affairs is being described. If we profess to accept it, according to this argument, we are misleading ourselves and being hoodwinked by words—words which at first sight appeared to mean something, but which we can recognize after reflection to be meaningless.

Now it is very difficult, it seems to me, to formulate the verification principle in such a way that it is free from difficulties and complications. Some may feel, for instance, in the case of Ayer's formulation, that the words 'factual', 'verify', and 'observation' present altogether too many problems to make easy acceptance possible. I myself share this hesitation, and I certainly do not regard this wholesale rejection of Bradley's metaphysical system as justified. To discuss difficulties in detail at this stage, however, would divert us from our main purpose, which is one of exposition. What I am concerned to do here and now is to make

---

[1] See his *Language, Truth, and Logic*, p. 35. This book was first published in 1936. Page numbers refer to the 2nd edition (Gollancz, 1949).
[2] *Appearance and Reality* (Macmillan, 1908), p. 499.
[3] *Language, Truth, and Logic* (1949), p. 36.

explicit just what it was that Ayer and those who thought like him were trying to achieve.[1]

Another way of expressing the logical positivist contention would be by the analogy of the 'dud cheque'. It might be said that metaphysicians of the past have done something comparable to writing a cheque without adequate funds in the bank. They have used words without proper 'cash' to back them; they have been unable to give their words 'cash-value' in terms of states of affairs.[2] 'The Absolute is incapable of evolution and progress' is a grammatically correct sentence; but the words are like a dud cheque, and cannot be 'cashed'.

A third way of throwing light on what the logical positivists were trying to do is to bring in the notion of *operational definitions*. There are many terms in science that are said to be 'operationally definable'; that is, their meaning can be explained in terms of the operations involved in determining whether the statements containing them are true or false.[3] For example, the psychological term 'intelligence quotient' is defined in terms of a person's performance on a particular intelligence test. 'X has an intelligence quotient of 120' can be shown to be true or false by going through a series of operations—in this case the operations of giving him a particular test. Some might wish to say that the right question is not '*What is* an intelligence quotient?' but 'How do you measure one?' Similarly it might be said that we should ask, not '*What is* electricity?', but 'How do you detect the presence of an electric current?', and that electricity just *is* what is detected. This links up with the demand that words should be given 'cash-value' in terms of states of affairs. The 'cash-value' of 'X has an intelligence quotient of 120' lies in the results of the test. Similarly the 'cash-value' of 'This is two feet long' lies in the results that we obtain when we measure. Now the logical positivist claim is that all assertions, if they are to be regarded as factually significant, must be operationally definable (or capable of being 'cashed') in the required way. Thus the 'cash-value' of 'There is a cat in the cupboard' lies in the operations which we go through to determine whether or not there *is* a cat in the cupboard.

[1] It may be of interest to observe, in passing, that Ayer has modified his views very considerably since *Language, Truth, and Logic* was first written. In fairness it should be added that he has shown himself quite as aware as his critics of the difficulties in formulating an adequate version of the verification principle.

[2] For further explanation of the words 'cash-value', see William James, *The Varieties of Religious Experience* (Longmans, Green and Co., 1941), p. 443.

[3] For a more technical discussion of this point, see P. W. Bridgman, *The Logic of Modern Physics* (Macmillan, 1927).

## Logical positivism. The verification principle

In the case of technical terms, like 'intelligence quotient', the operations are specified with a fair degree of precision; in the case of words of common speech, like 'cat' and 'cupboard', the matter is somewhat different. In the particular case of 'There is a cat in the cupboard' no detailed list of operations is given.[1] We are dependent on what we take to be the rules implicit in ordinary speech. These rules are imprecise; indeed there are all sorts of different operations which we could perform to test the truth or falsity of 'There is a cat in the cupboard'. Although, therefore, there is this difference between words of ordinary speech and specifically defined technical terms, for purposes of the present argument this difference is unimportant. In both cases we are left in no doubt as to the *sort of* operation that we are being invited to perform. On the other hand, if I were to say to you 'There is a disopholus in the cupboard', you may suspect from the context that I mean some strange animal—like the Jabberwock, perhaps; but unless criteria are given for recognizing a disopholus you will be at a loss. In this case no such criteria exist, for 'disopholus' is a word which I have invented. 'The Absolute is incapable of evolution and progress' is similar to 'There is a disopholus in the cupboard' in that in neither case are we told what operations to perform. The verification principle, when applied in these cases, can be thought of as a kind of protest. It is as though someone said 'You are using words as if you knew how to give them "cash-value" when it appears suspiciously as though you do not'. If someone asks, 'How would you verify whether the Absolute is incapable of evolution and progress?', he is making a request, not for advice on procedure, but for information on the meaning of words. Sometimes 'How would you verify?' is asked rhetorically, with the suggestion that the words in question mean nothing at all.

If 'The Absolute is incapable of evolution and progress' referred to a state of affairs, that state of affairs—so long as we are not told how to recognize it—would be for ever unknown and unknowable. If we choose, we may think of the verification principle as an attack on 'permanently unknowables'. The point can best be illustrated by referring to the views of Berkeley.[2] His target was the notion of 'material substance'. This was a technical term used by the physicists of his day,

---

[1] For a further discussion of this point, see F. Waismann, 'Verifiability' (*Aristotelian Society*, Supplementary Volume XIX for 1945), reprinted in *Logic and Language* (ed. A. G. N. Flew, Blackwell, 1950).
[2] See especially his *Principles of Human Knowledge* and *Three dialogues between Hylas and Philonous*.

and was supposed to refer to something lying behind or beyond the things which we normally observe such as chairs and tables. Such a 'something' would be for ever unknown and unknowable. The world would appear exactly the same in all respects whether it was present or not; and no purpose is served by bringing it into our discourse. 'Let me entreat you to consider', says Berkeley, 'whether it be like a philosopher, or even like a man of common sense, to pretend to believe you know not what and you know not why'.[1]

Three further points may be mentioned in the exposition of the verification principle, all of which, however, give rise to philosophical complications. In the first place, in order to eliminate 'permanently unknowables', some philosophers have said that we can know nothing except our own sense-impressions or sense-data. When, for instance, we set about finding out if there is a cat in the cupboard, we can, on this view, be aware of nothing except our own sensations—visual sensations, that is, of colour and shape, perhaps tactual ones of furriness, auditory ones of miaowing, and so on. It has therefore been said that 'There is a cat in the cupboard' means 'If an observer were to look, listen, feel, etc., he would have certain sense-data'. It has even been suggested that sense-data—or 'phenomena' as they are sometimes called—are the ultimate constituents of the universe, or at any rate that sentences about ordinary objects, if they are to be meaningful, must be capable of 'translation', or must be given 'cash-value', in terms of sense-data. This is the philosophical viewpoint known as *phenomenalism*. Although phenomenalism has received considerable discussion in philosophical journals, much of what has been said is of a technical kind and need not for present purposes be considered in detail. It is certainly not essential for the argument in this book that phenomenalism should be accepted.

Secondly, Berkeley sometimes raises his problem by asking 'Can you form an "*idea*" of what the words mean?' He says that he himself can form no idea of what 'material substance' would be like. 'Idea' here seems to mean 'mental image', and we can quite well see what Berkeley means. But, once again, it is an unnecessary complication to ask people to examine their mental imagery. Individuals vary considerably in this respect, and many can understand what words mean without forming any image at all.

Thirdly, the verification principle has at times been formulated by saying that 'The meaning of a proposition is its method of verification'.[2]

---

[1] *Second dialogue between Hylas and Philonous.*
[2] F. Waismann, 'Verifiability', *op. cit.*

This is enigmatic and difficult, and involves a questionable use of the word 'meaning'. For present purposes this formulation can be ignored.

Logical positivists allowed that mathematical assertions such as '$37 \times 5 = 185$' were meaningful, and also assertions such as 'Bachelors cannot be married'. In both these cases, it was claimed, the very meaning of the words or symbols used is sufficient to guarantee the truth of what is said. (We do, of course, make mistakes in arithmetic, and people may use words such as 'bachelor' incorrectly; but this does not affect the force of the argument.) Such assertions, it is claimed, are 'true by definition' and do not purport to tell us what the world is like. The general viewpoint is similar to that found in the philosophical writings of Hume. Hume agreed that there could be demonstrative certainty in the case of mathematics—the science of 'quantity and number'. 'All other enquiries of men', he continues, 'regard only matter of fact and existence; and these are evidently incapable of demonstration. . . . When we run over libraries, persuaded of these principles, what havoc must we make? If we take in our hand any volume; of divinity or school metaphysics, for instance, let us ask: Does it contain any abstract reasoning concerning quantity or number? No. Does it contain any experimental reasoning concerning matter of fact and existence? No. Commit it then to the flames: for it can contain nothing but sophistry and illusion.'[1]

It is important to note that, strictly speaking, neither Berkeley nor Hume nor their modern counterparts should be interpreted as *denying the existence* of anything. They are saying that certain combinations of words are pointless. 'Where there is not so much as the most inadequate or faint idea pretended to', says Berkeley, 'I will not indeed thence conclude against the reality of any notion or existence of any thing: but my inference shall be that you mean nothing at all: that you employ words to no manner of purpose, without any design or signification whatsoever.'[2]

The foregoing discussion will, I hope, throw some light on what those who have applied the verification principle were trying to achieve. I have tried to present the case as forcefully as possible, without reservations or modifications.

Difficulties arise, however, if the verification principle is used indiscriminately, and this is just what some of the logical positivists did.

[1] Hume, *An Enquiry concerning Human Understanding*, section XII, Part III.
[2] Berkeley, *Second dialogue between Hylas and Philonous*.

If we apply the principle to every sentence that we meet, we reach some rather shocking conclusions. In the first place, many traditional philosophical problems appear to be meaningless, such as 'Do universals have a separate existence?' and 'Is reality something "mental" or do things exist independently of the mind?' Clearly no observations will settle whether or not universals have a separate existence, and no criteria can be given for recognizing whether or not things exist independently of the mind. It seems to follow that philosophers in the past have devoted much of their time to the production of nonsense.

Worse is to come. Moral assertions such as 'It is wrong to kill' or 'Men ought to love their enemies' are not verifiable or falsifiable in the requisite way. The same seems to hold of many sentences containing the word 'God', such as 'God is love'[1] or 'The Godhead of the Father, of the Son, and of the Holy Ghost is all one'.[2] It would seem, therefore, that the utterances of moralists, preachers, and theologians must all be meaningless.

Such a view constitutes what I should call a thoroughgoing or 'pure' form of logical positivism. It is a view which is philosophically exciting, but scarcely tenable, and I do not know of any philosopher who has seriously held it. From the very beginning reservations and qualifications were being added. Some of these have been of such a fundamental kind that very little of the original viewpoint remains.

In the next three chapters I shall consider some of the ways in which the original logical positivist beliefs require to be modified. I shall not attempt any historical or chronological account of how particular philosophers made modifications, but I shall try to show why these modifications were thought necessary.

One final warning should be given in connection with *labels*. We have noted already that the words 'logical positivism' are a sort of battle-cry label, suggestive of a special very militant 'party-line'. But in this case so many modifications and qualifications have been added that it is perhaps questionable whether the party-label should be retained. This is no more than a verbal point, however, and it is a mistake for us to become too excited over the matter of party labels. If pressed to give a ruling on the matter, I should recommend that the words 'logical positivism' should be reserved for the early formulations of the verification principle before any reservations or qualifications were added.

[1] I John iv. 8.     [2] Athanasian creed.

## Logical positivism. The verification principle

It follows that any present-day philosopher who accepts the reservations and qualifications (and I know of no one who does not) cannot correctly be labelled a logical positivist. But it is really unimportant whether this book is regarded as an attack on logical positivism or as a defence of an extremely modified version of it.

# CHAPTER 3

# Modifications and developments

I shall begin by referrring to four minor modifications of the original logical positivist position. They are of a technical nature, and are not, in my opinion, of any outstanding relevance to the main theme of this book, but they have given rise to controversy, and therefore deserve some brief mention.

In the first place, it was agreed to be necessary to distinguish verifiability in principle from verifiability in practice. We cannot in practice verify, for instance, whether there are mountains on the farther side of the moon. No one has been there, and from where we are now we cannot see. But the sentence 'There are mountains on the farther side of the moon' is nevertheless verifiable or falsifiable 'in principle'.[1] We know what state of affairs it purports to describe and what operations we should have to go through to investigate that state of affairs. A sentence is not meaningless merely because there are practical difficulties preventing investigation of its truth and falsity.

Secondly, there is a problem about certain sentences which are alleged to be indubitable—'This looks red', for example, or 'I have tooth-ache'. To apply the verification principle in such cases leads to difficulty. 'How would you verify whether it looks red?' seems rather a curious question, and 'How do you know you've got tooth-ache?' seems more curious still. We feel disposed to reply. 'It just *does* look red' and 'I just *have* got tooth-ache', and our answers suggest that verification and falsification simply do not enter into the matter. There is in addition a special difficulty, as we shall see more fully in Chapter 9, about knowing if other people have tooth-ache. It would seem from these examples that the indiscriminate application of the verification principle

---

[1] See *Language, Truth, and Logic* (1949), p. 36. The original example is taken from Professor M. Schlick.

is unsound policy; but it does not, of course, follow that the principle is of no use at all. It would still be said that 'This looks red' and 'I have tooth-ache' do at any rate refer to something that could come within the experience of an observer, whereas 'The Absolute is incapable of evolution and progress' does not.

Thirdly, there is a problem in connection with sentences about such entities as atoms and electrons. The tough-minded logical positivist appears to be in a dilemma here. His great concern is with advances in scientific knowledge and with the methods of science. And yet his fellow scientists have introduced into their discourse words such as 'atom', 'electron', and 'proton', all of which, on strict logical positivist principles, should be suspected. The grounds for suspicion are as follows. These words, as normally used, cannot be regarded as the names of familiar observable objects, in the way in which, say, 'marble' and 'tennis ball' are the names of familiar observable objects. It makes sense to say 'This box contains three marbles and six tennis balls', but it would be very odd to say 'This box contains so many marbles and so many electrons'. If the physicist explains his use of 'electron' by saying 'We do not know what electrons are like in themselves but we know about them from their effects', it would seem that 'electron' stands for something permanently unknown and unknowable. On strict logical positivist principles, therefore, assertions about electrons (and other such entities) would have to be jettisoned as so much metaphysical lumber—an intolerable conclusion for any system of thought which, like logical positivism, claims to set store by the methods of science. This problem, however, is not insoluble. It is agreed that sentences containing the word 'electron' etc. can be given 'cash-value' in terms of observable occurrences, particularly occurrences in the laboratory; and their undisputed value over a wide area of scientific inquiry should lead even the most hardened verificationist to admit their legitimacy. At most, therefore, the problem is one of formulation. The verification principle could perhaps be re-formulated by saying that a sentence is meaningful either if it refers to what is in principle observable or if it is capable of translation into other sentences which themselves refer to what is in principle observable. On this criterion sentences containing words such as 'electron' can readily be agreed to be meaningful.

Fourthly, it was found necessary to distinguish between 'strong' and 'weak' versions of the verification principle.[1] According to the 'strong'

---

[1] See *Language, Truth, and Logic* (1949), p. 37.

version, a sentence was meaningful only if it was possible to specify the observations which would *conclusively* verify the sentence in question. But it was then recognized that many sentences which are clearly meaningful cannot be conclusively verified in this way. Thus the sentence 'All metal expands when heated' is intended to cover an indefinite number of cases; and we can never be sure, however much metal we observe, that it will not at some time be falsified; in other words conclusive verification is out of the question. According to the 'strong' version of the verification principle, therefore, 'All metal expands when heated' is meaningless—a preposterous suggestion. To avoid this difficulty a 'weak' version of the verification principle was recommended, as a result of which a sentence was not required to be conclusively verifiable, but was agreed to be meaningful if certain specifiable observations were *relevant* to its truth or falsity.

For our purposes these difficulties and subsequent modifications are of relatively minor importance. There are, however, two modifications which are crucial. As a result of them, much of the militant truculency of logical positivism disappears. The first is the large-scale abandonment of the word 'meaningless', the second the realization that philosophers of the past were performing a perfectly reputable task and were not solely wasting their time producing nonsense.

(1) The word 'meaningless' needs to be examined with extreme care. One of the first points that should be brought out is that, as commonly used, it is a term of abuse. To say that utterances about God or exhortations as to how we ought to live are meaningless is in effect to condemn such talk, to imply that it is not worth saying. It follows that nothing that is worth saying should be labelled 'meaningless'.

Now it is clearly grotesque to say that 'Men ought to love their enemies' is meaningless, or that moral exhortations in general are illegitimate pieces of linguistic muddle. What is needed, according to the modified view, is to distinguish such talk from *empirical* assertions, i.e. from those assertions whose truth or falsity is settled by observation. Empirical assertions, on this view, refer to facts and are 'factually significant';[1] but an assertion such as 'Men ought to love their enemies' does not purport to refer to any facts, and it is futile to condemn it for not being what it does not profess to be. This general conclusion—that

---

[1] For use of the phrase 'factually significant', see *Language, Truth, and Logic* (1949), p. 35. The passage is quoted on p. 19 of this book.

statements of value require to be distinguished from statements of fact—was no novelty; it had been widely held by philosophers long before the influence of logical positivism made itself felt.[1] But the verification principle lent additional emphasis to an already familiar distinction.

Not only, then, was moral discourse agreed to be legitimate after all; but there was a general relaxing of the original logical positivist stringency. Since the word 'meaningless' is a term of abuse, anyone who uses it is in effect taking sides on the question of what should or should not be said. As time went on philosophers became extremely hesitant to do this. Sentences can be worth saying for many different reasons; and it is certainly not obvious, as the 'pure' version of logical positivism seemed to imply, that the only worth-while assertions are those of the mathematician, the logician, the scientist, and the common-sense observer. Moreover it was recognized that the word 'meaningless', like other words, had 'blurred edges'; and if our criterion is the ordinary usage of this word, there may be cases where we are not sure whether to use it or not. Is Lewis Carroll's 'Jabberwocky' meaningless, for instance? Is it meaningless to say 'The music of Bartok is purple'? The rules thought to be clearly implicit in the word 'meaningless' are not as clear as was supposed.

Now since sentences can be worth saying for many different reasons, there re-emerged the idea of different sorts of truth—factual truths, moral truths, poetic truths, and so on. It was realized that one is not superior to the others, but that in many ways they are different. Thus 'There is a cat in the cupboard' is not superior to 'Thou shalt not kill', but its truth or falsity is established in different ways.

Despite the readmission of moral assertions, it does not follow that sentences containing the word 'God' can simply return into currency as though they had never been criticized. Some of us may feel disposed to say, 'If there can be moral and poetic truths, why should there not be theological truths?'; but this is no solution unless some positive account of theological language is given. Moreover there is the special difficulty that at least some sentences containing the word 'God' seem at first glance to be purporting to be factually significant, in which case the problems of verification and falsification still need to be faced. The whole question, however, of theological language is too complicated to be discussed here, and will be reserved for Part III.

[1] See, for instance, G. E. Moore, *Principia Ethica* (Cambridge, 1903).

(2) The second major modification—by which the work of philosophers of the past was not simply swept aside as futile—went hand in hand with a new emphasis on the need for a careful study of *language*. It was then suggested that the function of the philosopher was to do 'linguistic analysis'. The phrase 'linguistic analysis' is not a very satisfactory one, but a few examples will show the sort of thing that is meant. Metaphysicians of the past were concerned, among other things, with questions such as 'What is truth?' and 'What is the nature of the Self?' The fashion after the logical positivist era was to treat these problems *linguistically*. Thus philosophers would now tend to ask, not 'What is truth?'—for that sounds like a queer and recondite question of fact—but 'What are the different functions of the word "true", and what are the correct rules for the use of this word?' Again, the suggestion might be made that the correct question is not 'What is the nature of the Self?'—which once more appears to be a peculiar question of fact— but 'What are the different functions of the word "I"?'?[1] To put questions in this linguistic idiom, so it was claimed, serves to dissolve queer metaphysical puzzles of the traditional sort such as 'Is the Self a substance?' The traditional problems are thus, after all, not meaningless; but equally they are not recondite questions of fact.

To say that 'Philosophy consists only of linguistic analysis', however, is liable to generate misunderstanding rather than illumination. The words 'linguistic analysis' suggest that the philosopher's task is like that of a philologist or grammarian, or that his best plan would be to take all the words in the dictionary beginning with A, analyse them so as to prevent muddled thinking, pass on to the words beginning with B, and so on. This fails to indicate that there are certain words, such as 'real', 'space', 'time', 'true', 'not', 'is', 'cause', and 'know', which are of particular philosophical interest, and that the study of these words does give us new insight—insight, it can plausibly be said, into the nature of reality. Also the words 'linguistic analysis' suggest a quite new line of inquiry and a complete break with the philosophy of the past. The break is much less than was supposed in the heyday of logical positivism. We cannot say that there is nothing at all which is new in present-day treatment of philosophical problems; but, if we insist on using the phrase 'linguistic analysis', we must in all fairness recognize that the great philosophers of the past were doing 'linguistic analysis' too. Plato,

[1] Compare H. H. Price, 'Clarity is Not Enough' (*Aristotelian Society*, Supplementary Volume XIX for 1945) p. 21. For much of the present argument I am indebted to Professor Price.

for example, in his dialogue *The Sophist*, gives a detailed examination of sentences of the form 'A is not B', with the purpose, so it might be said in the modern idiom, of dissolving metaphysical puzzles about the existence of 'not-Being'; in the same way Aristotle, in his doctrine of the *categories*, can be interpreted as exhibiting the different senses of the Greek word for 'is'.

The traditional name for such inquiries is 'metaphysics'. Whether the name should continue to be used is a not very important matter of verbal decision. One possible usage is to say that 'What is the nature of not-Being?' should be labelled a metaphysical question only if it is regarded as a recondite question of fact, and to insist that the new questions which philosophers nowadays ask should be labelled not 'metaphysical' but 'linguistic'. On this usage, 'What is the nature of not-Being?' is a metaphysical question and stands condemned, whereas, 'What are the possible meanings of "is not" in "A is not B"?' is a linguistic question and admits of being answered by agreed methods. An alternative usage is to say that 'What are the possible meanings of "is not" in "A is not B"?' and 'What is the nature of not-Being?' are in effect the same question and should both be labelled 'metaphysical'. On this usage we can no longer say that metaphysical questions are meaningless, but rather that recent philosophy puts metaphysical questions in something of a new light. Yet a third usage would be to distinguish 'traditional' metaphysics from modern 'linguistic' metaphysics. On this usage problems do not cease to be metaphysical through being expressed in the linguistic idiom, but they are no longer metaphysical in the traditional sense.

In traditional metaphysics no special importance is attached to inverted commas. In modern metaphysics they are all-important. For example, the traditional question 'What is the nature of not-Being?' requires no inverted commas; but if we ask instead 'What are the functions of the word "not"?' the word 'not' goes in inverted commas. The statements of the philosopher are thus said by some to be 'second-order' statements. He does not, as it were, start conversations off, but discusses what is said by others. These others may be scientists, mathematicians, poets, preachers, or even ordinary people who talk about cats and cupboards. It is they who provide the first-order assertions, which the philosopher then proceeds to discuss. To put the matter another way, the philosopher *mentions* words which other people *use*. Here is an illustration. If an ordinary person says 'There is a cat in the cupboard' he is using the word 'cat' (and other words); when the philosopher says 'The word "cat" is logically different from the word "if"', he is *mentioning* the words 'cat' and 'if', and his statement is a second-order one. In the current technical sense of the word 'philosophy', first-order statements are not part of philosophy at all.

Despite these two major modifications—the large-scale abandonment of the word 'meaningless' and the realization that traditional metaphysicians were not simply writing nonsense—the verification principle can still be regarded as a useful philosophical tool. Its value, I would suggest, is threefold. (1) In the first place, it forces us to make a distinction between those assertions which are factually significant and those which are not. (2) Secondly, it serves to expose assertions which appear at first glance to be factually significant but which can be seen on examination to be meaningless. (3) Thirdly—and this is a point which will be discussed at length in the next chapter—it helps us to recognize a widespread mistake which has arisen over the usage of the words 'exist', 'true', and 'facts'. These points will now be explained in further detail.

(1) We have already noted how moral assertions, such as 'Men ought to love their enemies', require to be readmitted as meaningful. Such language is not vulnerable under the verification principle since it does not purport to be giving factual information; the problem of empirical verifiability and falsifiability does not therefore arise. In the same way, when Shelley tells us that

*Life like a dome of many coloured glass*
*Stains the white radiance of eternity,*[1]

we need not be in any way perturbed because the truth or falsity of what he says cannot be determined by observational methods. Shelley is making no attempt to give us factual information here. This is precisely the point which the verification principle forces us to recognize—namely the difference between those assertions which are factually significant and those which are not.

It cannot be too much emphasized, however, that we are *not* entitled to reject all assertions as meaningless simply because they fall into the latter group. The question certainly arises as to *what* such assertions mean; but a glib dismissal and a supercilious comment of 'meaningless' is likely on many occasions to be both inappropriate and unscholarly.

[1] From Shelley, *Adonais.*

## Modifications and developments

A further example will serve to illustrate this. A militant logical positivist, on the look out for meaningless assertions, would certainly find a happy hunting-ground among the works of those continental writers who are commonly labelled 'existentialist'. Thus when Heidegger tells us that 'Das Nichts selbst nichtet'—'The Nothing nihilates of itself'[1]—or when Marcel says that 'Man is the shepherd of Being',[2] we may well be puzzled. But one suspects a failure of communication between so-called 'existentialist' philosophers and philosophers in the British tradition. The correct procedure, I would suggest, is not to proclaim glibly, 'I have a principle which proves these assertions of Heidegger and Marcel to be meaningless', but rather to study them in their context, to examine if they are supposed to allow of verification or falsification by empirical means, and, if they do not, to examine what other legitimate function they might have. Only if all legitimate functions had been ruled out should we be entitled to regard them as meaningless.

(2) If assertions are clearly intended to provide factual information, and are nevertheless unverifiable and unfalsifiable, we are on safer ground in condemning them. There are a number of would-be scientific hypotheses, particularly in the field of psychology, which are vulnerable in this way. Thus it has been a common belief among psychologists that, when we remember, traces of past events are stored in the mind. I am not denying that this belief has given rise to some useful ideas. But if 'Traces of past events are stored in the mind' is intended as a literal factual assertion, we have every right to be puzzled. What does 'stored in the mind' mean? How does one tell whether something is, or is not, 'stored in the mind'? If no answer can be given, then it seems clear that the words 'stored in the mind' serve no useful purpose. Similarly it seems futile to discuss whether or not the mind occupies space, since the words 'The mind occupies space' are clearly intended to be factually significant, and yet no tests, whether in the laboratory or elsewhere, can provide appropriate verification or falsification; we should have no idea what tests to carry out.[3] The general danger against which the verification principle protects us is that of misleading ourselves, of supposing that our words make sense when reflection would reveal that they do not.

The verification principle serves also to warn us against generalizations

---

[1] M. Heidegger, *Was ist Metaphysik* (Bonn and Cohen, 1930), p. 19.
[2] Public lecture, 1954. Compare *L'homme problématique* (Aubier, 1955), p. 50, and Heidegger, *op. cit.*, p. 389.
[3] For the expression of a similar view, see R. H. Thouless, *General and Social Psychology* (London, 1925), p. 18.

which have been so qualified that they are proof against refutation. It is difficult to give examples which are uncontroversial; but as a possible illustration let us take the assertion 'All human beings are basically selfish'. This sounds like an assertion whose truth or falsity can be settled by a simple appeal to the facts; it would be falsified if a sufficient number of actions were discovered which were agreed to be altruistic. Let us suppose, however, that, whenever an apparently altruistic action occurs, the person who claims that all human actions are basically selfish replies, not, 'Yes, I agree; I was wrong', but 'No; that was really a selfish action the whole time.' If this reply was made on one single occasion, or even on two or three occasions, it might conceivably be convincing; but if the reply is produced on every single occasion when an apparently altruistic act occurs, then 'All human beings are basically selfish' has become so qualified that it is proof against refutation. The more qualifications are needed, the more uncomfortable the original generalization becomes.[1] In the last resort it ceases to be a genuine empirical generalization at all. We cannot in that case say that it has become meaningless; rather it has become something akin to a proposal or stipulation—a proposal that we should look at the world in a particular way. Often such proposals are of an evaluative kind. In this case the suggestion is perhaps that we can gain a useful 'slant' on the world by looking for selfish motives wherever possible. In such cases the verification principle enables us to distinguish the genuine generalization from what may be called an 'evaluative proposal'.

A further merit of the verification principle is that it enables us to treat with caution the remarks of the popularizing scientist. Thus when Sir James Jeans writes, 'The universe begins to look more like a great thought than a great machine',[2] we may well ask how one verifies whether or not something *'looks like* a thought' (my italics). Yet clearly this is supposed to be factual information of a sort. There is thus an extremely strong case for regarding Jeans' words as meaningless.

(3) We said also that the verification principle helps us to recognize a widespread mistake which has arisen over usage of the words 'exist', 'true', and 'facts'. The culmination of the whole attack on traditional metaphysics lies in the uncovering of this mistake. Discussion of this crucial problem will be reserved for the following chapter.

To sum up. First of all in this chapter we mentioned four minor

[1] Compare the attempts to qualify the Ptolemaic system of astronomy by postulating additional 'epicycles'.
[2] *The Mysterious Universe* (Cambridge, 1930), p. 148.

modifications in the original logical positivist position. These were, (i) the acceptance of verifiability in principle as opposed to verifiability in practice as the criterion of significance; (ii) the acceptance of statements of immediate experience as significant (such as 'I have toothache'); (iii) the acceptance of sentences containing words such as 'atom', 'electron', and 'proton' as significant; (iv) the acceptance of the 'weak', as opposed to the 'strong', version of the verification principle. Next we considered two major modifications; the first was the large-scale abandonment of the use of the word 'meaningless', and the recognition that there could be many different sorts of truth; the second was the realization that philosophers in the past had not simply been wasting their time producing nonsense. This realization was accompanied by a special technical study of *language*, known in some quarters, perhaps misleadingly, as 'linguistic analysis'. Finally, it was suggested that the verification principle could still be regarded as a useful philosophical tool, first because it forces us to make a distinction between those assertions which are factually significant and those which are not, secondly because it serves as a protective device against combinations of words which masquerade as factually significant assertions when they are not, and thirdly because it serves to disclose a fundamental mistake in connection with the words 'exist', 'true', and 'facts'.

# CHAPTER 4

# *'Absolute' existence*

The attack on traditional metaphysics has as its culmination the exposure of a long-standing mistake that has arisen in connection with the words 'exist', 'true', and 'facts'. In the present chapter I shall try to indicate where this mistake lies.

I shall begin by considering an objection to what has been said so far. Many readers may wish to challenge my use of the words 'factually significant'.

The objection might be formulated somewhat as follows: 'Although your approach to the verification principle is not that of the extreme logical positivist, you still seem to assume that the only factually significant assertions are those which admit of verification and falsification by empirical means. But you do not seem to have considered whether this assumption is *itself* supposed to be factually significant. If it is not, it must presumably be some sort of linguistic recommendation —a recommendation, perhaps, that the words "factually significant" shall be treated as synonymous with "empirically verifiable or falsifiable". Even as a linguistic recommendation, however, such procedure is surely questionable, since the words "fact" and "factual" are used in many different ways in ordinary speech, and you have no business to advocate a departure from ordinary speech without giving reasons for doing so. Quite apart from this, you clearly cannot base a whole new approach to philosophy on such a linguistic recommendation. If "factually significant" is to mean the same as "empirically verifiable or falsifiable", then it is scarcely surprising that you conclude that the only factually significant assertions are those which are empirically verifiable or falsifiable; but this tells us precisely nothing. If, however, your claim is intended to tell us something and to be factually significant, what possible grounds have you for making such a claim? Your claim clearly cannot be supported empirically, and on your own showing it must therefore be meaningless. Are you not hoist with your own petard?'

We may agree with the objector that the words 'fact' and 'factual' are used in ordinary speech in a variety of ways. Thus questions of fact are frequently contrasted with questions of law, questions of opinion, and so on. There is, moreover, a perfectly good use of 'fact' in which any true assertion may be said to 'state a fact'; and 'It is a fact that . . .' can be a preamble to many different types of assertion. None the less there is a good case for using 'factually significant' to mean the same as 'empirically verifiable or falsifiable'. This is a definition, a linguistic recommendation, certainly; but it is a recommendation which I believe can be justified, as I shall try to show later.

Let us allow the objector to press his point further. 'All you have really proved,' he may say, 'is that, in your sense of "factually significant", factually significant assertions are factually significant. Quite clearly, however, this is not all that you want to claim. Indeed I can see quite well what has happened. You may pretend that your definition of "factually significant" is harmless, but it is rather what I should call a "definitional joker"[1]—an apparently harmless appeal to the meaning of words, but an appeal which you can use, joker-like, for taking a trick to which you would not otherwise be entitled. I agree that we need a word to refer to those assertions whose truth or falsity can be settled by observation, but why should we not call them "empirical" assertions, instead of using the question-begging phrase "factually significant"? You need to widen your conception of what constitutes a fact. Otherwise what you are doing, albeit unobtrusively, is to introduce an ontological presupposition into your system, a presupposition which is atheistic and materialistic. To put the matter another way, you are an empiricist— that is, you are saying that the only assertions which refer to what really exists are empirical ones. You are thus in effect denying the existence of anything except what is empirically observable. This is surely a momentous metaphysical assertion of what you would call the "traditional" sort. On your own showing such an assertion must necessarily be meaningless.'

This objection can, I suggest, be met. Indeed the answer to it is of crucial importance for the main theme of this book.

We have admittedly no right simply to appeal to a definition or take

[1] I owe the phrase 'definitional joker' to Professor A. G. N. Flew. See his article, 'The Justification of Punishment' (*Philosophy*, Volume XXIX, no. III, October 1954), p. 292.

our stand on some allegedly 'correct' use of the word 'factual'. Moreover, as we shall see further in Chapter 14, the warning over 'definitional jokers' needs to be taken seriously in discussing the legitimacy of sentences containing the word 'God'. If our objector were wholly in the right, however, it would be reasonable to conclude that the attack on metaphysics had achieved nothing of major importance. I do not believe this account of the matter to be correct. What is called for is a further examination of the words 'exist', 'true', and 'facts'. This examination we must now attempt.

(i) *'Exist.'* I shall try to argue in what follows that the objector's central thesis depends on a mistaken use of the word 'exist'.

At the outset we need to clear up a point of a somewhat technical kind which may otherwise confuse the issue. It is not always realized that some questions—even if only a minority—of the form 'Is there' (or 'Does there exist') 'a so-and-so?' are matters for verbal decision rather than straightforward investigation. This holds particularly in the case of scientific technical terms—'the unconscious', for instance, or 'the superego'. 'Is there really such a thing as the unconscious?' is in effect a request for a verbal decision. What is being asked is, 'Is it scientifically valuable to introduce the concept "the unconscious" into our discourse?' According to the principle of Occam's razor—Entia non sunt multiplicanda praeter necessitatem—we should not encumber our discourse with such terms (or such 'entities', if you prefer) unless it is necessary. 'The unconscious' or 'the superego' can be said to exist, therefore, only if it is scientifically valuable to talk in that way. The matter is not one for observational investigation except in so far as the result of such an investigation influences our decisions.

Let us return to our objector. He need not dispute this last point; but it does not affect his main argument. 'The questions I am interested in', he will say, 'are not questions relating to linguistic decisions but straightforward questions about what actually does exist. You appear to assume that the only things that really exist are those which can in principle be observed. By this means you eliminate values, you eliminate God, and you eliminate the human soul.[1] And quite apart from realities of this sort there are other possible claimants to existence with which philosophers have been concerned in the past—universals, for instance, and propositions, and numbers. It is perfectly obvious, in my opinion,

---

[1] A letter in *Theology* (June 1951) speaks of 'What is still at bottom a materialistic and atheistic theory of the universe'.

that numbers do not exist, and that the things which we observe, like cats and cupboards, do exist. I would gladly believe that universals do not exist, except that philosophers have given us grounds for supposing that they do. Whether God exists is just the sort of problem which I expect philosophers to discuss. To say that the only assertions which refer to what really exists are empirical ones is a thinly disguised form of atheistic materialism'.

The sense of 'exist' in which the objector uses the word in this context is what I shall call the 'absolute' sense.[1] What exists in the absolute sense is somehow thought of as being part of the furniture of the universe in much the same way, perhaps, as chairs, tables, and bookcases are part of the furniture of a room. This analogy must not, of course, be pressed, since the existence of chairs, tables, and bookcases can be determined empirically by simple observation, whereas philosophers are supposed to give us information about God, universals, and numbers by some special non-empirical means. But the general assumption behind the notion of 'absolute existence' is that one can legitimately ask 'what there is' in the universe,[2] in much the same way as one can ask what there is in a room. In what follows, I shall attempt to reply to our objector by trying to convince him that this basic assumption is mistaken. The final outcome of the attack on traditional metaphysics is that the notion of 'absolute existence' is unintelligible.

I cannot hope to produce knock-down arguments in support of this view; but the following considerations may serve to throw further light on the matter.

(a) Things that exist do not form a class distinguishable by special characteristics from things that do not exist. 'Why are chimeras like golden mountains? Because neither exist' is clearly nonsense. In the same way it is nonsense to suppose that chairs, values, and numbers would be alike in that all have the characteristic of existence. Yet those

[1] The phrase 'absolute existence' occurs originally in the writings of Bishop Berkeley. What follows is not intended as any sort of exposition of Berkeley, but I do not think it is far-fetched to claim support from Berkeley for the views expressed. See especially his *Principles of Human Knowledge*, section CXLII.

[2] Compare W. V. Quine, *From a Logical Point of View* (Harvard, 1953). The first essay in this book (reprinted from the Review of Metaphysics, II, no. 5, September 1948), is entitled 'On What There Is'. I am not suggesting that Quine's discussion in this essay is without value, but he has, I think, misconceived the problem which he is attempting to solve. The question 'What is there?', as asked by Quine in this context, seems to me a meaningless one. Compare G. J. Warnock, 'Metaphysics in Logic' (*Aristotelian Society Proceedings*. Volume LVI for 1950–1).

who ask about the constitutents of the universe are making precisely this mistake. We all agree that 'chairs, tables, bookcases' is a legitimate conjunction, and that the objects referred to form a valid class. Where the mistake lies is in the assumption that 'chairs, values, numbers' forms a comparable group. Chairs, tables, and bookcases have in common the attributes of solidity, tangibility, extension etc., but chairs, values, and numbers do not have in common the attribute of existence. The phrase 'constituents of the universe' is misleading because it suggests that they do.

(b) If we apply the verification principle to the assertion 'Numbers have (or have not) a real existence' we reach some strange results. This sentence can be made intelligible, as we shall see later, if it is understood as an assertion or a denial that number-words, such as 'three', are 'thing'-words, i.e. the names of 'things'.[1] But so long as it purports to be a contribution to our knowledge of 'what there is' in the universe we are bound to be puzzled by it. The verification principle brings out, at the very least, that it is not an empirical assertion. Yet if it is not an empirical assertion, just what sort of an assertion is it? If 'Do numbers exist?' means, in effect, 'Are number-words, such as "three", names of things?', it is a second-order question, to be solved in the same way as e.g. 'Is "if" a thing-word?' But if 'exist' is used in the absolute sense, then 'Do numbers exist?' is clearly a first-order question, and we need to ask what first-order methods are appropriate for solving it. For purposes of comparison let us consider some straightforward first-order existence-questions, such as 'Do dodos still exist?' 'Do there exist any prime numbers between fifteen and twenty-five?' 'Do there exist any duties which are absolutely overriding?' In all three cases there is no difficulty over classification. Whether there still exist dodos is an empirical question, and the person to answer it is the explorer; whether there exist any prime numbers between fifteen and twenty-five is a question for the mathematician; whether there exist duties which are overriding is a question which concerns any of us who are interested in moral issues. But to whom can questions about the ultimate constituents of the universe be referred? Whose methods are appropriate for solving them? How do we know whether our answers are right or wrong? Assertions about the ultimate constituents of the universe do not refer to what is empirically observable; they are not scientific generalizations

[1] For the moment I am deliberately leaving the word 'thing' vague. For further discussion, see pp. 41–2.

or mathematical formulae; they are not moral exhortations; they are not poetry. If we try to classify them they seem to belong nowhere at all. Someone who disputes our whole argument may wish to reply that they are specifically metaphysical questions of the traditional sort, and that the person who must solve them is the traditional metaphysician. But how does a traditional metaphysician of this sort set to work? By what methods does he determine if numbers are, or are not, among the ultimate constituents of the universe? What grounds can there be for an assertion either one way or the other? There are admittedly many questions on many different subjects to which the answers are in dispute or doubtful. But it is not disputes and doubts that are the trouble here. It is the complete lack of any agreed method of solution. This lack points inevitably to the view that 'absolute existence' assertions—assertions about the ultimate constituents of the universe—are meaningless. The phrase 'ultimate constituents of the universe' is nothing, I suggest, but a vast philosophical mistake.

An important qualification, however, must now be added. I do not wish to suggest that questions such as 'Do numbers really exist?' 'Do universals really exist?' etc., can simply be dismissed without further discussion. As we saw in the last chapter, it is a curious characteristic of many metaphysical problems, which are alleged to have been finally disposed of, that they re-emerge in a somewhat different guise. 'Do numbers exist?' is, I think, of this variety. A helpful re-statement of this question is, 'Is "three"—or any other number-word—a *thing*-word?' This is clearly a legitimate question of the second-order philosophical variety, and, if asked in this way, it is clearly different from the first-order, absolute-existence questions which we rejected as meaningless.

I have left the word 'thing' deliberately vague. In principle, however, the second-order question admits of solution provided we agree on the criteria to be used for deciding whether a word is or is not a thing-word. There is room for disagreement here on points of detail; but an attempt will now be made to indicate some of the criteria which seem implicit in our ordinary thinking.[1] Roughly speaking a word is a thing-word if that for which it purports to stand satisfies the following conditions, (*a*) if it can act and be acted upon, (*b*) if it lasts through periods of time, (*c*) if it has spatial boundaries, (*d*) if it is solid, and (*e*) if to regard

[1] Compare the *Oxford English Dictionary*, 'Thing . . . whatever exists or is conceived to exist: any separable or distinguishable object of thought.'

it as a unity is for any reason thought valuable or important.[1] In the case of numbers these conditions are scarcely fulfilled at all, and we therefore feel disposed to say that numbers 'don't really exist'. In other cases we find some of the criteria satisfied and not others. Thus clouds, rainbows, and shadows have shape, but not solidity; in the case of our own self-awareness, we are aware of something which occupies space and can inaugurate action, but the 'I' or 'self' cannot be thought of as a solid object. In other cases a certain unity of structure leads us to think in terms of things. Examples of this sort would be 'The Choral Symphony', 'The British constitution', 'market prices', and 'a depression moving over Iceland'. All these are *things* in a sense, and yet they are not. What is required in each case is a ruling or decision, in part analogous to a decision in a court of law. An action, for instance, counts as trespass if enough of the conditions which go to make up trespassing are satisfied. In the cases we have cited our ruling will depend on our purposes and values. Thus A may say that the Choral Symphony is 'nothing but a collection of vibrations in the air' while B may insist that it has a 'real existence' of its own. In this case A's remark has a derogatory ring, while B's remark sounds more favourable. Those who wish to emphasize the unity of the Choral Symphony as a work of art will side with B, while those who wish to commend the viewpoint of the physical scientist and treat it as more important than the viewpoint of the music critic will side with A. A similar problem of values is what separates a Platonist type of philosopher from a so-called 'empiricist'. Plato makes the point[2] that the mathematical formula for determining the course of the planets is more important than the visual observations which we make of the skies. He therefore speaks of the real (i.e. mathematical) movements of the planets, and ascribes an inferior status to the visible heavens. To put the matter in modern terms, one might say that, according to Plato, the great scientist is the person who has the good ideas, and that the trying out of these ideas in the laboratory or elsewhere is more akin to routine hack-work. In contrast an empiricist philosopher would say that the mathematical formula is a mere device, and that the observed events are the 'real' ones. Empiricism thus assigns a privileged status to those assertions which refer to what can actually be observed, Platonism to assertions stating general scientific laws. It is not the purpose of this book to take sides on the Platonism versus

[1] For a further discussion of the first three criteria, see K. Koffka, *Gestalt Psychology* (New York, 1935), pp. 70–2.
[2] *Republic*, Book VII, section 529.

empiricism controversy. We are concerned only to show that these questions about 'real existence'—e.g. 'Do numbers have a real existence?' 'Is the world of our senses the real world?'—are second-order questions, and that they are meaningless only if asked as if they were first-order, absolute-existence questions. To ask if numbers have a real existence is to talk about number-words, not to use them, and to ask if the world of our senses is the real world is to talk about empirical assertions, not to make them.

Those who want to insist that there is something real in human personality over and above the physical components of the body are in effect insisting that human personality is something of value, and those who wish to insist that values themselves have a real existence are in effect saying that judgments of value require to be taken seriously.

To make clear our central point it may be helpful at this stage to introduce a further distinction. We noted earlier how the word 'exist' could appropriately be used in sentences of several different types, e.g. 'Do dodos still exist?', 'Do there exist any prime numbers between fifteen and twenty-five?' 'Do there exist any duties that are absolutely overriding?' In all these cases it is possible to tell what sort of question is being asked by studying the context. Let us refer to such questions, then, as 'contextual existence-questions'. In contrast 'Do the objects of sense-perception exist?' 'Do values exist?' 'Do universals exist?' and 'Does the Choral Symphony exist?' may be labelled 'metaphysical existence-questions'. Our main conclusion can now be expressed by saying that metaphysical existence-questions are second-order questions. The absolute-existence mistake consists in treating them as though they were first-order questions, and as though they could be asked in vacuo independently of the context which gives them their meaning.

(ii) *True*. If our central claim about 'absolute existence' can now be taken as established, the words 'true' and 'factual' can be discussed more briefly. It is not a matter of major importance for this book what ruling is given for the correct use of the word 'true'. Sometimes the word 'true' is used as a general term of commendation for assertions of many different sorts; sometimes it is taken to mean 'true of something that really exists'. If we take this second usage seriously, then for every true sentence we must postulate a reality or a world of which the sentence is true. Thus if '$37 \times 5 = 185$' can be labelled 'true', it must be true of the world of mathematics; and if 'It is wrong to kill' is true, it must be true of the world of values, and so on. This talk is harmless

43

provided we do not take the words 'reality' or 'world' too seriously, or more explicitly, provided we do not make the 'absolute-existence' mistake and suppose that these worlds exist side by side, so to speak, as part of the universe. In such a context we have no more right to deny the existence of a world of mathematics or of values than to assert it.

It may be mentioned in passing that, though the word 'true' has come to be used widely, so as to cover many different types of assertion, the word 'verification', which means literally 'making true', has come to be used only in a narrow sense. As used in a philosophical context, 'verification' has come to mean 'verification by empirical means'. This usage is harmless provided we take note of the resultant lack of parallelism between the words 'verification' and 'true'.

(iii) *Factual.* The same general principles hold in connection with the word 'factual'. Whatever decision we make on the question of how widely this word should be used, no major consequences follow. The only point of importance is to avoid the 'absolute-existence' mistake. If someone says that there may be facts other than empirical ones—facts, for instance, to which moral or mathematical sentences refer—this is just the mistake that he is making. To say that the only factually significant sentences are empirical ones may be regarded as a justifiable protest against the notion of 'absolute existence'.

We are now in a position to answer the objection which was raised at the start of this chapter. The objection was this. When we insisted that the only factually significant assertions were empirical ones, it seemed that we were smuggling in a presupposition which was atheistic and materialistic, and that we had ruled out non-empirical realities simply by the glib manipulation of a 'definitional joker'.[1]

The answer to this objection is now clear. If we speak of 'non-empirical realities' at all, we are in serious danger of making the 'absolute-existence' mistake. No claim will be made in this book about 'what really exists', since the words 'really exists' in this context are unintelligible. We have begged no question by using 'factually significant' to mean the same as 'empirical', since the question which we are accused of having begged is a meaningless one. If someone says that the important question is whether there really are facts to which moral and mathematical sentences refer, he is making the 'absolute-existence' mistake, and he should be challenged to say what he means by 'really are' in this context. This counter-challenge seems to me unanswerable.

[1] See p. 37.

More will be said on the subject of materialism in Chapter 8. All that need be said here is that, if 'materialism' is understood to mean acceptance of the assertion 'Nothing exists except matter', then materialism is untenable, since it commits the 'absolute-existence' mistake. The charge that our presupposition is atheistic can, I believe, be answered too. But the subject is too complicated to be discussed here since it raises the puzzling question of the applicability of words such as 'entity', 'real', 'exist', etc. in the case of 'God'. This is a matter which will be discussed more fully in Part III.

It should be emphasized again that the present views cannot correctly be labelled 'empiricist'. There is no need to make a fetish over the word 'empiricism'. If an 'empiricist' is one who says that only empirical assertions refer to what really exists, then, despite the empiricist origin of the attack on metaphysics, empiricism itself must be abandoned as a meaningless theory. It is possible, however, as we noted earlier, to take up a modified version of empiricism, in which the label is used to express acceptance of a particular system of values. To say that only empirical assertions refer to what really exists (or that only empirical assertions can be labelled 'true' or 'false') could be interpreted as saying that empirical assertions have in some way a privileged status, and that other assertions, e.g. those of the moralist, are less important. Now admittedly the early versions of logical positivism may have been empiricist in this sense. Logical positivism has commonly been regarded as the handmaid of science, and its central beliefs arose in a climate of opinion where 'scientific method' was certainly a watchword. But there is nothing empiricist about the present viewpoint, since no claim is being made that one type of assertion is more important than another. Indeed it seems to me rather futile to discuss whether an observational truth such as 'There is a cat in the cupboard' is 'more important' than a moral truth such as 'Men ought to love their enemies', since the function of each is entirely different. I conclude that we are not necessarily committed by the present argument to being empiricists in the sense of believing that empirical truths have some privileged status.

Finally, I would suggest that the important criterion of whether a person takes present-day philosophical techniques seriously is his avoidance of the 'absolute-existence' mistake. Such avoidance, we need to remember, does not come easily; on the contrary, it involves a changed outlook, a fresh orientation. Some may have supposed that those who adopt this outlook do so in order to seem intellectually superior, or perhaps in order to be perverse or difficult. The truth is rather that reflection *forces* this change of outlook upon us; it is a challenge which cannot be ignored.

The main arguments of this book will be based on the assumption that sentences involving reference to 'absolute existence' are meaningless.

# CHAPTER 5

*Moral assertions and their legitimacy*

Mention was made in Chapter 2 of the view that moral assertions were meaningless.[1] Whether such a view was ever seriously held is very doubtful.[2] The fact remains, however, that many laymen interested in philosophy are still suspicious that modern philosophers do not take their moral problems seriously. In so far as this criticism is directed against individual philosophers, it need not be answered; but if the suggestion is that modern philosophy, as such, compels us to regard moral problems as unimportant, it is essential that the layman's suspicions should be removed.

I shall argue in this chapter that moral assertions have a perfectly legitimate status, and that there is nothing whatever in modern knowledge to prevent us from taking moral problems seriously.

The claim that moral assertions are meaningless is clearly so grotesque that it can be dismissed without discussion. But those who take the progress of science seriously may still be tempted to suppose that moral assertions have in some way an inferior status as compared with the assertions of scientific or common-sense observation. A special difficulty in connection with moral problems is that there does not appear to be an established body of knowledge comparable to the knowledge available to the astronomer or physicist. Scientists may disagree with each other on questions such as the age of the earth, but in all cases there is at least agreement on the sorts of method relevant to settling such questions. Scientific assertions, it might seem, have a respectability which moral assertions lack. Such a claim, however, if it is meaningful at all, clearly

[1] See p. 24.
[2] Possibly Professor Ayer, in a fit of youthful exuberance, came at one time somewhere near such a view. See *Language, Truth, and Logic* (Gollancz, 1949), chapter VI.

cannot itself be settled by methods appropriate to science, since it involves some sort of evaluation; and, as we shall see more fully in the next chapter, empirical observation cannot tell us what values we ought to hold.

It is also objected, sometimes, that the world at the present day is crying out for a lead on moral matters, and that professional philosophers are failing to give the requisite guidance. It is said that they 'fiddle and play tricks while the world burns',[1] that they split hairs, and waste time discussing the meaning of sentences such as 'This rocking-horse is covered with pink spots.'[2] When people are yearning to know, in Tennyson's words, 'what God and man is', philosophers seem to turn a deaf ear, and in place of the bread of moral exhortation they offer only the stones of linguistic analysis. This criticism of modern philosophy, however, although it merits sympathy, is the result of misunderstanding. If most technical philosophers at the present time do not give a lead on moral matters, this is not necessarily because they are indifferent to morality and its problems; it is rather that they regard it as outside their terms of reference to give such a lead. The technical philosopher, they would say, has no special right to assume the rôle of prophet or preacher; to blame him would be like blaming, say, a numismatist or a mathematician for failing to give a lead. *Qua* numismatist, or *qua* mathematician, it is simply not his job. This does not mean that philosophers are committed to the view that a moral lead is not needed, nor is there the least justification for saying that those who feel called to give such a lead are wasting their time. The point is rather that if we wish to write a political or religious pamphlet on world problems, a technical philosophical journal is not the place to have it published.

It may still be objected that there is a special branch of philosophy, namely moral philosophy, which ought specifically to be concerned with moral problems. As we shall see in a moment, however, there is a difference between doing moral philosophy and taking sides on particular moral issues. It is not clear that moral philosophers in their technical work are expected to do the latter.

A final difficulty, of a more serious kind, remains to be discussed. It may still be said that philosophers should defend 'absolute' or 'objective' standards of value, and that present-day 'linguistic' philosophers have

---

[1] So writes Father M. J. d'Arcy, reviewing Ayer's *Language, Truth, and Logic*. See *Criterion*, 1936.

[2] For an eloquent complaint along these lines, see C. E. M. Joad, 'Appeal to Philosophers' (*Aristotelian Society Proceedings*. Volume XL for 1939–40), p. 35.

failed to do this. To examine the force of this objection, let us consider further what such philosophers are trying to achieve.

A decade or two ago a number of philosophers accepted the so-called 'emotive' theory of moral terms. According to this theory the function of words such as 'ought', 'right', 'wrong' etc. was to express emotions. Thus 'Stealing money is wrong' was taken to be the expression of the speaker's unfavourable emotions towards stealing money.[1]

The word 'expression' needs to be emphasized. According to the more convincing versions of the emotive theory, a moral assertion is not simply a piece of autobiography; in saying that something is good the speaker is not just reporting that he has certain emotions, but is actually expressing or giving vent to these emotions.

This theory has been nicknamed the 'Boo-hoorah!' theory, on the grounds that it treats the words 'ought', 'right', and 'duty' as comparable to interjections such as 'Boo!' and 'Hoorah!' This, however, is perhaps something of a caricature, and should not be taken too seriously.

It is now widely agreed that this reference to the speaker's emotions is unnecessary; and, according to more recent views, emotions do not enter into the matter. The 'emotive' theory has in fact largely been superseded by what may be roughly called the 'imperativist' theory.[2] On this theory one of the main functions of moral terms is to regulate conduct, to tell us what to do. Sentences in the indicative mood, it seems, may in some contexts have the force of imperatives. Thus, 'It is wrong to kill' means the same as 'Do not kill', and 'Men ought to love their enemies' is simply another way of saying 'Love your enemies'.

The great advantage of the imperativist theory, in comparison with the emotive theory, is that it makes sense of moral disagreement. If A says that killing is always wrong and B says that killing is sometimes justified, then on the emotive theory there is no disagreement between them. A's words express A's emotions and B's words express B's emotions. There is no contradiction here, any more than there would be if A said 'I have black hair' and B said 'No, my hair is brown'. On the imperativist view, however, they are advocating different policies, and the disagreement between them is therefore serious.

The ways in which moral assertions are like and unlike imperatives

[1] Compare Ayer, *Language, Truth, and Logic* (1949), p. 107.

[2] For a treatment of the subject along 'imperativist' lines, see R. M. Hare, *The Language of Morals* (Oxford, 1952). A combination of 'emotivist' and 'imperativist' views is to be found in C. L. Stevenson, *Ethics and Language* (Oxford, 1944). I use the word 'imperativist' in a deliberately loose sense to cover a wide range of prevalent views.

is a technical matter which need not concern us. All that we need note is that imperativism, in the inexact sense which I have given to the word, involves a large number of technical developments, and that these developments show that language functions with far greater complexity than earlier theorists had indicated. Language can be used e.g. for commending, disparaging, expressing agreement or disagreement, conveying congratulations or regrets, arranging in order of merit, giving vent to indignation, inviting others to share indignation, advising, persuading, and for many other purposes. The straightforward distinction between 'factual' language and 'moral' language, like many philosophical classifications, is an over-simplification, since many assertions do not fall unambiguously into either group. 'The theory of evolution is well-founded', expresses commendation of a particular scientific theory; 'The town drains are in an appalling condition' gives vague factual information on what people would find if they inspected the drains, invites us to share the speaker's attitude of disapproval, and perhaps also carries the suggestion that something ought to be done. These different functions of language may be combined in all sorts of ways in the same sentence, and it is not always clear which function predominates. Thus a person who says that the states in eastern Europe are 'democratic' may conceivably be intending to convey information about the constitution and election-procedure of such states, but it is quite likely that he is using 'democratic' as a general word of commendation and not as a descriptive word at all.

A further technical problem which has come under discussion is the difference between the specifically moral 'ought', as in 'Men ought to love their enemies' and other uses of 'ought', such as 'You ought to have led the knave of spades'. It is outside the scope of this chapter to suggest possible answers to this question. My purpose is simply to indicate the general range of problems with which present-day moral philosophy is concerned.

What, then, is it that philosophers have allegedly failed to do? What are these 'absolute' or 'objective' standards which they are accused of having abandoned?

I should like to say at once that I do not myself unreservedly endorse an 'imperativist' viewpoint. Even if we assume, however, that this imperativist viewpoint is substantially correct, there is no justification for accusing philosophers of doing something morally disreputable.

This can be shown, first and foremost, by pointing out that moral philosophy, as carried out by philosophers with imperativist leanings, is a second-order activity. The moral philosopher's job, on this showing, is to *discuss* moral terms rather than actually to use them. To say that 'It is always wrong to kill' is in some ways like an interjection, or that it is in some ways like an imperative, does not commit us one way or the other on the question whether it always *is* wrong to kill. To do moral philosophy, as we said earlier, is not to take sides on any moral issue.

When people speak of 'absolute' standards, the word 'absolute' is ambiguous. The claim that moral rules are absolute could be taken to mean that they admit of no exception. Thus if 'It is wrong to tell a lie' is absolute, then there can never be occasions when lying is justified. Whether any moral rules are absolute in this sense may perhaps be questioned. In the case of lying many people would agree that there could conceivably be circumstances when lying was not merely justified but actually a duty. If, for instance, they found themselves in a position where answering a sick person's questions truthfully would seriously undermine his health or would subject him to a near-fatal shock, many people would consider it their duty to tell a lie. Whatever the rights or wrongs of this controversy, however, it has no bearing on the accusation that present-day moral philosophy constitutes a threat to moral standards. Those whose professional task is to reflect on moral assertions are not necessarily committed either to the view that lying is always wrong or to the view that lying is sometimes justified.

Those who say that philosophers should defend 'absolute' standards of value may, however, be using 'absolute' as synonymous with 'objective'. What is right and wrong, the critics would say, must be objective in the sense of being grounded in the nature of things. On certain moral issues, in other words, we must admit that there is an objectively right and an objectively wrong answer. It is objectively wrong, for instance, for certain tribes to practise cannibalism or ritual murder, and we in Europe who abhor such practices are objectively justified in doing so. Imperativist philosophers, on the other hand, according to this argument, are reduced to saying that cannibals issue imperatives in one direction, Europeans in a different direction, and that, since imperatives and interjections cannot be labelled 'true' or 'false', there can be no question of discovering the *true* answer as to which side is right.

The immediate reply which an imperativist philosopher might make to this criticism would be to say that 'true' and 'false' can be used as terms of commendation for many different types of assertion, moral assertions included. To say that a moral assertion is true or false is, on the imperativist view, to take sides on the moral issue in question; to say that 'cannibalism is wrong' is true or to say that cannibalism *really is* wrong is to take sides on the issue of cannibalism.

The defender of objectivism, however, may regard this concession as a sop rather than as a genuine reassurance. He may want to insist that 'true' should be used to mean 'true of objective reality', and that some moral assertions are true in this strict sense.

The case for objectivism does not seem to me by any means discredited. It is true that we cannot regard goodness and rightness as the names of mysterious 'non-natural qualities', as some earlier writers apparently did;[1] but it is by no means impossible that some more adequate version of objectivism will come to be reinstated in the not too distant future.

Whether this is so or not, however, there is no good ground for regarding imperativism as a dangerous or subversive theory. An imperativist is certainly not committed to the view that the imperatives 'Be a cannibal' and 'Perform ritual murder' have an equal claim on our respect to that of the command 'Thou shalt not kill'.

For final reassurance the following additional points may be made. First, the imperativist does not in the least dispute that there are important differences between 'You ought to try this new brand of coffee' and 'He ought to have led the knave' as compared with 'Men ought to love their enemies'. It can quite well be agreed that 'Men ought to love their enemies' has an importance which the other two lack, and that conversion to a moral principle is something quite different from conversion to a new brand of coffee or conversion to a new policy at bridge. Secondly, there seems no good reason for supposing that imperative sentences are less important than indicative ones. One of the

[1] G. E. Moore (*Principia Ethica*, Cambridge, 1903, chapter 1) speaks of goodness as a quality, and wants to refer to it as a 'non-natural' quality. That Moore's view is mistaken can, I think, be shown if we consider a group of phrases such as 'a good action', 'a good girl', 'a good kick', or 'a good hot cup of tea'. On Moore's view we should have to say that there is a special non-natural quality which a good action, a good girl, a good kick, and a good hot cup of tea all have in common. According to the imperativist, on the other hand, the function of the word 'good' is to commend; and the qualities for which we commend an action, for instance, may be quite different from those for which we commend a cup of tea. For a fuller development of this argument, see R. M. Hare, *The Language of Morals* (Oxford, 1952), section 7. Compare also Aristotle, *Nicomachean Ethics*, Book I, chapter VI.

central demands of Christianity, 'Repent ye', is couched in the imperative mood, and it would be futile to argue that it therefore has no special claim on our allegiance. Thirdly, we should do well to remember that a central theme in Kant's moral philosophy is the notion of a 'categorical imperative';[1] and no one could suggest that Kant did not take moral problems seriously.

From the foregoing arguments we may conclude that, even if the imperativists are wholly right, there are no obvious grounds for supposing that moral assertions should not be taken seriously. On the contrary, they have a perfectly legitimate function, whose importance there is not the slightest ground for disputing.

This conclusion has a special relevance to any discussion of the claims of religion. Much religious language is concerned in one way or another with moral decision. Thus 'Repent ye' is a call to make a fresh set of moral decisions; acceptance of 'God is love' commits us, among other things, to the moral policy of always showing love to others; and the 'I do' of the confirmation service and the 'I will' of the marriage service are actual declarations of moral commitment. I am not suggesting that religious language is simply moral exhortation in disguise. Both 'God is love' and the language of commitment ('I do', 'I will') will be discussed in some detail later in the book. All that need be noted here is that there is a clear connection between such talk and the language of moral assertion.

In the case of 'I do' and 'I will', this connection is straightforward. In the case of 'God is love' some further explanation is called for. Assertions such as 'God is love' constitute what I shall call in Part III 'the language of parable'. In general we may say that no moral assertion necessarily entails a parable-assertion, but moral assertions can be the consequence of parable-assertions, and parable-assertions can therefore be cited as the reason for particular behaviour. Thus 'Men ought to love their enemies' does not entail any conclusion about God, and could be accepted by someone who had no beliefs about God at all; but it is part of the meaning of 'God is love' that it carries certain moral assertions as consequences, and it would be self-contradictory to say 'God is love and it does not matter whether men show love or not'. Again, if a person saw a firing-squad about to open fire on its victim, he might say 'Don't shoot!—God is love', where 'God is love' is given as the reason for not shooting.

[1] See *Fundamental Principles of the Metaphysics of Morals*, second section.

One final point. I would like to suggest tentatively that imperativism, though not a dangerous or subversive theory, is none the less mistaken. If moral assertions follow from parable-assertions about God, then they must be no less 'objectively valid' than these parable-assertions. Whether parable-assertions about God can be said to be 'objectively valid' in any worthwhile sense is a difficult problem, which will be discussed in Part III. For the moment I offer no more than a tentative suggestion that an 'objectively valid' moral assertion is one that follows from an objectively valid parable.

Nothing has been said yet by way of vindication of these parable-assertions such as 'God is love'; but by establishing that straightforward moral assertions such as 'Men ought to love their enemies' have a legitimate function, we have done something to prepare the way for other sorts of religious language. In so far as religion is concerned with the question, 'How ought I to live?' there is not the slightest ground for treating religious language disparagingly, or for supposing that it is less important than the language of the scientific investigator.

# CHAPTER 6

## *How moral assertions are validated*

The question which I want to ask in this chapter is, By what arguments can we discover whether our moral beliefs are right or wrong?

The answer which philosophical reflection supplies is that the matter in the last resort is one for individual conviction rather than rational argument. There is no question of mathematical certainty—the sort of certainty that is legitimate for the assertion that $19 \times 21 = 399$; nor is there the certainty that we have in the case of simple empirical assertions such as 'There is a cat in the cupboard'. There can be argument on moral matters, certainly, but there may sometimes be basic disagreement which no amount of argument can resolve.

If the moral assertion in question is of a very general kind, such as 'It is wrong to kill' or 'We ought to try to promote the greatest happiness of the greatest number', it is often appropriate to use an appeal to consistency. Thus, if a person claims to be acting on the principle that it is wrong to kill, he might ask himself or be asked whether he considers euthanasia invariably wrong; and, if he does not, then he cannot consistently accept the principle that it is *always* wrong to kill. Similarly, if someone professes to believe that we ought to try to promote the greatest happiness of the greatest number, he might be challenged to say whether he attaches importance to the way in which happiness is distributed. If he agrees that a slightly smaller amount of happiness evenly distributed is more desirable than a greater amount of happiness unevenly distributed, he cannot consistently accept the principle that we ought *always* to try simply to promote the greatest happiness of the greatest number. It does not, of course, follow that general principles such as 'It is wrong to kill' and 'We ought to try to promote the greatest happiness of the greatest number' are of no use in regulating conduct it is more satisfactory, however, to treat them, not as absolute obligations to which there is no exception, but as so-called *prima facie* obligations, which hold good if other things are equal, but which allow of exceptions if conflicting obligations point strongly in another direction.[1] Sometimes if we are in doubt about our duty in a particular situation, consideration of general principles may be of help; quite often, however, it is the other way round, and we are better able to say what our duty is in particular situations than to formulate any general principle. In either case an appeal to consistency is entirely appropriate.

If two people disagree on some particular problem of policy, this disagreement may simply have arisen through failure to agree on the facts of the case. Thus if two N.S.P.C.C. officers disagree as to whether a child ought to be removed from its home, this may well not be a moral disagreement at all; it may simply be that they disagree as to what would be the consequences of keeping the child at home as compared with removing it. In such a case, if accurate knowledge of the facts were obtainable (which of course it may not be), this is quite sufficient to resolve the dispute. In other cases there may be a fundamental difference in moral outlook. In other words, two people may have altogether incompatible ideas as to what is important for children. In such cases rational argument has its limitations.

Let us illustrate this point with a particular example, that of whether the death-penalty should be retained as the punishment for murder. Disagreement here seems in part due to disagreement over the facts and in part due to a genuine difference in moral outlook. If A and B disagree over whether the death-penalty should be retained, what sorts of argument are they likely to use?

First of all, they may perhaps discuss the relative consequences of retention and abolition. This is a factual question; and it may be that the difference in their views is simply due to disagreement over the facts. A may maintain, let us say, that the death-penalty is not the only adequate deterrent to would-be murderers, whereas B may disagree. The obvious course in this case is to try to reach agreement on the facts. There could be examination of statistics, particularly, for example, to see whether there was an increase in the number of murders in countries where the death-penalty was suddenly removed. There could be consultation with those who have made a special study of the mentality of criminals. In practice, no doubt, even those who have studied

[1] For the phrase '*prima facie* obligation', see Sir W. D. Ross, *Foundations of Ethics* (Clarendon Press, 1939), chapter 5.

the matter are fallible, and statistics are notoriously hard to interpret; but it is quite easy to see how in principle agreement could be
reached.

It might transpire, however, that A was taking his stand against the
death-penalty on the grounds that human life is sacred and that killing
is therefore morally wrong in itself. If he takes the extreme position that
killing is *always* morally wrong, then no factual evidence will be
logically sufficient to make him change his view on the death-penalty;
and even if he takes the less extreme position that it is *prima facie* wrong
to kill, he would still need to be satisfied, before supporting the death-
penalty, both that it was a unique deterrent, and that the obligation to
protect others outweighed the obligation not to kill.

Again it might transpire that B's support of the death-penalty was
not based on the belief that it was an effective deterrent, but on the
general principle that a person who has taken another's life deserves to
suffer the same fate.[1]

In this case argument between A and B would be unlikely to have
much effect. Something could perhaps be done by an appeal to consistency, but there is nothing blatantly inconsistent either in A's view
or in B's. In the last resort we should be forced to say that there was a
basic difference of moral outlook.[2]

In general, however strong our convictions on moral matters, there
is no question of our being able to prove that they are right by a
demonstration, nor of their having the same sort of certainty as the
things which we know about from sense-experience. Experience can
tell us that this or that is the case, but it can never tell us that something
*ought to be* the case. No set of 'is'-sentences on their own can constitute
the proof of an 'ought'-sentence.

This general conclusion has four consequences which are specially
relevant to the theme of this book.

[1] The original *lex talionis*—'an eye for an eye and a tooth for a tooth'—seems
to have been designed as a check on primitive savagery. If you deprive me of my
eye, then I must limit myself to depriving you of yours, and must not e.g. take
your life or take vengeance on your family. According to Jesus' teaching, even
depriving you of your eye would be going too far. (See Matthew, v, 38, 39.)

[2] In practice, of course, our arguments on moral issues are frequently
influenced by primitive, irrational factors of which we are quite likely to be
unaware, and the reasons which we give for our moral decisions are sometimes
'rationalizations', i.e. attempts to justify by reason conclusions which we have
already decided to support. (Compare chapter 12.) For the moment I am
concerned not with the psychological question of the ways in which people argue
about moral decisions, but with the logical question of how moral decisions can
be justified.

# Religion and the scientific outlook

(a) In the first place it need not surprise us if the question 'How ought I to live?' has been answered by different people in different ways. There is no agreed body of knowledge for answering this question, comparable to the agreed body of scientific knowledge that has grown up in the past few centuries; and it is a mistake to think of the philosopher as a special technician who can produce a set of right answers from up his sleeve. If anyone hopes for demonstrative certainty on what way of life is best, nothing can be done except to tell him that such certainty is just not available. Eminent thinkers do in fact disagree, and if anyone thinks differently from ourselves he is not necessarily either a knave or a fool.

(b) Once it is realized that no 'is'-sentences can prove the truth of an 'ought'-sentence, it is possible to dispose once for all of any so-called 'scientific ethics'—that is, any attempt to give our moral beliefs the same secure status as the findings of science. It has sometimes been thought that we can tell from biology the general direction in which species are evolving, and it has been argued that we ought to promote anything that furthers this 'evolutionary trend'.[1] But to say that we *ought to* promote etc. is not itself a biological assertion. Any would-be 'scientific ethics', before it can even start, must smuggle in one of these 'oughts' or some other word indicating what is morally desirable. Sentences containing a reference to what is morally desirable cannot be accepted or rejected solely as a result of the findings of 'science'.

(c) Some have wished to draw a favourable contrast between the humility of the scientist who is prepared to revise his theories in the light of new evidence and the dogmatic self-assurance of the religious thinker or moralist who is not. But if a 'dogma' is understood to mean a view which is held as a matter of conviction rather than as the result of evidence or rational argument, then there is certainly no ground for supposing that all dogmatism is to be deplored. It would, of course, be quite inappropriate to profess belief in a scientific theory without having attempted to consider the evidence on which it is based, but it would be equally inappropriate to regard an assertion such as 'Men ought to love their enemies' as a provisional truth comparable to a scientific law.

Many would say (rightly, in my opinion) that moral beliefs should be

[1] Thus C. H. Waddington, in *Science and Ethics* (Allen & Unwin, 1942), p. 135, writes: 'The ethical system which has a general validity for mankind as a whole . . . must be that ethical system which has actually been effective in guiding the evolution of man as a whole.'

held with humility, and that we should be ready, in Oliver Cromwell's words, to 'think it possible (we) may be mistaken'. Certainly if the word 'dogmatic' suggests total unwillingness to reconsider, moral beliefs should not be held dogmatically. But this is not the whole story. Most people would agree that moral convictions which are not held strongly are worth very little. If we saw a man acting with wanton cruelty to a child, for instance, most of us would unhesitatingly condemn such action on moral grounds; and if a third party were to plead in the name of 'liberalism' and 'tolerance' that the man was entitled to his opinion on how the child should be treated, and that we ought not to be 'dogmatic' on the subject, most of us would treat such a plea with contempt. Inevitably moral assertions involve something of the 'I-am-right-you-are-wrong' attitude, and it is certainly a difficult problem in practice to combine moral conviction with humility. But we are not justified in using this difficulty as a ground for making an unfavourable contrast between moral assertions and 'scientific' ones.

(*d*) We frequently hear it said that man's moral progress has not kept pace with his scientific progress—that he has learned to control the power of the atom, but has not learned the wisdom to use his discoveries beneficially. The general contention is one which I do not wish to dispute; but we need to remember that the adoption of a changed set of moral values is something very unlike the acquisition of technical skill as a scientific investigator. There can be expert technicians, but there cannot be expert moralists, and education in sound values, if possible at all, is something very different from technical education. Any fresh start, whether moral, political, or religious involves a change of heart, a new orientation, a new way of looking at things. We become converted; we see something which we had not seen before. In the last resort this is not a matter for rational argument but rather for personal conviction. As was noted earlier, there may come a time when rational argument simply breaks down. If A sees a particular issue in one way and B sees it in another way, there may simply be no common ground between them. Agreement can be reached, in such cases, only if one of them undergoes a fundamental change of heart.

*       *       *

The main purpose of the last two chapters has been to place moral assertions 'on the map', so to speak—that is, to establish their legitimacy and to call attention to the grounds on which they can be supported.

This is an essential preliminary to our discussion of specifically religious assertions in Part III. The central conclusions of the last two chapters are (i) that moral assertions have a perfectly legitimate status, and (ii) that their truth or falsity is a matter in the last resort for personal conviction rather than rational argument.

# CHAPTER 7

# The scope of philosophy

To conclude Part I of this book I propose to offer some remarks of a more general kind on the scope and limitations of present-day philosophy.

Traditionally the philosopher tends to be thought of as a person who teaches us how to live,[1] and who gives us what is commonly called a 'philosophy of life'. He is a person who gives us a general 'world-picture' or perhaps of other worlds and other realms of existence. In the light of recent developments it seems to me that we need to treat this traditional conception of philosophy with caution. Questions about how we ought to live, as we have seen in the last chapter, are not a matter for 'experts'; and, though we may have confidence in the advice of trained, clear-headed thinkers of all kinds, it is a mistake to regard the professional philosopher as a person whose job it is to know all the answers to our moral and religious difficulties. Moreover there is danger, if we suppose that the philosopher knows all about different 'realms of existence', of making what I called in Chapter 4 the 'absolute-existence' mistake; in other words, there is danger of supposing that such realms exist side by side, so to speak, as part of the ultimate constituents of the universe. The main outcome of the so-called 'attack on metaphysics', as has already been indicated, is the realization that the notion of 'absolute existence' is unintelligible. It becomes unhelpful, therefore, to think of the philosopher either as a moral teacher or as an informant about special 'realms of existence'.

It does not, of course, follow that moral problems are unimportant or that the question 'How ought I to live?' is unanswerable; but there is at least a possible case for saying that such problems lie outside the scope of philosophy in the strict sense of the word.

[1] Compare Plato, *Republic*, Book I, section 352, where Socrates is made to say 'We are debating no trivial question, but the manner in which a man ought to live.'

One suspects at times that nothing is in dispute here except the question of how widely the word 'philosophy' should be used. If moral assertions are not to be included as part of philosophy, then the branch of study to which they belong can simply be given some other label; there seems no need to quarrel over words.

There is a complication, however, in that the word 'philosophy' has strong persuasive force. To argue that a certain procedure 'isn't really philosophy' is in effect to condemn. Discussions on what is or is not philosophy are thus more heated than they would be if it was simply a matter of how the word 'philosophy' should be used. On the one hand people have wished to condemn what present-day philosophers are doing as trivial. On the other hand, the people engaged in such activity would no doubt reply that their investigations are fascinating, at any rate for those with a bent in that direction. If anything is to be condemned, on their view, it is the pseudo-philosopher who makes sweeping generalizations about the world's evils and then advocates sweeping remedies. It is this procedure, they would argue, which 'isn't real philosophy'. There seems a basic disagreement here on what is worth while.

There is no need, however, to be drawn into this dispute. As far as the verbal point is concerned, we could perhaps distinguish between 'technical philosophy', which limits itself to these technical second-order investigations, and philosophy in some wider sense. As for the basic disagreement, it seems rather futile to say that technical philosophy is just not worth while or that those who do it 'ought to be doing something else'. On the other hand, no one has any right to disparage the efforts of moralists, preachers, and social reformers just because their assertions do not constitute 'philosophy' in the technical sense.

Even if we agree, however, to use the word 'philosophy' only in a narrow technical sense, it is still not easy to give a straightforward account of what philosophy is about. Perhaps it may be helpful to say that one of the main concerns of the philosopher is with *epistemology* or *theory of knowledge*. The question par excellence which he asks is, 'How do we *know*?' Thus '$8 \times 8 = 64$' is not known in the same way as 'There is a cat in the cupboard' and neither are known in the same way as 'Men ought to love their enemies'.

An important advantage of saying that philosophy is concerned with theory of knowledge is that this formula supplies a much-needed link between traditional and modern philosophy. The question 'How do we know?' is certainly one which has been central in the thought of most of the great philosophers of the past. Thus Plato was in effect pointing out that the truths of mathematics are not known in the same way as the truths of common-sense observation;[1] Descartes discusses the sort of knowledge we can have of ourselves, God, and the external world,[2] and Kant makes clear that truths about God, freedom, and immortality are not known in the same way as the truths of Euclidean geometry and Newtonian physics.[3] Moreover to say that philosophy is concerned with theory of knowledge would be acceptable also to a modern philosopher, for it is a formula which makes explicit the second-order character of philosophical investigation. The questions 'How do we know this?' and 'What arguments can be used in support of it?' are appropriate only when someone has already made a first-order assertion.

Traditionally it has been supposed that the philosopher takes, as it were, a bird's-eye view of a large range of territory, in contrast with the specialist—say a scientist or mathematician—who covers a small area in great detail. We can now work out how far such a picture is informative and how far misleading. It is misleading in that it suggests separate 'worlds', as though the 'world' of mathematics, the 'world' of common-sense, and the 'world' of values all existed in some 'absolute' sense. It is helpful, on the other hand, in that it serves to bring out that the philosopher is not a specialist in the same way that the mathematician or the scientist are specialists. The philosopher does not limit himself to a few different types of assertion; he is interested in everything that people say, whether they say them at home, in the laboratory, in church, at an art gallery, or anywhere else. The idea of a 'bird's-eye view' stresses the comprehensive nature of philosophical investigation.

Various other suggestions have been made in recent years on the rôle of philosophy. For example it has been compared to psycho-therapy. A philosophical worry such as 'Can I really know if anything exists except myself?' is on this view comparable to a neurotic worry; it requires to be 'treated', rather than answered with an unambiguous 'Yes' or 'No'.[4] Wittgenstein is reported to have suggested that his purpose was to 'dissolve' philosophical problems rather than solve

[1] See e.g. *Republic*, Book VII, sections 529–30, and *Phaedo*, section 64, c.
[2] See e.g. his *Discourse on Method* and *Meditations*.
[3] See *Critique of Pure Reason*, Introduction, section III.
[4] Compare John Wisdom, *Philosophy and Psycho-Analysis* (Blackwell, 1953), pp. 169–81. B. A. Farrell (*Mind*, Volume LV, no. 217, for April 1946) speaks of 'therapeutic positivism'.

them.[1] No doubt many have found this remark illuminating; but such *obiter dicta* should not be regarded as more than suggestive. All sorts of parallels may illuminate the philosopher's activity, but no one formula should be regarded as the last word on the subject.

The emphasis on 'theory of knowledge' will be retained throughout this book. In Part II I shall be concerned largely with the claims of science, in Part III largely with the claims of religion. In both sections alike, however, and whatever the particular assertion which is being examined, I shall be continually returning to the fundamental questions 'How do we know this?' and 'What arguments are relevant to establishing its truth or falsity?'

[1] See *Mind*, Volume LXI, no. 242, for April 1952, p. 259.

# PART TWO

PART TWO

# CHAPTER 8

## *Materialism*

In popular belief the issue of materialism used to be regarded as a focal point in the conflict between 'science' and 'religion'. The physical scientist has frequently been thought of as a tough-minded individual who insists that materialism is true, in contrast with the tender-minded religious person who believes that it is false. In the last few decades this type of controversy has tended to die down, but one's impression is that of an uneasy armistice rather than of a final resolution of the conflict.

The chief meaning of the word 'materialism', according to the *Oxford English Dictionary*, is 'the opinion that nothing exists except matter and its movements and modifications'. If these words are interpreted literally, it seems clear that their purport is to give us information about the nature of the universe. What they are telling us, in effect, is that there might have been more than one sort of entity in the universe, but in fact there is only one sort, viz. matter.

I shall argue in the first part of the present chapter that this literal version of materialism is neither true nor false but meaningless. Later I shall discuss two other versions of materialism, both related to the literal one, but requiring to be distinguished from it. I shall suggest that neither of these two versions is meaningless, but that neither presents the religious believer with any serious problem.

I

The argument in Chapter 4 will have made clear how, in my opinion, the claims of a literal materialism should be treated. They are claims about what 'exists' in the 'absolute' sense of exist, and require, therefore, to be rejected as meaningless. Counter-claims of an anti-materialist kind are meaningless also.

To make this rejection more convincing, however, let us examine the materialist thesis further by applying the verification principle. 'Nothing exists except matter' certainly looks as though it is intended to be a factually significant assertion; and in that case we must assume it to be verifiable or falsifiable by the methods of common-sense or scientific observation. We should therefore be prepared to form an opinion on the basis of existing evidence, and alter it if future evidence points to a different conclusion.

Now an unreflecting materialist might be quite willing to discuss the question in these terms. There are plenty of observations, he would say, which go to support the belief that materialism is true. Wherever we go, we see solid tangible objects—trees and gate-posts, houses and motor-cars. 'Matter' is commonly understood to comprise solid stuff of this sort, and the evidence shows that this is the stuff which goes to make up the world.

Now the commonly accepted way of attacking this version of materialism is to make counter-claims. It might be argued, for instance, that God, the soul, and values all have an independent existence, and that matter is therefore not the only reality.[1] This procedure, however, is bound to end in deadlock, with neither side able to convince the other; and though we may respect the motives of those who make these counter-claims, we are forced to conclude that their method is mistaken. The correct procedure is not to make counter-claims but to raise with the materialist the problem of falsifiability.

His argument, as we have just formulated it, is that we meet plenty of trees and gate-posts, but that we never meet non-material objects. This sounds comparable to, 'I've met plenty of sea-gulls but no dragons'; and just as we infer, after sufficient investigation, that there are no such things as dragons, so, it seems, we are invited to infer that there are no non-material objects. The difficulty, however, is this. In the case of dragons we at least know what we are supposed to be looking for. We know exactly what it would be like to meet one, even though

---

[1] C. E. M. Joad, in *Philosophical Aspects of Modern Science* (Allen & Unwin, 1932), p. 259, writes: 'I hold that the universe contains at least three different orders or realms of being. There are the material constituents of which the physical world is composed . . .; there are the minds which are aware of them; and there is a third order' (of changeless objects). He speaks on p. 260 of 'the realm of changeless and eternal objects, truth, goodness, beauty, and, it may be, deity, which are neither mental nor material.' C. S. Lewis in *Miracles* (Geoffrey Bles, 1947) argues for the existence of 'Reason'—an entity which 'is not inter-locked with the great interlocking system of irrational events which we call Nature' (p. 33).

none of us has ever done so. But do we know in a comparable way what it would be like to meet a non-material object? Let us for the moment put aside the examples of 'God' and 'the soul', since they are too controversial to be discussed briefly. Let us suppose that the materialist is challenged over the two examples, 'thoughts' and 'beauty'. Now he need not deny that people think. His reply can simply be that what is really happening is a series of physico-chemical changes in the brain. In the same way he need not deny that e.g. pictures or pieces of music are beautiful; all that he need deny is that beauty has a 'real existence' independently of the physico-chemical composition of the picture, or independently of the sound waves that occur when the piece of music is played. Yet if the materialist makes a reply along such lines his stock one, if, *whatever* instances are offered, his rejoinder is always 'But that is something material too', his original claim that 'Nothing exists except matter' loses its point. It is irrefutable, certainly, but it has been made irrefutable at the cost of being meaningless. The crucial objection to this version of materialism is that it ignores the need for falsifiability.

To illustrate the point further, here is a fable. Let us suppose that a young sailor, whom we will call Sinbad, had been born at sea, and had lived all his life on one particular ship without ever having come near land. One day he heard the captain of the ship using the word 'shore'. On being told what this word meant, Sinbad shook his head in a puzzled way, and said 'Nothing exists except sea'. Now the captain was a person who did not like ignorance to go unchecked, and he was seriously worried about the limitations of Sinbad's viewpoint. 'Sea is not the only thing that exists,' he said. 'There is shore as well. It is a wonderful place full of excitement; indeed there are things to do on shore far more exciting than the things you do in your humdrum life on the ship. I quite appreciate that this may sound strange to you, since you have had no experience of the shore. But do not be narrow-minded. Have faith, and believe in something for which, here and now, there is no direct evidence.'

I have deliberately given the captain's words a special flavour of a quasi-religious kind. Similar language is frequently used by religious apologists in attacking materialism. The materialist, it seems, is like Sinbad in that he has *left something out*—something allegedly very important. Inspection shows, however, that the dispute between Sinbad and the captain is totally unlike the dispute between the materialist and his opponent. 'Nothing exists except matter' is grammatically similar to 'Nothing exists except sea', just as it is grammatically similar to 'Nothing exists except flowers' or 'Nothing exists except snow'. But it is different from all three in a way in which they are not different from each other. Simple observation tells us that there are things other than sea, that there are things other than flowers, that there are things other than snow. 'Nothing exists except sea' is falsifiable. The way to falsify it is to discover some land. Confronted with land, Sinbad would agree that 'Nothing exists except sea' was mistaken. Sinbad and the captain are, so to speak, playing the game according to the same rules; the method of resolving their disagreement is not in question. In contrast, the rules for determining the truth of 'Nothing exists except matter' seem altogether uncertain. In the case of the materialist and his opponent there is the same information available to both. Both know what it is like to think; both can look at pictures and listen to music; both, if they take the trouble, can learn what is known about the human brain and what is known about the production of sound-waves. Confronted with alleged evidence against materialism, the materialist does not say, 'Yes, I realize I was wrong', but refuses to accept it as valid evidence. 'Nothing exists except sea' is falsifiable empirically; 'Nothing exists except matter' is not.

It may be objected that, in this section, I have been attacking a man of straw, since no one nowadays holds such a crude version of materialism as the one which I have outlined. I agree that the tough-minded scientific materialist is a figure of the past; but I would suggest that there are still plenty of people who are ready to assimilate 'Nothing exists except matter' to 'Nothing exists except sea', and this is the mistake which I have been attempting to rectify. 'Nothing exists except matter', if interpreted in this literal way, requires to be exposed as meaningless, not to be contradicted by an equally unjustified counter-assertion.

2

It would be a mistake, however, to regard what has been said as the last word on the subject of materialism. We noted in Chapters 3 and 4 how, time after time, apparently meaningless questions re-emerged as questions of a rather different sort. Thus 'What is the nature of the Self?' re-emerged as a request for discussion of sentences containing the word 'I'. In what follows I shall try to show that the problem of materialism re-emerges in a similar way. The question at issue is that of evaluating the language of traditional physics.

'A symphony or a sunset', so the materialist might say, 'is really nothing but a collection of particles of matter in motion.' This is in effect to say that the physical scientist's account of symphonies and sunsets is the only true one, that it is the physical scientist who tells us about 'what really exists'. 'What really exists' requires in this context to be interpreted, not in the 'absolute' sense, but as a means of evaluation. Materialism, in this version, is in effect *a commendation of the world-picture of traditional physics*. In what follows I shall refer to this world-picture as 'the model of the enclosed billiard-table'.

The word 'model' has been somewhat overworked in recent philosophy, and requires explanation. The suggestion is that, in talking about some state of affairs, we can helpfully introduce a 'model'—that is, some sort of picture or likeness, something which we hope resembles our original in an important way. If the model is a good one, we gain useful insight, since what holds of the model may also hold of the original. If the model is a bad one, it may generate strange puzzles and perplexities. For example, it may be helpful, in thinking of the central nervous system, to use the model of an elaborate network of telephone lines. This model is to a large extent helpful, since the existence of a telephone implies the possibility of messages, and we are thus encouraged to look for something analogous to messages passing through the central nervous system. The model is also misleading since it encourages people to hope that one day they will find a mysterious telephone-operator. Puzzles of this sort require to be disposed of by making explicit the ways in which the model is misleading.

Traditional physics, then, can helpfully be thought of as using the model of an enclosed billiard-table. By 'traditional' physics I have in mind the work of Newton and his successors down to the end of the nineteenth century. I am not suggesting that any one person explicitly accepted all that the model involves, but there can be no doubt that the general 'world-picture' which this model gives us has been extremely influential.

The billiard balls are, of course, the atoms of physical theory, the 'little bodies'[1] of John Locke, his 'minute and insensible parts'.[2] These were thought of as existing in space and time, as having position and

---

[1] See e.g. *An Essay Concerning Human Understanding*, Book II, chapter XXIII, section 26.

[2] Locke, *op. cit.*, Book IV, chapter III, section 11.

motion, but as being without colour, smell, and warmth.[1] The total amount of energy within the enclosed system was assumed to remain constant, and no movement was possible except as a result of previous movement.[2] Finally, it was taken for granted that there were no jumps in nature[3]—a principle which excluded the possibility of action at a distance.[4]

The analogy with the game of billiards must not be pressed too far. In particular we need to remember that, in a game of billiards, there are human beings who set the billiard balls in motion, whereas in a model it is presupposed that there can be no interference from outside. It is for this reason that we have referred to it as an *enclosed* billiard-table— enclosed, so it may be helpful to imagine, in a glass case, with no possibility of interference from outside. Better still, we should think of a system of solid bodies which does not have an 'outside' at all.

When it is said that whatever exists must exist in space and time, that the total amount of energy remains constant, and that there can be no action at a distance, we must not think of these assertions as empirical hypotheses to be tested by experiment. As such, they would be un-falsifiable and therefore meaningless. They should be thought of rather as principles inherent in the model, as assertions whose truth is guaranteed from the very nature of the model which we are using. Their contradictory is regarded not as false but as 'inconceivable'.[5] If action appears to have taken place at a distance, we are required to assume that there *must have been* some intervening medium; if an object appears to

[1] Colour, smell, and warmth were known as 'secondary' qualities. For a discussion of the difference between 'primary' and 'secondary' qualities, see the above passage in Locke, and Berkeley, *Principles of Human Knowledge*, section X, and *First Dialogue between Hylas and Philonous*.

[2] Compare Kant, *Critique of Pure Reason*, First and Second Analogy. Much of the early part of the *Critique of Pure Reason* is a working out of what the model of the enclosed billiard-table involves. For a more recent discussion of similar problems, and for an expression of views rather different from those of Kant, see W. T. Stace, 'The Parmenidean Dogma' (*Philosophy*, Volume XXIV, no. 90, July 1949). By 'the Parmenidean dogma' Professor Stace means the view that 'something cannot come out of nothing'—a view which is, of course, an integral part of what I have called 'the model of the enclosed billiard-table'.

[3] Compare Kant, *Critique of Pure Reason*, Third Postulate.

[4] The fact that gravity acts at a distance might seem an insuperable objection to this principle. Yet it is a principle which even Newton found it difficult to reject. In a letter to W. Bentley he writes: 'It is inconceivable that inanimate brute matter should without the mediation of something else which is not material operate and affect other matter without mutual contact.' (Published in *Works of W. Bentley*, ed. A. Dyer (1838), III, p. 221.) Newton was not a materialist in our first sense of the word; he did not subscribe to the view that 'Nothing exists except matter'.

[5] Compare Newton's letter to Bentley, quoted above.

have vanished, we are required to assume that the particles making up that object *must have gone somewhere*. There is no question, if we are using the model at all, of discounting the principles that are inherent in the model, and no question of arguing on empirical grounds that such principles are mistaken.

If it is assumed that there can be no movement except as a result of previous movement, it would seem to follow that everything that happens must be causally determined. In that case there is no possible room either for acts of free choice on the part of human beings, or for acts of intervention, in the form of miracles, by God. The materialist claim, according to this version of materialism, is not that there is *no* God and *no* such thing as the soul; it is that the words 'God' and 'soul' cannot be regarded as the names of causal agencies. It is not that the materialist has looked for a God and cannot find one; it is not that he has failed to discover the soul. It is rather that he knows beforehand that neither the word 'God' nor the word 'soul' will serve his purposes. They explain nothing, and can play no part in his general system.

Moreover it makes no sense to argue that there must have been a 'first' cause, lying outside the system, and not itself caused by anything else. This form of reasoning constitutes one version of the so-called 'cosmological' argument for the existence of God. But the inference to God as first cause is invalid. The principle that every event must have a cause holds only when we are explaining the movement of one billiard ball in terms of the movement of others. There can be no question of arguing for the existence of a causal agency lying outside the whole system.[1]

If by 'materialism', then, we mean an attitude which takes seriously the model of the enclosed billiard-table, then no simple answer can be given as to whether materialism is true or false. On the one hand it can be pointed out that relativity theory and the growth of quantum physics have led to a gradual abandonment of the model of the enclosed billiard-table,[2] and that, quite apart from the revolution in modern physics, the model has obvious limitations if we apply it to simple electrical phenomena or to some of the intricacies of human and animal behaviour. On the other hand it cannot be denied that the model has

---

[1] Compare Kant, *Critique of Pure Reason*, Transcendental Dialectic, Of the Impossibility of a Cosmological Proof of the Existence of God.

[2] A billiard ball must be in a particular place at a particular time, and to reach a new place it must traverse the intervening distance. Physicists, however, want to say that this is not necessarily true of an electron.

had an enormous influence on the history of thought and has contributed in an outstanding way to the progress of science. No final verdict is possible. Models of this sort are not normally shown to be true or false by crucial experiments; it is rather that they work well or badly for particular purposes, and when they work badly they gradually fall into disuse.

Even, however, if we are unhesitating in our commendation of the model, there is no question of any resultant threat to any important religious belief. There is admittedly an apparent difficulty in that, if we take the model seriously, we must insist that the word 'God' cannot legitimately be introduced as the name of a causal explanation such as would advance scientific knowledge; but this difficulty does not constitute a genuine threat, since, as we shall argue in Part III of this book, sentences containing the word 'God' cannot normally be regarded as quasi-scientific explanations of empirically discovered events. In general it is true to say that a decision on whether or not to accept the model of the enclosed billiard-table is a decision for the scientist. If he finds the model helpful he is entitled to use it; if developments in modern physics or elsewhere make it untenable he is entitled to reject it. To choose or reject a particular model for scientific purposes, however, does not commit us in any way to taking sides on a religious issue.

3

It remains to consider a third sense of the word 'materialism'—the sense in which we might say that a person has a very materialistic outlook or is very materialistically inclined. The suggestion here is that the person attaches particular importance to so-called 'material' goods, to such things as food, clothes, and houses, rather than to such things as religious and aesthetic experience or the pursuit of knowledge for its own sake. Since such a set of values is widely believed to be mistaken, 'materialism' in this sense frequently figures as a term of abuse.

The relationship to our second sense of 'materialism'—in which 'materialism' stood for an attitude of commendation towards the model of the enclosed billiard-table—is not entirely straightforward, but there is certainly a link. If we assume not merely that the model of the enclosed billiard-table is a good and valuable way of looking at the world, but also that it is the one and only correct way of doing so, then the language of the mystic, the poet, or the art critic must be regarded as having an inferior status. As an example let us take the following account of Beethoven's Choral Symphony. 'In the first movement . . .', writes Tovey, 'an already long and spacious development has settled down to a quiet conversation which shows no sign that anything will disturb its gentle pathos, until quite suddenly the heavens are on fire and the foundations of the earth are shaken.'[1] Such language, according to this view, is inferior compared with an account of the Choral Symphony in terms of sound waves and their amplitudes and frequencies; to be concerned with the beauty of the Choral Symphony as a piece of music is to waste our time with unrealities. There is thus a link between the materialism which carries commendation of the model of the enclosed billiard-table to extremes and the materialism which regards 'material' goods—food, clothes, and houses—as more important than appreciation of beauty.

There is nothing, however, in the 'scientific outlook' to compel us to adopt values of this sort. Few, if any, of the great scientists were materialists in this third sense. A pure scientist need not be concerned with material well-being at all, and even an applied scientist is not committed to holding that material well-being is the only important thing in life. For all of us the matter is one of personal decision; the issue is a moral one rather than a factual one. As we saw in Chapter 6, factual discoveries may influence our moral decisions, but they cannot demonstrate conclusively that a particular set of values is the right one. The scientist who professes to reject materialism in this third sense of the word is guilty neither of inconsistency nor of self-deception.

To sum up. If 'materialism' is understood to be belief in the literal truth of 'Nothing exists except matter', then materialism is a meaningless theory and can make no demands on our allegiance. If 'materialism' is understood as an attitude of commendation towards the model of the enclosed billiard-table, then there are good grounds for taking materialism seriously. There can, however, be no possible conflict with any assertion made in the name of religion, so long as such assertions are not pieces of would-be science. Finally, if 'materialism' is understood to mean the view that only 'material' well-being is important, i.e. such things as food, clothes, and houses, then there is nothing in the 'scientific outlook' which compels us to be materialists.

[1] D. S. Tovey, *Beethoven* (Oxford, 1944), p. 103.

# CHAPTER 9

*Behaviourism*

Our next task is to consider the influence of materialistic ways of thinking on attempts to understand human personality. It has traditionally been assumed that human beings possess or comprise two things, a mind and a body. Our bodies are solid, spatial, and material; our minds are none of these things. There are various sciences—such as physics, chemistry, and biology—which are concerned with body or matter, and there is a science, psychology, which is concerned with the mind.

Even psychology, however, can be studied from a materialist viewpoint. The outcome of the materialist approach to psychology is the system known as 'behaviourism'. A 'behaviourist', in the commonly accepted sense, is one who denies the existence of mind or consciousness. On this view the subject-matter of psychology is not mind but behaviour.

Behaviourism appears at first sight to be an anti-religious creed. Religion, so it might be supposed, is interested in the mind and, more especially, in the soul. If we can assert, with the authority of science behind us, that there is no such thing as mind or soul, then the claims of religion about the soul would seem to be discredited. The only crumb of comfort for a religious person is, on this showing, that not all psychologists profess to be behaviourists.

I shall try to show in this chapter that a literal behaviourism is open to the same objections as a literal materialism, and that, in professing to believe in either, we are making the 'absolute-existence' mistake and thus misleading ourselves with words. I shall then suggest that the behaviourist position, like the materialist one, can better be understood as the commending of a particular policy. I shall argue, however, that even if this behaviourist policy is fundamentally sound—as I believe it to be if properly formulated—there is no justification for using behaviourism as a weapon with which to attack religious beliefs. It follows, of course, that fears on the part of religious people that behaviourism is a threat to religious belief are unjustified.

The person who first coined the label 'behaviourism' was the American psychologist, J. B. Watson.[1] I shall not attempt in this chapter to examine Watson's arguments in detail, nor indeed the arguments of any one thinker. Instead, I shall try to set out what, in my opinion, a behaviourist could say or might say, irrespective of whether anyone has actually said it.

I

Let us start by assuming that the words 'There are no such things as minds' are to be given a simple, literal interpretation. Understood in this way they constitute a claim about what does and does not exist. The implied suggestion is that there might be such things as minds but that in fact there are not.

It has been argued in Chapter 8 that 'Nothing exists except matter', if interpreted literally, is a meaningless form of words. Exactly the same objection holds of 'There are no such things as minds'.

Once again let us apply the verification principle, and ask ourselves how anyone would settle whether there are or are not such things as minds. We see at once that disagreement over this matter is not like disagreement over e.g. whether there are living beings on Mars. This latter question can be settled by evidence, and if there is any doubt on the matter it is because the evidence is insufficient. But if we ask whether there are such things as minds, there is no question of our having insufficient evidence; the point is rather that no indication seems possible even of what would count as valid evidence. The difficulty with 'There are no such things as minds' is not whether it is true or false, but what constitutes its 'cash-value'. If no 'cash-value' can be indicated (as is inevitable if the words are understood at their face-value), then there can never be more than futile assertion and counter-assertion, with no

---

[1] See his *Psychology from the Standpoint of a Behaviourist* (Philadelphia, 1919) and his *Behaviourism*, (Kegan Paul, 1925). Chapter 1 of the latter shows obvious hostility to traditional religion, but the grounds for this hostility are not made at all clear. In suggesting (p. 17) that there should be a 'behaviourist ethics', Watson has failed to realize that moral assertions are not deducible from empirical assertions. (Compare p. 57 of this book.) Since on his own showing psychology must concern itself with what is empirically testable, any moral (or, as he would say, 'ethical') assertion must lie outside the scope of psychology.

final solution and no means of obtaining one. From the arguments in Part I it will be clear that to discuss in these terms whether there are or are not such things as minds is to discuss a meaningless question.

The behaviourist position, however, like the materialist, requires to be reformulated. Unless we wish to set up a man of straw, in order to give ourselves the satisfaction of 'proving behaviourism wrong', there is no point in interpreting the word 'behaviourism' as belief in the literal truth of 'There are no such things as minds'. It is preferable to use the label to refer to views which at least require to be taken seriously; only so can we be sure that we have put the case for behaviourism at its strongest.

2

The best way to interpret the label 'behaviourism' is as a commendation of certain policies. What we need to consider next, therefore, is the question of what policies the label 'behaviourism' serves to commend.

There is no one answer to this question. In general, the behaviourist is commonly thought of as a person who likes to approach psychology from the physiological side. He would rather, for instance, measure the rate of your heart-beat than listen to what you tell him about your feelings of fear. Reports on how a person feels, how things look or sound to him, or what steps he took to solve a problem are known as 'introspections'; and part of what is commonly understood by the word 'behaviourism' is the belief that it is bad policy in psychology to rely on people's introspections. Valid scientific findings, it might be claimed, should be expressed in measurable terms, and they should be something which any observer can check. If you introspect, there is no public check on the information which you give, and you cannot express the amount of your fears etc. in measurable terms. The behaviourist is in effect demanding that psychology should imitate where possible the methods of chemistry and physics and present its findings quantitatively.

Another part of behaviourist policy is its characteristic approach to the problem of learning. At the start of the present century (some years before the word 'behaviourism' was coined) the Russian investigator Pavlov had studied the phenomenon of salivation in dogs.[1] He had discovered that if a buzzer was sounded just before a dog was given food, the dog came in time to salivate at the sound the buzzer, before

[1] See I. P. Pavlov, *Conditioned Reflexes* (Oxford, 1927).

the food actually appeared. The process of training the dog in this way came to be known as 'conditioning', and the resultant response (in this case salivation at the buzzer, instead of the food) has commonly been called a 'conditioned reflex'. One characteristic of behaviourism is the belief that all learning can best be understood as a process of conditioning, and that the Pavlov type of investigation is the best or only possible way of investigating learning.

These matters, however, are simply issues of practical policy. They cannot be regarded as having any significance for religion. Not all psychologists look upon the method of introspection as necessarily undesirable; and, to add to the complications, some self-professed behaviourists might be willing to re-admit introspection by the back-door, labelling it 'verbal behaviour'.[1] In addition there is a good case for supposing that concepts other than that of the conditioned reflex are helpful to our understanding of the learning process. We know, for instance, from psycho-analysis, that the relationship of the person learning to his teacher is an all-important factor in the situation. But there is nothing in behaviourist policies, as we have described them so far, which would commit us to abandoning any particular set of religious beliefs. The problems which we have considered concern the psychologist only; the question at issue is how best to do psychology.

In examining the relevance of behaviourism to religion, what we need to consider is a special version of behaviourism, the chief characteristic of which is the refusal to use the word 'mind' as though it was a 'thing'-word.[2] This version of behaviourism will now be explained.

To treat the word 'mind' as a 'thing'-word is what Professor Ryle has called a 'category-mistake'.[3] The whole subject of classifying words into 'categories' and determining what constitutes a 'category-mistake' is difficult and raises problems; but the main point can perhaps be illustrated as follows. The word 'if' is clearly not a 'thing'-word, and it would therefore be a category-mistake to speak in the same breath of 'a body and an if'. The words 'body' and 'if' belong to different logical categories. In the same way, 'hope' is not a 'thing'-word, and it is therefore a sort of category-mistake to say, as Lewis Carroll does in

[1] J. B. Watson writes: '*Saying* is doing—that is *behaving*. Speaking . . . is just as objective a type of behaviour as baseball'. *Behaviourism* (1925), p. 6.

[2] For a discussion of what is meant by a 'thing'-word, see pp. 41–2.

[3] See G. Ryle, *The Concept of Mind* (Hutchinson, 1949), chapter 1. The views which follow are not intended as an exact reproduction of those expressed by Ryle, but anyone familiar with *The Concept of Mind* will appreciate how much I owe to him.

*The Hunting of the Snark*, 'They pursued it with forks and hope.' The word 'mistake' should, of course, not be pressed. Such talk is quite harmless as a witticism, and it is part of the greatness of Lewis Carroll that he deliberately made category-'mistakes' for the fun of it. Similarly it is a delightful touch by P. G. Wodehouse when he speaks of 'a police-man with nothing on his mind but his helmet'.[1] But people have wanted in all seriousness to speak of 'minds and bodies' in the same breath. The behaviourist contention is that this way of talking is misleading and gives rise to unnecessary problems.

Recently a man whom I met in the train started to tell me about his smoking habits. 'When I am away from home,' he said, 'my pipe never enters my mind, let alone my mouth.' On Professor Ryle's view this again would constitute a category-mistake. Here it makes good sense to ask 'Which side of your mouth do you normally have your pipe?', but it would make no sense to ask 'Which side of your mind do thoughts normally come in?'

If the word 'mind' is regarded as a 'thing'-word, it must refer, presumably, to some recondite ghost-like 'thing'. Professor Ryle speaks of 'the dogma of the ghost-in-the-machine'.[2] This witticism should not be taken too seriously, but it effectively serves to challenge our un-critical ways of thinking about human personality. If the word 'mind' stood for some recondite, ghost-like object occupying and controlling the body, then minds, if they existed at all, would be altogether mysteri-ous entities, unknown and unknowable. More strictly, sentences purporting to give information about people's minds would be 'uncashable' and therefore meaningless. These were precisely the grounds on which, earlier in this chapter, it was argued that, on a literal interpretation, it was equally meaningless both to assert and to deny the existence of minds. But it is clear, according to this new version of behaviourism, that in fact we frequently do discuss people's minds and mental processes. We describe people as 'intelligent', 'alert', or 'quick-witted', for instance; and we know how to correct our assessments. We study people's hopes, fears, and aspirations; if we are psychologists we study their dreams and day-dreams. We do all this, however, not by peering at some recondite ghost living inside their bodily machinery, but by studying the ways in which they behave. In general, sentences which contain the word 'mind' or refer to mental powers or qualities

---

[1] *The Code of the Woosters* (Herbert Jenkins), p. 89.
[2] *The Concept of Mind* (1949), p. 15.

require to be translated into sentences about behaviour. Only so can appropriate 'cash-value' be given to them.

There are many types of sentence in which this behaviourist principle works with no difficulty. Thus 'He has an astute mind' and 'His mind was wandering' are clearly sentences which require to be 'cashed' in terms of behaviour. The function of such sentences is not to refer to ghostly happenings in a ghostly world, but to refer in a special way to familiar happenings. There are many ways of telling if a person has an astute mind, for instance—ability to make appropriate remarks in a discussion, ability to solve difficult problems, and so on. 'X has an astute mind' tells us what sort of behaviour to expect from X in these and similar circumstances. Moreover the behaviourist is undoubtedly right in insisting that the word 'mind' cannot legitimately be brought in when we are at a loss for alternative explanations. Thus it is no answer to the question, 'Why did he suddenly remember the message at that moment?' to say that *his mind* enabled him to do so. To bring in the word 'mind' in such a context would be vacuous and uninformative.

It may still be objected that the behaviourist case is hopeless from the start, since it takes no account of sensations and images, and no account of thinking. It is an undoubted fact, it would be said, that people have sensations and experiences which they recognize as in some way 'internal' or 'private'—feelings of tooth-ache, for instance, or awareness of tickles. Again many people have vivid mental imagery; they can form what we call 'pictures in the mind's eye', and can call up auditory, tactual, and other sorts of image.[1] These images are undoubtedly recognized as 'internal' in contrast with such things as houses and trees which we recognize as 'external'. Similarly thought, which involves operation with verbal and other images, can correctly be considered as an 'inner' process. It does not seem unreasonable, therefore, to regard tooth-ache, tickles, and mental images as something 'ghostly', in the sense of having a position in space but not being accessible to the sense of touch.

This objection can be strengthened by an appeal to recent neurological findings. Clinical investigation suggests that our awareness of the space occupied by our own bodies—awareness, that is, of our body-image or 'body-schema', as it has been called[2]—is far more complicated than is commonly realized. It has been found that patients with brain lesions

[1] See Francis Galton, *Inquiries into Human Faculty* (first published 1883).
[2] The term 'body-schema' was invented by Sir Henry Head. See his *Studies in Neurology* (London, 1920), II, pp. 605-8 and 722-6.

are sometimes unable to recognize parts of their body as 'belonging', while it frequently happens that those who have had limbs amputated feel so-called 'phantom-limbs' in the space that was occupied by the missing member. In both cases the patient receives a faulty impression of the space which his actual (tangible) body is occupying. These findings serve to bring out that, so long as the brain is intact, we are aware of what, by analogy with phantom-limbs, may be called the 'phantom-body'.[1] We are aware privately, so to speak, and from within, of our body-image, and are not dependent, like an outside observer, on using the visual and tactile cues which relate to our actual tangible body. We are aware, in other words, of 'ourselves' independently of our tangible body; and it would seem therefore that to speak as though there were something 'ghostly' inside this body is not just the misguided blunder that the words 'ghost-in-the machine' suggest.

This whole argument, however, does not weaken the case for behaviourism in the version which is now being put forward. We need not dispute that it feels as if there is something 'ghostly' inside us. Still less need we dispute that people have tooth-ache and tickles, or that they have mental images and think. The point is rather that assertions such as 'I have tooth-ache', 'My imagery is very clear and distinct', or 'This feels strange' are in many ways quite different from empirically verifiable assertions such as 'There is a cat in the cupboard'. We touched on this problem in Chapter 3;[2] but it now requires to be discussed in more detail. We can tell if someone else has tooth-ache by studying his behaviour—by seeing if he goes about groaning and holding his jaw, and in particular by observing what he says when we ask him if he has tooth-ache; but there are no comparable tests in the case of ourselves. Indeed it is doubtful if it even makes sense to say 'I'm not sure if I've tooth-ache, but I'll go and apply a few tests to find out'. To suggest that we discover if we ourselves have tooth-ache only when we find ourselves telephoning to our dentist is clearly grotesque. Even in the case of other people, it cannot be said that the 'cash-value' of 'X has tooth-ache' is identical with the 'cash-value' of 'X is holding his jaw, X is announcing that he has tooth-ache' or any combination of such assertions. The behaviourist need not dispute this. His reply to the whole objection is that if 'X has tooth-ache' cannot be 'cashed' in terms

---

[1] See J. O. Wisdom, 'The Concept of Phantom-Body' (*Actes du XIème congrès international de philosophie*, Volume VII for 1953).

[2] See p. 26.

of X's behaviour, then it is an assertion whose truth or falsity lies outside the scope of a scientific investigator. He need not take the extreme position of denying that people have tooth-ache. His point is rather that, for practical purposes, 'X has tooth-ache' must either be 'cashed' in terms of behaviour or else means nothing at all.

This point is of considerable importance when laboratory experiments are being described. Let us suppose, for instance, that an investigator rotates a multi-coloured disc in front of his subject, and that, when the rotation has reached a particular speed, the subject reports that the disc looks white. The behaviourist can legitimately insist that the result should be described, not as 'It looked white to the subject' but rather as 'Subject reported, "This looks white".' This description focuses attention on the actual laboratory occurrence, and there is no question of anyone's having to surmise about the 'private' experiences of the subject, since, from the investigator's point of view, those experiences are for ever unknown and unknowable.

We can, of course, on this showing, make inferences from one publicly observable datum to another. Thus from direct examination of a tooth or from X-rays we could infer that the verbal report 'I have tooth-ache' was likely. What the behaviourist is objecting to is an inference to things which are for ever unknowable, as other people's experiences appear to be.[1]

To put the behaviourist's point in a general way one might say that sentences which refer to the immediate experience of the person who utters them (such as 'I have tooth-ache', or 'This looks white') cannot occur in the psychologist's vocabulary unless they occur as a verbal report.

This version of behaviourism clearly cannot be proved wrong by calling attention to the obvious fact that people have immediate experiences such as tooth-ache.

One final argument against behaviourism requires brief mention. 'Psychology' means by derivation 'study of the psyche'—'psyche' being the Greek word commonly translated as 'mind' or 'soul'. It would seem, therefore, that a behaviourist—one who wishes to reformulate sentences containing the words 'mind' and 'soul'—cannot legitimately claim to be studying psychology. To be a behaviourist is apparently to give up psychology altogether.

[1] For a fuller discussion of this type of puzzle, see John Wisdom, *Other Minds* (Blackwell, 1952).

This argument, however, does not prove that psychology (in its normal sense) has no future. At most it would prove that the label 'psychology', since it suggests 'ghost-in-machine' ways of thinking, is inappropriate, and should be abandoned. Against this proposal, however, it could be said that this change of terminology would create more trouble than it was worth. On this view the things which are done in psychological laboratories and clinics are so clearly agreed by long-established usage to constitute 'psychology' that any change of label is unjustified.

Our general conclusion on the behaviourist issue should, I think, be something as follows. The label 'behaviourist' is too imprecise to justify us in saying that all psychologists ought to be behaviourists. On the other hand, provided the word 'behaviourist' is interpreted along the lines suggested, the behaviourist arguments require to be taken seriously, and are not just foolish aberrations.

### 3

So much, then, for the behaviourist case. It remains to consider to what extent, if at all, there is conflict between behaviourism and religion. The conclusion for which I shall argue is that, although in the light of the behaviourist argument some rethinking about human personality is called for, there is no need for any head-on conflict.

In the first place we need to remove the discussion from the crude level in which the question at issue is whether the universe does or does not contain such things as souls. According to this crude view religion teaches us that it does, behaviourism that it does not. Here, certainly, there is conflict, but it is a conflict which need not concern us, since both parties are beating the air over a meaningless question. 'Has man a soul?' does not admit of verification or falsification by observational means, and cannot therefore be the factually significant question which it purports to be.

What is required is a detailed examination of the uses of the word 'soul' in religious contexts. Behaviourism forces upon us the recognition that sentences in religious contexts containing the word 'soul' must not be interpreted as giving factual information. They have a perfectly legitimate function, but this function is of a different kind.

# Behaviourism

'God . . . breathed into his nostrils the breath of life; and man became a living soul'. Such is the biblical account of the creation of man's soul.[1] Now it is certainly possible to take these words in a crude, literal sense. If they are so interpreted, it makes sense to ask, 'When and where did this happen?' It may well be that there are Christians who would be willing to conduct the discussion in these terms, and who would be prepared to assign a particular date and place. In doing so, they might not necessarily commit themselves to accepting the literal truth of the Genesis narrative; they might be willing to say instead that at some stage in his evolution and in some part of the world man acquired a soul. But they would insist that, since that time, whenever a baby is conceived, a new soul is created by God.

This constitutes what may be called a 'para-physical' account of souls. We know to some extent how in the human embryo a particular organ develops such as the brain; and the suggestion seems to be that, besides these 'physical' occurrences there is also a non-physical occurrence, the creation of a non-physical entity, namely the soul, by a non-physical agency, namely God. Whether this 'para-physical' account of the creation of souls has been implicitly accepted by Christian theologians is a debatable question. Some of the official statements are at least suggestive of a 'para-physical' view. Thus we read in *Humani Generis*[2] that the doctrine of evolution is an open question, so long as we confine our speculations 'to the development, from other living matter already in existence, of the human body'. We are then told: '*That souls are immediately created by God* is a view which the Catholic faith imposes on us' (my italics). A contrast seems implied here between the empirical assertion that bodies have (or have not) evolved, and another apparently empirical assertion to the effect that souls were created by God. Bodies, it seems, are 'physical' objects, souls 'para-physical' ones. But it would be unfair to attribute a 'para-physical' view to theologians in general, since the views expressed in *Humani Generis* would not necessarily be accepted as valid by theologians of every denomination, and in any case the passage in question may allow of a different interpretation. My point is simply that wherever language *is* being used in a 'para-physical' way, the outcome is not a true or false assertion, but a meaningless one.

If the purpose of talk about creation of souls were to give empirically

[1] Genesis ii. 7.
[2] Encyclical letter of Pope Pius XII, section 36, 1950.

85

discoverable information, what strange information this would be! We are being asked to believe, apparently, that a totally unknown and unknowable event took place, namely the creation by unknown means of an unknown entity. If this is intended as an empirical hypothesis, it is small wonder that psychologists and physiologists should profess no interest in it.

Once we realize, however, that the purpose of introducing the word 'soul' in a religious context is not (or should not be) to give factual information, the difficulty disappears. Those who say 'Man has a soul' are not saying anything comparable to 'Cows have horns', despite the grammatical similarity between the two sentences. 'Man has a soul' requires rather to be assimilated to 'Men are children of God'. Such language is what I shall call in Chapter 16 'the language of parable'; and more will be said in that chapter on the sort of justification that can be given for accepting or rejecting it. Two points, however, may be made here. In the first place, 'Men are children of God' does not purport to be a literal factual assertion. There is no question of taking a random sample of people and collecting data on their parentage. This being so, there is no need to be disturbed because methods of empirical verification and falsification are lacking. Secondly, an important function of such talk is to safeguard the sanctity of human personality. If human personality is to be taken seriously and if human beings really do matter, it is not altogether foolish to express this by saying that there is a special *part* of the personality which is sacred, namely the soul. It is this sacred part of ourselves which is rewarded when we act well and punished when we act badly. We can perjure it, save it, and lose it. The spatial metaphor of a 'part' of the personality is in many ways inappropriate, and it is, of course, perfectly possible to feel reverence for human beings without believing that there is something ghostly inside them; but if we object to ghost-in-machine terminology in such a context, all that follows is that some alternative terminology is needed. It certainly does not follow that human personality must be regarded as unimportant. Indeed, such a conclusion is quite unwarranted, since 'Sentences containing the words "mind" and "soul" require reformulation' does not entail the falsity of 'All men are children of God' or any parable-language of such kind. It is therefore quite unjustified to accuse the behaviourist of having 'taken away the soul' or of having 'reduced' human beings to 'mere bundles of matter'.

A further argument sometimes made against the view that 'man has a soul' is that based on the existence of self-regulating machines. A machine having the same physico-chemical make-up as the human body, and behaving in all relevant respects like a human being, is perhaps a matter of fantastic speculation rather than a serious likelihood in the near future, but there is no self-contradiction in postulating its existence, no obvious absurdity in supposing that one might be made. Now such a machine, it might be argued, would clearly be able to carry out appropriate responses without the aid of a 'soul'; and it is therefore unnecessary to postulate a soul in the case of human beings either. Even on its own terms this argument does not seem to me fully justified, since, when we cause things to happen, we are aware of the 'phantom-body' or 'body-schema' playing a part;[1] the feeling is of something 'ghostly' inside us. Let us set aside this difficulty, however, and agree that the soul should not be thought of as a recondite entity which 'aids' human beings to carry out bodily movements. (So long as we are considering things from the point of view of an external observer we are, of course, perfectly right to admit this.) Even so there is no question of 'discrediting the soul' in any important sense. If one of the main functions of the word 'soul' is to safeguard the sanctity of human personality, considerations about the possibility of man-like machines do nothing whatever to establish whether or not man has a soul. Human personality is not discredited just because it is misleading (or partly misleading) to think of the human body as inhabited by a recondite 'ghost'.

Thus although it is necessary for the behaviourist to insist that sentences containing the words 'mind' and 'soul' require reformulation if we are to understand them properly, he is in no way committed to advocating that these words should never be used. For purposes of everyday assessment, or even for the more systematic reports on personality made by psychologists, it would be quite appropriate to say, for instance, that a person had an astute mind. To insist that this sentence requires to be 'cashable' in terms of behaviour does not commit us to saying that the 'cash-value' need actually be given on any particular occasion; it is quite enough if the funds are, so to speak, in the bank, and can be produced when necessary. Similarly, when 'mind' and 'soul' are used in religious contexts, we may legitimately insist that paraphrase in terms of the sanctity of human personality should be

---

[1] For an explanation of these terms, see pp. 81–2. Compare also A. Michotte, *La Perception de la Causalité* (Louvain, 1954), p. 211.

possible in principle, but we need not insist that the paraphrase should always be given. Thus when Wordsworth says,

> *Thy friends are exultations, agonies,*
> *And love, and man's unconquerable mind,*[1]

it would no doubt be possible to rewrite these lines in such a way that the word 'mind' was avoided, e.g. by referring to human indomitability under duress; but there is nothing in our argument to suggest that the result would necessarily be an improvement, still less that Wordsworth had no business to express himself in the way that he did. It is an unfair caricature of the behaviourist to suggest that he is a Philistine whose methodological blinkers make him want to exchange fine poetry for mediocre paraphrase.

It might still be said, however, that there is a conflict between behaviourism and religion on the question of immortality. Some forms of religion, according to this claim, require us to believe that the soul survives death and is immortal, whereas the behaviourist, since he does not genuinely believe in the soul at all, cannot therefore believe in its immortality.

It is questionable whether a behaviourist, in our sense, can be correctly described as 'not genuinely believing in the soul'; certainly those who take the behaviourist arguments seriously are not committed to believing that, in a religious context, sentences containing the word 'soul' are always false. But to say this does not remove all possibility of conflict. It is certainly the case that problems connected with life after death have been couched in 'ghost-in-machine' terms. Thus, when Hamlet says,

> *I do not set my life at a pin's fee,*
> *And for my soul, what can it do to that,*
> *Being a thing immortal as itself?*[2]

the soul is being directly compared to a ghost, and the whole effectiveness of the poetry depends on the contrast between what will happen to Hamlet's body and what will happen to his soul. But it does not follow, however great our objection to 'ghost-in-machine' language, that the religious truths which such language attempts to convey are discredited. Just what these truths are is a matter which will be discussed more fully

---

[1] W. Wordsworth, *Poems dedicated to National Independence and Liberty*, Part I, no. viii.

[2] *Hamlet*, Act I, scene 4.

in Chapter 19. Two points only will be made here. The first is that 'Death affects the body but not the soul' cannot simply be assimilated to 'Paralysis affects the limbs but not the heart'; it is comparable rather to the words of the psalmist—'Therefore will we not fear, though the earth be moved: and though the hills be carried into the midst of the sea.'[1] Secondly, we need to remember that many thinkers in the Christian tradition have fought shy of 'ghost-in-machine' terminology; the official doctrine is not 'immortality of the soul' but 'resurrection of the body'. Such a viewpoint, so far from being in conflict with behaviourism, is in full accord with it.

In summary, we may say that the picture of behaviourism as a tough, anti-religious creed is misguided. If the case for behaviourism is put at its best, then behaviourism requires to be taken seriously; but in taking it seriously we are not thereby committed to any views which constitute a threat to religion.

## 4

Finally a few words should be said on the so-called 'mind-body' problem. This problem is usually raised in the form 'What is the relation between mind and body?', and the possible answers are (i) interactionism, the view that mind and body interact, (ii) psycho-physical parallelism, the view that mental and bodily events do not interact, but that for every mental event a physical event runs parallel, and (iii) epiphenomenalism, the view that mental events are 'epiphenomena' (by derivation 'things appearing on the surface') and that only bodily or physical events can be causes.

Now it might be supposed that one stroke of the verification principle can sweep all these theories aside as meaningless. Certainly it would seem that sentences such as 'Mind and body interact' or 'Mind and body do not interact' do not admit of verification or falsification by observational means, and that a controlled laboratory experiment would get us nowhere. We cannot, however, reject all three views as meaningless; it is not as simple as that. The problem, once again, is one of these metaphysical ones which appear at first sight to be meaningless, and yet later re-emerge in a new light. Roughly speaking, these three theories are proposals that we should order our language in particular ways. Here is an example of one of the

[1] Psalm xlvi, v. 2.

problems involved. If we regard feelings of worry and feelings of pain as typically 'mental', the sort of question that can profitably be asked is whether the words 'worry' and 'pain' stand for causal agencies. Interactionism says that they can be regarded as both causes and effects; and an interactionist might defend his thesis by an appeal to ordinary language, where we do in fact say that worry causes indigestion and that pressure on an exposed nerve causes pain. On the other hand, if we insist that nothing can be a cause unless it is a solid body like a billiard ball, then neither 'worry' nor 'pain' can be 'cause'-words. They can only be the effects of what happens in our brain and elsewhere in our bodies. In that case we have shifted from interactionism to epiphe-menalism. The programme of psycho-physical parallelism is rather different. It urges us to look for physical events which run parallel to feelings of pain or worry. For every such feeling, it would be said, there must be its physical accompaniment.

The above is not more than a passing glance at some of the problems at issue, but it serves to make plain that, whatever answers we give, these answers can have no particular religious significance. It is sometimes thought that epiphenomenalism, in assigning some sort of inferior status to mental events, is necessarily opposed to religious ways of thinking. There is no justification for such a view. If we consider once again a typically religious assertion such as 'All men are children of God', we can see at once that its truth or falsity is not in the least influenced by the truth or falsity of '"Pain" is not a "cause"-word'. Where language is being put to such completely different uses, there is no question of conflict; and indeed, if we look in general at the differences of function between the language used in scientific contexts and the language used in religious contexts, we shall be less likely to imagine conflicts where none exist.

# CHAPTER 10

# *Determinism*

By 'determinism' is meant the view that all events are causally determined. Since, however, the words 'causally determined' admit of different possible interpretations, some clarification of terminology is necessary before we proceed to our main discussion.

Since the time of Hume many philosophers and scientists have supposed that 'A is the cause of B' means exactly the same as 'B regularly follows from A in accordance with a law or rule'.[1] Throughout this chapter, however, I shall be using the words 'cause' and 'causally' in their popular, non-Humean sense. In this sense a cause is thought of as something which *produces* its effect or *makes* this effect occur. Events which are causally determined are thus events which are produced or made to happen by some other event. If it is in fact true that all events are causally determined, this must apply to those events which go to make up human actions; and if human actions are causally determined, it follows that none of them can be freely chosen. According to this usage, therefore, belief in determinism and belief in free choice, or free-will, are incompatible.

An exhaustive treatment of the many problems raised by the notions of 'free-will' and 'determinism' would be too long and difficult a task to be attempted here. I shall therefore limit myself to a discussion of those points which are relevant to the main theme of this book.

The central difficulty for many people is this. Acceptance of a 'scientific world-outlook', so it is thought, compels us to be determinists. Religion, on the other hand (or at any rate the Christian religion), lays stress on the notions of sin, atonement, and redemption. Now since it

[1] Compare Hume, *A Treatise on Human Nature*, Part III, and *An Enquiry Concerning Human Understanding*, section VII.

is inappropriate, and, indeed, morally repugnant, to regard a person as a sinner and in need of redemption if his actions are not freely chosen, it is necessary to insist on religious grounds that man has free-will. There thus appears to be a basic conflict between 'science' and 'religion' on this issue; and, on the assumption that the methods of science have a validity which cannot be called in question, it would seem that the only honest course is to side with 'science'.

This conflict can to a large extent be resolved if we make explicit just what the demands of 'science' really are. I shall try to show in this chapter that acceptance of such demands does not commit us to abandoning any religious beliefs of importance. I agree that a modification of our more self-righteous attitudes towards sin and moral shortcoming is called for; but there are insufficient grounds, in my opinion, for saying that the problem of free-will presents an insuperable difficulty to a religious person.

In Section 1 of this chapter I shall examine the argument against free-will based on the principle that every event must have a cause. In Section 2 I shall discuss the argument that where there is predictability there cannot be free-will. In Section 3 I shall consider whether belief in free-will can be attacked on empirical grounds.

I THE ARGUMENT AGAINST FREE-WILL BASED ON THE
PRINCIPLE THAT EVERY EVENT MUST HAVE A CAUSE

It is commonly taken to be a fundamental scientific principle—one inherent in the model of the enclosed billiard-table—that every event must have a cause. If the principle is a valid one, it follows that there must be a cause for every single piece of human behaviour—a cause which is sufficient to furnish a full and complete explanation. If everything that everyone does is part of the causal chain, then it is 'unscientific'[1]—a violation of an apparently sacrosanct scientific principle —to suppose that any act can be uncaused or free.

This argument, however, does not present the believer in free-will with an insoluble problem. In the first place modern physicists have

[1] Compare Freud, *Introductory Lectures on Psycho-Analysis* (lecture 6). According to Freud, belief in free-will is 'quite unscientific, and . . . must give ground before the claims of a determinism which governs even mental life' (p. 87 of Joan Rivière's translation, Allen & Unwin, 1922). Freud is not here basing his attack on free-will on any empirical findings, but is, in effect, merely professing uncritical acceptance of the model of the enclosed billiard-table.

largely abandoned the model of the enclosed billiard-table.[1] Too much should not be made of this, since even if modern physics were wholly 'materialistic', sentences containing the words 'the soul', 'free-will' etc. would not thereby be proved to be false. It remains true, however, that the change in outlook over the last fifty years serves to emphasize that the model has not the sacrosanct status that some may have attributed to it.[2]

Even, however, if the validity of the model were unchallenged, the result, as far as free-will is concerned, would not be a genuine difficulty, but rather what may be called a 'puzzle'.[3] To illustrate the difference between a difficulty and a 'puzzle' let us consider the assertion 'X cannot really know what Y is thinking'. If this is to be regarded as a genuine difficulty, its solution clearly lies in a request to Y; he should cease to display that baffling 'poker-face' and should become more communicative. But when philosophers say 'X cannot really know what Y is thinking', they are formulating a 'puzzle'—a puzzle which in this case centres round various possible uses for the words 'really know'. There are uses for 'really know' such that *it makes no sense to say* that we really know what other people are thinking; there is also the familiar usage in which this can perfectly well be said. What I am suggesting is that, in some contexts, the assertion 'No acts are freely chosen', like 'X cannot really know what Y is thinking', involves a 'puzzle' rather than a genuine difficulty. If the model of the enclosed billiard-table is assumed to be operative, there is *no room* for the assertion. 'He did it of his own free-will.' This assertion is ruled out from the start.

The believer in free-will, on the other hand, is implicitly making a claim which can be tested empirically. His belief, therefore, is not threatened unless the empirical evidence shows him to be mistaken. As far as he is concerned, an argument based on considerations of what the model of the enclosed billiard-table does or does not allow us to say is an argument at cross-purposes.

This point can be brought out fully by applying the verification

[1] For a fuller explanation, see p. 73, footnote.

[2] It is sometimes thought that Heisenberg's 'Uncertainty Principle' provides us with a special extra reason for believing in free-will. (For a brief account of this principle, see L. de Broglie, *The Revolution in Physics*, Kegan Paul, 1954.) I agree that Heisenberg's discovery involves a departure from the model of the enclosed billiard-table, and that it emphasizes the need to substitute statistical generalization for complete predictability. But to suppose that it allows for free-will in the sense of proving electrons to be free agents (as though they were people!) is to replace legitimate philosophizing by fantasy.

[3] I owe this distinction to Professor John Wisdom. See his *Other Minds* (Blackwell, 1952). Professor Wisdom distinguishes (p. 1) between 'natural doubt' and 'philosophical doubt'.

principle. 'No acts are freely chosen' clearly sounds as though it is intended to be factually significant. The assumption in that case is that there is a difference between acts which are freely chosen and acts which are not freely chosen, and the factual claim is that acts of the former sort never occur. Whether there is any good empirical evidence for this claim will be discussed in Section 3 of this chapter. If we take a common-sense view the claim is patently false.

To show that this is so it is enough to point out that when I went for a walk yesterday my act was freely chosen; I was not acting under any compulsion. Now clearly a determinist would not agree that this evidence refuted him. He would have to reply that I mistakenly thought I was free when in fact I was not. This might be convincing in the case of the first few examples of apparently freely chosen acts that were quoted to him; but if, *whatever* evidence is produced, the determinist invariably replies, 'No; the act was not really freely chosen', he is so qualifying his original claim that it has become unfalsifiable and has ceased to be a genuine empirical assertion at all.[1] To go for a walk when one is not compelled to do so is precisely what is meant by a freely chosen act in our sense; and we may safely say to the determinist that if such an action is not to count as freely chosen, then he is using 'freely chosen' in some new and unexplained sense. What looked at first glance like a factually significant assertion has turned out to be something more akin to a proposal or stipulation.

This is just what the determinist is in effect doing. He is making a stipulation in the interests of scientific methodology—a stipulation that we are not allowed to say 'He did it of his own free-will'.

Within the context of certain sorts of investigation this stipulation is perfectly sound. Thus, if someone asks 'Why did so-and-so kick the cat?' it is no answer to be told that he did so of his own free-will. Yet it is a stipulation which clearly cannot be adopted universally. In some contexts the difference between freely chosen actions and those done under full or partial compulsion is all-important. Thus, for instance, artificial stimulation of the 'speech-area' of the brain can produce involuntary speech-movements; in such cases the person is certainly not free to choose whether he speaks or not.[2] In general it is essential

---

[1] For a fuller explanation of this argument, see pp. 33–4.

[2] W. Penfield and T. Rasmussen tell of a patient who, when stimulated by this means, was asked to try not to make a noise. They report that, although he did his best, 'the cry followed stimulation just the same'. (From *The Cerebral Cortex of Man*, New York, 1955, p. 89.)

for the neurologist to distinguish acts which his subjects can perform at will from involuntary, reflex, or automatic ones. To suppose that all actions are of this 'forced' or artificially stimulated variety is clearly grotesque.

I have argued in this section that although the principle that every event has a cause may give rise to 'puzzles' about free-will, it cannot give rise to any genuine difficulty.

Any claim that we must seriously abandon belief in free-will can be justified, if at all, only by appealing to the empirical evidence.

## 2 THE ARGUMENT THAT SCIENCE INVOLVES PREDICTABILITY, AND THAT WHERE THERE IS PREDICTABILITY THERE CANNOT BE FREE-WILL

One of the central tasks of the scientist is to frame general laws. He is not content merely with observing particular phenomena; he is interested also in classification and prediction. A general law is a sentence of the form 'If events of type A occur, then events of type B regularly follow'.

Most scientific procedures involve the deliberate setting up of events of type A, in order to test empirically whether events of type B do or do not occur.[1] Sometimes it is found that events can be predicted with virtually a hundred per cent certainty—eclipses, for instance, or the boiling of water when heated; in other cases we have to be content with varying degrees of probability, as, for instance, in the case of the marriage-rate for a particular country or the result of a general election.

Let us now apply this notion of predictability to individual behaviour. If X knows how Y is going to behave tomorrow, then it might seem that Y's behaviour is already determined and that Y himself has no free choice in the matter. To put the matter in general terms, it might seem that where there is predictability there cannot be free-will. If this is so, it follows that in so far as the psychologist (or any other investigator who is interested in studying individual behaviour) is able to frame laws and make predictions, to that extent there cannot be free-will. The psychologist who is also a Christian is thus forced, apparently, to regard progress

[1] Compare Kant, *Critique of Pure Reason*, Preface to the second edition: 'Reason must approach nature . . . in the character of . . . a judge, who compels the witnesses to reply to those questions which he himself thinks fit to propose.'

in his science as something of a mixed blessing. The more he is contributing to our knowledge of psychology, the more damage he is apparently doing to belief in free-will.

The argument from predictability gives rise to a complicated group of philosophical problems, which I cannot hope to discuss exhaustively. The following remarks, however, will serve, I hope, to indicate that even when a person's behaviour is completely predictable it is still possible for him to be a free agent.

In passing, we may note that a similar problem is sometimes raised, not on the basis of predictability by scientists, but on the basis of predictability by an omniscient God. It might seem that if all our future actions are foreseen by God (or eternally known to him), we cannot be free to choose them. As far as the present argument is concerned, it does not matter whether the person with the appropriate foreknowledge is assumed to be God or some highly skilled scientist. The same considerations will apply in either case.

If a person's behaviour were to be fully predictable in accordance with established laws, we might feel disposed to say that he 'couldn't have acted otherwise', and to conclude that therefore he was not free. The word 'couldn't', however, in this context, is ambiguous. All that can legitimately be meant here is that, had he acted differently, this would have been totally unlike him, totally foreign to his nature, and in conflict with the 'laws' or generalizations that might otherwise be made about his behaviour. Where a wrong act is wholly out of character in this way, we are in fact less inclined to blame. We say of the person that he was 'not himself', or that something outside his control must have influenced him. Conversely acts that we might have expected of a person are those for which we are most inclined to hold him responsible. If X knows that Y would never steal money belonging to someone else, it does not follow that Y merits no praise for resisting this temptation when it comes, nor is Y absolved from blame just because he is known to be the sort of person who steals whenever he can.

We may therefore conclude that, even when his behaviour is predictable, a person does not cease to be a moral agent.

There is, however, a further version of the 'predictability' argument which at first glance has such horrifying possibilities that it cannot be ignored.

In general, if X were to predict all the details of Y's future, and if, one by one, all the predictions were fulfilled, then Y might well feel that some terrible fate was hanging over him.[1] This, indeed, is the impression we receive, for instance, in Sophocles' *Oedipus Rex* and Shakespeare's *Othello*. Oedipus has been powerless to avoid the prophecies, and the full extent of his powerlessness gradually becomes revealed during the play. Similarly we feel that Othello is sure to realize in time that Desdemona is innocent; and yet we know, throughout, that his fate is unavoidable, and that he does not discover the truth until it is too late.

Even in real life we can give ourselves the impression of this 'drama-situation' by simple reflection on past events. Things have happened, inevitably, in the one way that they did happen, and we seem powerless to alter them in much the same way as Othello is powerless to avoid murdering Desdemona.

Further reflection, however, shows that the problem is not really the horrifying one which it appears to be at first glance. As far as the present argument is concerned, the important feature in the drama-situation is that the result is inevitable. Thus Oedipus does not avoid fulfilling the prophecies despite the fact that he has been told about them. Othello is not, of course, told in advance how he will behave, but the audience knows the full outcome, and that is enough to produce this feeling of inevitability. The question which we need to ask is, Do such things happen in real life? Is it in fact the case, when we are told how we shall behave or when it is well known how we shall behave, that we are powerless to behave otherwise? Certainly if someone *knows* and *foretells correctly* that I shall act in a particular way at a particular time, it will always be found that I do act in that way; but there is nothing disconcerting in this, since the conclusion follows as a matter of logic from the meaning of the words 'know' and 'foretell correctly', and if I did not behave in the way that was predicted, the words 'know' and 'foretell correctly' would not have been appropriately used. The crucial question is whether real life is or is not like the drama-situation, and whether people, after being told of their future behaviour, are or are not powerless to prevent it. This is a matter which can be settled only by an appeal to evidence; and so long as we are satisfied that we are not ignoring important empirical discoveries we are perfectly justified in concluding that real life is sometimes *unlike* the drama-situation, and that in real life people are sometimes *able* to avoid dangers about which they have been warned. If someone asserts that 'the whole of reality is like a

[1] I am grateful to Professor A. G. N. Flew for some pertinent comments on this problem. Compare his paper, 'Can an Effect Precede its Cause?' (*Aristotelian Society*, Supplementary Volume XXVIII for 1954), especially pp. 61-2.

drama-situation', he is either saying something which is questionable on empirical grounds, or else making one of those claims which turn out on examination to be unfalsifiable and therefore meaningless.

I conclude, therefore, that the 'drama-situation' argument, interesting though it is, cannot be regarded as a valid argument against the existence of free-will.

I have not attempted in this section to supply an exhaustive treatment of the problems raised by predictability. I suggest, however, that enough has been said to indicate that 'All actions are predictable' and 'Some actions are freely chosen' are not incompatible. It follows that if 'All actions are predictable' were ever found to be true, in other words, if the scientific ideal of universal predictability were ever realized, nothing would follow as to whether people had or had not free-will. At least on this score the psychologist who is a Christian can be satisfied that there is no problem for him to resolve.

### 3 CAN BELIEF IN FREE-WILL BE ATTACKED ON EMPIRICAL GROUNDS?

The evidence which I propose to discuss will be classified under two main headings, (*a*) physiological, and (*b*) psychological. Under (*a*) I shall refer to knowledge obtained from the study of the endocrine glands—glands which secrete chemicals, known as hormones, into the blood-stream—and knowledge obtained from the study of the central nervous system and of the brain in particular. Under (*b*) I shall refer to the results of psychological research into juvenile delinquency and also to some of the discoveries brought to light by psycho-analysis. No comprehensive survey of evidence will be attempted, but attention willl be called to a number of recent empirical findings which appear to be relevant to our problem.

(*a*) A child whose thyroid gland fails to develop becomes what is called a 'cretin'—a misshapen dwarf incapable of any rational thought. Other glandular disorders may result in precocious sexual behaviour, listlessness, moroseness, and similar traits usually frowned upon by society.[1] Operations on the brain are sometimes followed by loss of

[1] For fuller discussion and further references, see R. S. Woodworth, *Psychology. A Study of Mental Life* (Methuen, 1940), chapter VI.

social responsibility.[1] A surprising number of those awaiting trial for murder, though not certifiable 'insane', have been found by the use of the electro-encephalograph to have abnormal brain-rhythms.[2]

(b) At a certain 'approved school' for delinquents, it was found that many of them had apparently had recourse to anti-social behaviour as a means of avoiding a situation in the home which had become emotionally intolerable.[3] Children who have no mother or mother-substitute during the early years of life are liable to suffer severe personality disorders and may in many cases take to stealing.[4]

Moreover psycho-analysis has made clear that human beings are not as rational as some of us in our more optimistic moments may have supposed. Our behaviour is frequently influenced by the bizarre reasonings of infancy no less than by adult attempts to deal on a realistic level with genuine problems. Primitive impulses and irrational fears and phantasies seem in many cases to be right outside a person's control.

To say what all this evidence proves, from the point of view of moral responsibility, is far from easy. I began by citing what would be agreed to be a clear-cut case—that of the cretin. Glandular deficiency makes it quite impossible for the cretin to show normal rationality, and there is no question whatever of holding him morally responsible for his shortcomings. The problem is one of deciding how closely the other cases approximate to the clear-cut standard case where we agree that there is no moral responsibility. If a person is sexually precocious or morose, and we know that he has a particular glandular disorder or has undergone some operation to the brain, most of us would say either that this exonerates him fully or at least that it partially exonerates him. In other cases the issue is not so clear-cut. It is difficult to argue that a person who has killed someone is not a moral agent simply on the basis of an abnormal electro-encephalograph record; but the fact that his record is abnormal at least makes us hesitant in supposing him to be fully accountable for the killing. Moreover, since abnormalities of the endocrine system or the brain are not obvious to a casual observer, there is a possible case for saying that these types of abnormality are more frequent than is commonly realized. The outcome seems to be

[1] Woodworth, op. cit., pp. 278–9.
[2] See the Report of the Royal Commission on Capital Punishment, especially paragraph 400.
[3] See D. H. Stott, Delinquency and Human Nature (Carnegie Trust, 1950).
[4] For further discussion and detailed statistical evidence, see John Bowlby, Forty-four Juvenile Thieves (Baillière, Tindall, & Cox, 1946).

that in any individual case we are at least extremely hesitant in ascribing moral praise and blame. It may, of course, be quite appropriate to use words of commendation or disparagement, such as 'You did well' or 'You ought not to have done this', in order to train a person, but this is not the same as regarding him as a responsible moral agent.

Psychological investigations present the same sort of problem. Thus in the case of delinquents whose crime appears to be the result of an emotionally intolerable situation, it is perhaps going too far to say that they had no choice in the matter at all, but most of us would hesitate before ascribing full moral responsibility to them. Similarly, where a person is clearly under the influence of unconscious phantasy, we might not go so far as to say that he cannot help acting as he does, but most of us would agree that he is in part being influenced by circumstances outside his control. Moreover the clinical evidence shows that people are influenced by unconscious phantasies far more often than is commonly realized.

In addition we need to take into account the phenomena connected with post-hypnotic suggestion. Let us suppose that a person has been hypnotized, and, while under hypnosis, has been instructed to act in a certain way when he wakes up. The instruction might be, for instance, 'Ten minutes after you wake up you will open your umbrella'. Now the interesting thing is that in many such cases the person does precisely as he was instructed, and, what is more, *believes that he is acting perfectly freely*. This seems to suggest that, even when we think we are free, there may be occasions when we are not free at all, or at least are under strong pressure to act in a particular way.

We cannot, of course, argue from this that something comparable to post-hypnotic suggestion is operative the whole time; but if our behaviour can be influenced, even part of the time, in this way without our realizing the fact, there is at least the possibility that we may be the victims of outside influence more often than we suppose.

As a result of empirical findings, then, we may conclude that people are not invariably the free agents which they appear to be at first glance. The truth seems to be rather that there are varying degrees of power to make free choices. The situation, I suggest, is comparable to that in which a person required to act in a particular way is cajoled, threatened, and perhaps tortured, until he finally breaks down. In extreme cases a person could claim that he was not a free agent at all; in other cases we may suppose him to be partly free, but in any individual instance we are hesitant in saying that someone could have or ought to have held out longer than he did.

There is, however, no justification for the conclusion that acts are *never* freely chosen; indeed such a conclusion is grotesque and paradoxical. Thus it is of particular importance in a neurological examination to distinguish between acts which can be executed at will and acts which are not freely chosen at all. Any neurologist would agree that some acts come into the former class. Similarly in the case of psycho-analysis it is always assumed that when the need for displaying neurotic symptoms is removed, the person will be able to help himself. Analysts speak, in technical jargon, of 'ego-strength'. As we shall see in Chapter 12, the purpose of psycho-analysis can plausibly be regarded as the removal of the need for irrational behaviour, the whole assumption being that the person will then be free to act in whatever way he thinks best.

In addition it should be said that practising psycho-analysts do not doubt their own freedom and their own moral responsibility. To fail to keep an appointment with a patient without good reason would undoubtedly be regarded as a breach of professional standards. Talk of 'professional standards' would lose its point if there were no freedom of choice.

We may conclude, therefore, that acceptance of a 'scientific world-outlook' does not force us to be thoroughgoing determinists. There is considerable evidence, however, suggesting that people are not altogether the free agents which they appear to be at first glance. If we take this evidence seriously, we are often likely to feel hesitant in ascribing moral praise and blame.

# CHAPTER 11

# Psychical research

The systems which have so far been considered in the present section of this book—materialism, behaviourism, and determinism—are commonly thought to constitute a threat to traditional religion. Psychical research, on the other hand, has often been supposed to provide the religious believer with a possible line of defence. Its methods appear to be impeccably 'scientific', and yet its conclusions appear to suggest that there is something 'spiritual' in man's nature after all.

I have argued in the last three chapters that materialism, behaviourism, and determinism are not the threat to orthodox religion which is commonly supposed. I shall argue in the present chapter that, just as these three systems cannot be made the basis for attacking religion, so also psychical research cannot be invoked as a means of defending it.

I shall argue that it is misguided to expect from psychical research any discovery that from a religious point of view would radically alter our conception of man and his position in the universe. With one qualification (which will be made at the end of the chapter), I shall maintain that the findings of psychical research, whatever their scientific value, have no relevance for religion.

A few words should be said, first of all, about the subject-matter of psychical research. Psychical research may be said to concern itself with so-called 'paranormal' findings. The distinction between what is 'normal' and what is 'paranormal' is agreed by many people to be a problematic one; and, in my opinion, there is no long-term justification for making such a distinction. Roughly speaking, however, phenomena may be regarded as 'paranormal' if they are in conflict with certain allegedly fundamental presuppositions of scientific method. Thus, if a person is able to see through a window what is happening in the next room, there is nothing paranormal about this, since such vision can be explained in terms of the established laws of optics. If, however, a person has 'seen' (or at any rate knows in some way or other) what is happening in the next room when there is a sound-proof wall in between, and when he is not in a position to infer or guess what is happening there, it might seem in such a case as though something had happened which no ordinary scientific principles could explain. Such an occurrence would then be classified as 'paranormal'.

For our purposes these paranormal phenomena can be divided into two groups. First, there are the so-called 'spontaneous' occurrences, such as premonitions of a person's death when that person is many miles away, apparent communication of messages to the living from the dead, and alleged activity by ghosts and poltergeists. Secondly there are the results obtained from systematic experiments on card-guessing and from systematic attempts to influence the fall of dice by 'willing' a particular result.

Ability to influence the fall of dice in this way is assumed to involve the occurrence of a process labelled 'psychokinesis' (PK)—i.e. movement by the mind independently of any physical medium. Ability to score highly in the card-guessing experiments is assumed to involve 'extra-sensory perception' (ESP)—i.e. perception by some means other than that of normal sense-perception. There are usually said to be three varieties of ESP. First, there is telepathy, defined in the *Oxford English Dictionary* as 'the communication of impressions of any kind from one mind to another, independently of the recognized channels of sense'; secondly, there is clairvoyance, defined as 'a supposed faculty possessed by some persons consisting in the mental perception of objects at a distance or concealed from sight'; thirdly, there is precognition, defined as 'antecedent cognition; foreknowledge'. As will be shown later in the chapter, the terms 'psychokinesis', 'extra-sensory perception', 'telepathy', 'clairvoyance', and 'precognition' give rise to difficulties; but they require to be mentioned here since they are widely accepted as basic terms in psychical research.

On the question of assessing the evidence, little need be said here. In the case of reports of 'spontaneous' phenomena, it is unavoidable that the evidence should fail to satisfy strict scientific standards. Accurate observation, unbiased observers, and undistorted verbal accounts are not easy to achieve, and in many cases have not been achieved. This is not to say that reports of spontaneous phenomena are necessarily false; it is only to say that we cannot be sure that they are true. It is not my intention here, however, either to commend any particular report as trustworthy or to condemn any alleged findings as invention. We can quite legitimately assume, for purposes of argument, that some of the 'spontaneous' occurrences reported e.g. in the *Proceedings of the Society for Psychical Research* and in their *Journal* took place as described. I shall argue that, *even if they did*, there is no justification for waving flags and claiming that religion has been vindicated after all!

In the case of the systematic experiments, there can be little room for doubt as far as the actual facts are concerned. For illustration purposes here is a fairly typical experiment of the card-guessing variety.[1] The experimenter, let us say, has a pack of twenty-five cards, consisting of five crosses, five circles, five rectangles, five stars, and five wavy lines. Like ordinary playing cards they are all the same on the back. After shuffling and cutting the cards he places them face downwards, and makes sure that his subject cannot see the symbols on them and is not given any accidental 'cues' to help him. The subject is asked to name the symbol on the top card, and when his choice has been noted down the card is removed. The procedure is repeated for all the twenty-five cards in the pack.

Now if it were merely a matter of chance, the person being tested would be expected to give, on the average, five correct answers out of twenty-five. The odds against higher and lower scores can be worked out mathematically. The claim is made that a small number of people have been consistently able to obtain average scores of seven, eight or even more correct answers in a run of twenty-five cards. Professor Rhine has described how in one experiment a person was taken through the pack twelve times. He therefore gave $12 \times 25$ answers, that is three hundred. By pure chance we should expect his total of correct answers to be 60. The actual number was 119. Perhaps this does not sound very spectacular. But the odds against scoring 119 by pure chance can be worked out mathematically. They are well over a million to one.

These odds are quite sufficient to exclude the hypothesis that such a score was obtained by lucky guessing. In statistical language the result is said to be 'significant'. There are no fixed criteria for deciding whether a result is significant. Much depends on the issues at stake in each particular case. In some cases investigators are quite satisfied with odds of a hundred to one against chance. But even if we insist on

[1] For further details of this type of research, see J. B. Rhine, *New Frontiers of the Mind* (Pelican, 1950).

something stricter—say, odds of a thousand to one—there are still plenty of results in psychical research which, even by this stricter standard, must be regarded as significant.

I propose to take it as established (i) that a number of the people who took part in the card-guessing experiments have consistently produced results which are statistically significant, (ii) that such results occurred for the most part without any deliberate hoax or collusion, (iii) that adequate safeguards were taken to exclude the possibility of using ordinary sensory cues, and (iv) that, in the relevant cases, no mathematical errors were made in the calculation of odds against chance. If anyone claims that the appropriate conditions have never been adequately satisfied, and that the experiments are vulnerable on one or more of these counts, the arguments of this chapter will not be seriously affected. They can be regarded in that case simply as an attempt to assess what the consequences would be for religion if the appropriate conditions at some future date actually *were* satisfied.

Two further facts of importance appear to have emerged from the research. The first is that no systematic differences in scores were observed when obstacles were placed between the person being tested and the cards which he was required to guess; the second is that the distance between the person being tested and the cards appeared to have no systematic effect. In view of these findings, it would seem that any theory in terms of light-waves, radiations, etc. is inadequate, since such waves would be deflected by obstacles, and would become weaker the greater the distance between the person being tested and the cards. Of course it is always possible to say that waves are operating which are of a special sort—able to pass through obstacles, too weak to be detected by normal apparatus, and so on; but in the absence of any confirmatory evidence, such a hypothesis serves no useful purpose.

Why, then, are these findings supposed to be revolutionary? The commonly accepted reason is that they are thought to constitute a refutation of materialism.

In discussing this claim let us begin by interpreting the word 'materialism' in its popular and literal sense. In this sense it may be taken to mean the view that 'nothing exists except matter and its movements and modifications'. (Compare Chapter 8, p. 67). There seems no doubt that some have supposed that psychical research, if its findings were established, would constitute a refutation of materialism in this sense of the word. Thus Professor Rhine writes, 'The clash between supernatural religion and the materialistic philosophy of natural science produced a crisis in the minds of thinking men. Most of the more scientific either abandoned their supernatural religion or came to a settled compromise by which they allowed the best of religion and science to occupy distinct mental compartments. A few, however, decided to have a closer look at Nature to see whether there were not in Nature itself evidence of reality that transcended physical explanation'.[1] A little later he writes, 'On the broad front of religion and its affiliates parapsychology has its major significance. All that is needed to see something of this significance is to recognize that in a universe in which it were clearly established that only physical forces exist, religion, morality, democracy, freedom, and many other function that make life meaningful would have no place or reality'.[2]

The issue, then, for Professor Rhine, seems to be whether 'only physical forces exist' or whether there is 'evidence of reality that transcends physical explanation'. Professor Rhine may not perhaps be thinking of a crude version of materialism, in which the only real objects are solid small particles of matter. But the version of materialism which he is considering is still a popular and literal one in the sense that it purports to be a theory about *what there is in the universe*.

His suggestion seems to be that, if it can be established (as he thinks it can) that there are nonphysical forces operating in the universe, this makes it reasonably sensible (or at any rate not just a stupid blunder) to believe in other nonphysical entities such as God and values.[3]

As we have seen already in Chapter 4, and again in Chapter 8, pp. 67 to 70, the issue under discussion is a meaningless one. Theories about 'what there is in the universe' involve the 'absolute-existence' mistake. We need to ask, By what criteria could it be established whether nonphysical entities or forces exist? If two people disagree as to the 'contents of the universe', by what possible method could such disagreement

---

[1] See his article in *The New Outline of Modern Knowledge* (Gollancz, 1956), p. 195. I have deliberately chosen to quote a popular, non-technical discussion of psychical research, since we are concerned here with popular beliefs rather than with any technical details of experimentation. Professor Rhine appears to share these popular beliefs, though not all research workers in this field would do so.

[2] *The New Outline of Modern Knowledge*, p. 210.

[3] For the word 'nonphysical', see p. 205 of Professor Rhine's article. No explanation is given but we may assume it to refer to forces other than those—such as waves and particles—which are recognized in orthodox physics. My own use of 'para-physical' on p. 85 and elsewhere is a deliberate attempt to expose the mistake of which I believe Professor Rhine and others to be guilty.

be settled? And if there is no method which would be accepted as the correct one for settling the question, what precisely is being asked?

It is unlikely, of course, that Professor Rhine would take this barrage of questions lying down. The methods which he relies on, as he would immediately point out, are empirical methods. He is concerned, therefore, not with 'absolute'-existence questions, not with 'metaphysical'-existence questions in the traditional sense, but with what we have called 'contextual'-existence questions[1]—the context being that of empirical observation. On this showing the question whether there exist nonphysical forces is settled by the same methods as the question whether there are physical forces, e.g. light-waves. Sentences about light-waves cannot, of course, be given 'cash-value' in the same straightforward way as sentences about e.g. chairs and tables; they are not observable entities like chairs and tables. It would be argued, therefore, by analogy, that we could not expect 'nonphysical' forces to be observable any more than are light-waves, but that the same arguments which justify our speaking of light-waves also justify our speaking of 'nonphysical forces'.

If this is the claim, however, it is hard to see, even if it were established, how it could justify high-faluting assertions about God and values. When Professor Rhine tells us that the results of psychical research make it easier for us to look with sympathy towards 'religion, morality, democracy, freedom', we may reasonably ask how empirical evidence, however well attested, could support such non-empirical assertions as 'Men ought to love their enemies', 'Democracy is the most suitable form of government for the U.S.A.' or 'All men have the right to freedom'. A scientist has every justification for being thrilled and fascinated by his investigations; but one feels that Professor Rhine, with his references to religion, morality, democracy, and freedom, has treated us to the wrong sort of thrills. The whole passage, like many others on psychical research, creates an atmosphere of mystification and excitement which seems to me quite inappropriate in an empirical inquiry.

We may conclude, then, that psychical research is a reasonably straightforward empirical investigation, and is not, as some have supposed, an esoteric means of enabling us to proclaim mighty truths about God and the universe.[2] By straightforward empirical methods we

[1] See p. 43.
[2] A recent letter to *The Observer* appeared to assume that the findings of psychical research, if established, would 'prove scientific humanism wrong'.

can study the conditions in which better-than-chance scores occur—whether fatigue, jealousy, or hypnosis influence the results, whether those who score highly on the tests are of this or that type of personality, whether they have this or that type of brain-rhythm, whether ability to score highly runs in families, whether it lasts over long periods of years, and so on. There are all sorts of questions of this kind, to some of which the answers are more or less known, on some of which no reliable information has yet been obtained. But whatever answers are given to such questions, there is no justification for high-faluting inferences about God or values.

The tendency to be high-faluting arises in part from an ambiguity in the key terms, 'psychokinesis', 'extra-sensory perception', 'telepathy', 'clairvoyance', and 'precognition'. All these terms are based on 'ghost-in-machine' ways of thinking,[1] and there is the same resultant difficulty in all of them. I am not saying that all sentences suggestive of a 'ghost in a machine' are *ipso facto* misguided; but we frequently need to be on the alert as to how such sentences are verified and falsified and what empirical facts would constitute their 'cash-value'.

It may at first sight seem rather surprising that scientists have failed to agree as to whether extra-sensory perception and psychokinesis are established facts. All that is needed, so it might seem, is a willingness to examine the evidence. If the evidence is unreliable, why should some obviously competent thinkers accept it? If it is reliable, why should other equally competent thinkers refuse to examine it? Blindness and prejudice may be responsible, of course; but it seems odd, in that case, that there is no comparable blindness and prejudice over relativity and quantum physics. The lack of agreement, I would suggest, has arisen not because there is any irremediable dispute as to the facts, but rather as a result of different views as to how the key terms should be given 'cash-value'.

Let us illustrate with reference to the word 'telepathy'. What is said here of 'telepathy' applies, *mutatis mutandis*, to the other terms also. We need to distinguish its dictionary meaning from what may be called its 'operational' meaning. 'Telepathy' according to the dictionary means 'the communication of impressions of any kind from one mind to another, independently of the recognised channels of sense'. If someone claims that telepathy in this sense occurs, the suggestion seems to be that the ghost inside one person has been communicating with the

[1] For an explanation of the phrase 'ghost-in-the-machine', see chapter 9, p. 80.

ghost inside another person without the operation of any 'physical' machinery. But how can we give 'cash-value' to such talk about the intercommunication of ghosts? How could the claim that such 'communication between minds' takes place ever be verified or falsified? Clearly, if such talk is taken seriously, we are indulging in misuse of 'ghost-in-machine' terminology, since we are postulating a process which is totally unknown and unknowable. 'Telepathy occurs', in this context, is neither a true nor a false assertion, but a meaningless one.

The defender of telepathy will not, of course, be satisfied with this. He will call our attention to the empirical evidence—in particular the fact that, under specified conditions, a number of people have scored 'better than chance' in card-guessing experiments. There is a complication here in that results under some conditions are compatible with clairvoyance or precognition no less than with telepathy; not all experiments point exclusively to one rather than to the other two. This, however, does not affect his basic argument, since all that is needed is to specify what conditions would constitute a telepathy experiment, what condition would constitute a clairvoyance experiment, what conditions would be compatible with all three explanations, and so on.[1] But if telepathy is being defended along these lines, what has happened to all the high-faluting talk about 'communication between mind and mind'? The defender of telepathy has shifted to an 'operational' account of the meaning of the word 'telepathy'. He is saying, in effect: 'All I mean when I say that telepathy occurs is that, if you carry out card-guessing and similar experiments on suitable subjects in specified conditions, you will get statistically significant results'.

The same considerations hold in the case of both the other varieties of ESP—clairvoyance and precognition—and also in the case of PK. There is an ambiguity in all cases between the 'dictionary' sense of these words and the 'operational' sense.

The results of this ambiguity are disastrous. In the first place it precludes the possibility of a straight answer to the question, 'Does extra-sensory perception occur?', since it is perfectly possible to agree that it does in the operational sense, while rejecting the view that anything analogous to perception is taking place, and while rejecting high-faluting talk about 'communication between minds'. Results of

---

[1] Detailed specification of the conditions is a complex matter and need not be attempted here. The experiment described on p. 104 would normally be taken as a clairvoyance experiment. There can be precognition only if the 'target'-card is not in existence at the time of the guess.

questionnaires asking people whether they are willing to consider ESP 'an established fact or a likely possibility'[1] are therefore vitiated from the start. Secondly, and more important, there seems considerable confusion as to whether, and in what sense, the concept of 'ESP' can be said to 'explain' the results. The passage of light-waves from an external object to the eye, and the resultant transmission of impulses along the optic nerve to the brain may be said to constitute an 'explanation' of visual perception. Many would be prepared to say that it constitutes a 'physical' explanation—an explanation, that is, in terms of 'physical' agencies or forces. Now it is tempting to suppose that significant results at the card-guessing experiments can be 'explained' in the same sense and along similar lines; the difference would appear to be that in such cases 'nonphysical' forces are operating. But such an 'explanation is vacuous and tells us nothing; in the appropriate sense of 'explain' it does not explain at all. The behaviour of light-waves is something which can be investigated independently of a person's report on what he perceives, and the explanation is scientifically helpful since it links together two distinct classes of event—the verbal report and the independently discoverable behaviour of light-waves. Talk of 'nonphysical' forces, on the other hand, provides no such link. It is no valid explanation to postulate the totally unknown operation of totally unknown forces; and to label such forces 'mental' and say that communication between minds 'explains' the card-guessing scores is to leave us as much in the dark as when we started. Certainly we can say that telepathy may be the explanation as opposed to precognition or clairvoyance, or indeed that any one of the three is the explanation as opposed to the other two; this is a legitimate sense of 'explain', since it adds to our knowledge of the conditions in which the results took place. Similarly it is legitimate to say that the results are due to ESP, if this means simply that it seems impossible to attribute the results to cues or inference or chance. What is quite illegitimate is to suppose that the operation of 'nonphysical' forces explains the successful card-guessing in the same sense as the operation of 'physical' forces, such as light-waves, explains visual perception. As an explanation the latter increases our knowledge, the former is vacuous.

If 'extra-sensory perception' and the other terms are understood in

[1] Professor Rhine (*The New Outline of Modern Knowledge*, p. 205) says that when this question was put to the Fellows of the American Psychological Association, over 16 per cent gave an affirmative answer. Since the question is ambiguous this evidence clearly cannot be taken at its face value.

their 'operational' sense—if they are taken simply as ways of describing the experimental results—then there is no ground for objecting to them. If they are understood in that way, however, no high-faluting eonclusions follow about the status of minds in the universe. The only possible basis for any high-faluting conclusions would be the discovery of the occurrence of ESP etc. in the 'dictionary' sense. The supposition, however, that ESP occurs in *this* sense is unintelligible. No account can be given of the 'cash-value' of this claim, and there is no means of knowing what we are supposed to be looking for. The whole idea of 'nonphysical' forces operating in the universe—except as a restatement of the experimental results—is unintelligible. In brief, if the terms 'ESP' etc. are understood in the 'operational' sense, no high-faluting conclusions follow; if they are understood in the dictionary sense, neither existing experimental evidence nor any other experimental evidence could ever prove that such 'nonphysical' events occur.

The main conclusion from the foregoing argument can now be stated. On the assumption that the word 'materialism' is understood literally, we cannot take seriously the claim that ESP, if established, would 'refute materialism'. If the general thesis of this book is right, then the claim is a muddled attempt to refute a meaningless theory. To this situation we can aptly apply some words used by Kant in another context; it presents 'the ludicrous spectacle, of one (as the ancients said) "milking a he-goat, and the other holding a sieve".'[1]

There is, however, a second sense of the word 'materialism', which now needs to be considered. A materialist in this sense is one who takes seriously the model of the enclosed billiard-table.[2]

So far we have considered only a literal-minded version of materialism. It should be stressed that the somewhat scathing conclusions of the last section are not intended as an attack on the genuinely scientific work that has been done in the field of psychical research. My argument was directed only against popular misconceptions of the relevance of psychical research to religion, and against high-faluting claims, unjustified by the evidence, about the status of 'minds' in the universe. We must now leave behind this literal version of materialism, and concentrate on the genuine challenge which psychical research appears to make to traditional ways of thinking.

[1] *Critique of Pure Reason*, Introduction to Transcendental Logic.
[2] See chapter 8 of this book, especially pp. 71–4.

When it is claimed that the findings of psychical research constitute a refutation of materialism, the most helpful way of interpreting this claim is to treat it as a claim that psychical research forces us to abandon the model of the enclosed billiard-table.

I am not prepared, myself, to assert that existing evidence is sufficient to do this. But if a satisfactory theory is finally built up to explain better-than-chance scores at card-guessing,[1] it is perfectly within the bounds of possibility that the model of the enclosed billiard-table might be found inadequate on these grounds no less than as a result of relativity theory.

According to the rules of this model, there cannot be action at a distance without an intervening medium. Yet it seems in successful ESP experiments that the person being tested is being acted upon in precisely this way. According to the rules of the model a later event cannot influence an earlier one, yet if precognition genuinely occurs, it might seem that this is precisely what is happening, since the subject is apparently being influenced by something which *has not yet happened*. The model teaches us to regard space and time in a common-sense way; yet it is not beyond the bounds of possibility that experimental results at some future date might lead us to revise our notions of both these concepts, just as relativity theory forces us to revise them.

Even, however, if some such revision is now called for, or is called for at some future date, as far as our main theme is concerned—the relevance of psychical research to religion—no important consequences follow. It is grotesque to suppose that any form of language justified by such developments could entail the truth or falsity of 'God is love',[2] or other typically religious assertions. Such developments, if they occurred, would simply be part of the progress of science—an interesting part, no doubt, but not such as would justify high-faluting language about minds or would-be religious flag-waving. It is precisely because the words 'paranormal' and 'para-psychology' create this 'flag-waving' sort of atmosphere (at any rate for the unwary), that I regard them as unsatisfactory. Findings described in terms of ESP are no more and no less paranormal than findings described in terms of relativity theory. Para-psychology is simply a branch of psychology; and if the evidence shows that man's ability to predict events or recognize what is happening

---

[1] If no such theory is discovered, psychical research will be regarded by future generations as something of a 'blind alley'. It is too early, in my opinion, to express views as to possible developments.
[2] 1 John iv. 8.

at remote distances is greater than we suppose, this is interesting, but does not provide us with an excuse for airing our views on God and the universe.

Finally it may be said that some of the 'spontaneous' phenomena— e.g. the apparent arrival of messages from the dead—have a direct relevance for religion, since they serve to provide experimental evidence in favour of immortality.

The evidence that such events happen is, of course, inconclusive. For purposes of argument, however, let us assume that messages are sometimes received at séances, perhaps in familiar tones, containing information which no one but the dead person could have possessed.

There are, of course, possible difficulties about the inference from 'This sounds like Mr X's voice' (where Mr X is someone who is dead) or 'Only Mr X could have known this' to 'This message was sent by Mr X'. In ordinary speech we do not say 'This is Mr X', unless there is bodily continuity between the person whom we are now meeting and the person whom we knew as Mr X. In the present case, therefore, it might seem that 'This message was sent by Mr X' could be true only if a person having bodily continuity with Mr X was later discovered by independent criteria to be sending the message—a condition which at an ordinary séance is clearly not satisfied. This difficulty, however, is perhaps not insuperable. A possible reply would be to say that such a message shows that Mr X is having experiences after death. It has long been recognized that 'cash-value' cannot satisfactorily be given to sentences relating to other people's experiences.[1] For all we know, it seems possible that a disembodied Mr X might be continuing to have experiences, and the message at the séance might seem to be a pointer to this fact much as a person's holding his jaw is a pointer to the fact that he has tooth-ache. If this argument is right, and if the objection about 'bodily continuity' is overruled, it seems not impossible that empirical evidence might provide support for the assertion 'People have experiences after death'.

This, then, is the qualification referred to at the start of this chapter.[2] It is conceivable that evidence from psychical research might be relevant towards confirming or refuting the assertion 'People have experiences after death'; and, if this is labelled a 'religious' assertion, then psychical research might conceivably have some relevance to religion. To make this reservation, however, is possibly to take the

---

[1] Compare pp. 82-3.     [2] See p. 102.

séance phenomena too seriously—more seriously, perhaps, than many scientific workers in the field of psychical research would wish.

Finally it should be pointed out that although 'People have experiences after death' might, at a pinch, be classified as religious language, it is certainly not the language of orthodox Christianity. Orthodox Christianity speaks of 'resurrection'. Talk of resurrection will be classified, in Chapter 19, as 'the language of parable'. A full account of what this involves cannot be given here, but we may say here and now of parable-language that nothing which happens in the séance-room or the laboratory is relevant to its truth or falsity. 'People have experiences after death' may be affected by observational evidence, but not 'God . . . hath begotten us again unto a lively hope by the resurrection of Jesus Christ from the dead.'[1]

My conclusion is that the findings of psychical research are of no major significance for religion.

[1] I Peter i. 3.

# CHAPTER 12

## *The contribution of psycho-analysis*

'Humanity has in the course of time had to endure from the hands of science two great outrages upon its naïve self-love. The first was when it realized that our earth was not the centre of the universe, but only a tiny speck in a world-system of a magnitude hardly conceivable. . . . The second was when biological research robbed man of his peculiar privilege of having been specially created, and relegated him to a descent from the animal world, implying an ineradicable animal nature in him. . . . But man's craving for grandiosity is now suffering the third and most bitter blow from present-day psychological research which is endeavouring to prove to the "ego" of each one of us that he is not even master in his own house. . . . We psycho-analysts were neither the first nor the only ones to propose to mankind that they should look inward; but it appears to be our lot to advocate it most insistently and to support it by empirical evidence which touches every man closely. This is the kernel of the universal revolt against our science, of the total disregard of academic courtesy in dispute, and the liberation of opposition from all the constraints of impartial logic.'[1]

This quotation from Freud illustrates not only the general atmosphere of hostility which his discoveries evoked, but also his own reaction to this hostility. Whether greater opposition to Freud came from his colleagues in the medical profession, from religious leaders, or from some other group need not concern us. What is clear is that early in the present century it was commonly thought that psycho-analytic theory and orthodox religious belief were totally incompatible.

As with the issue of materialism, the heat of the controversy has to some extent died down in recent years. Books have been written to

[1] From Freud, *Introductory Lectures on Psycho-Analysis* (translated by Joan Rivière, Allen & Unwin, 1922), pp. 240–1. For a brief discussion of the first two 'outrages' mentioned by Freud, see the footnote to p. 209 of this book.

show that psycho-analytic theory and orthodox Christianity are reconcilable;[1] and it has even been suggested that *unbelief*, rather than belief, is the more neurotic state of the two.[2] Even if nowadays, however, there is little open warfare between religious leaders and psychoanalysts, there is still a large amount of suspicion; and it is as though there were an uneasy armistice rather than a permanent peace-treaty. Perhaps religious leaders have doubts about psycho-analytic theory but are insufficiently sure of their ground to voice them; perhaps some analysts have simply taken for granted that Christian orthodoxy requires to be rejected, and feel no need to deliver provocative challenges on the matter. At any rate, the general position seems to be one of confusion; and an examination of possible sources of conflict seems urgently necessary.

This chapter is an attempt to answer the question whether acceptance of the essentials of psycho-analytic theory makes it inconsistent and dishonest to profess belief in Christian orthodoxy.

There is, of course, a difficulty over 'labels' here; there is no universal agreement as to what constitutes 'the essentials' of psycho-analytic theory and what counts as 'Christian orthodoxy'. For this reason it is very easy to formulate some caricature of psycho-analytic theory and then pronounce it totally unacceptable on religious grounds; and it is equally easy to formulate some caricature of religious belief and applaud psycho-analytic theory for ridding us of such nonsense. There inevitably follows some not very profitable argument as to how far the caricature *is* a caricature. Both sides then direct their attack against the more inept remarks made by members of the opposite camp; and these remarks are then assumed to be typical of all who bear the opposite 'label'. 'Label'-warfare serves only to impede clear thinking.

In what follows I shall argue that if both 'labels' are interpreted reasonably, psycho-analytic theory and orthodox Christianity are not in irreconcilable conflict. Some rethinking of our religious ideas is admittedly called for; but no major distortion either of orthodox Christianity or of orthodox psycho-analytic theory is required in order to make the two compatible.

Before we pass on to considering possible sources of conflict, a few preliminary points require to be cleared up.

In the first place some account is called for on the general question of

---

[1] See, for instance, R. S. Lee, *Freud and Christianity* (London, 1948).
[2] See H. C. Rumke, *The Psychology of Unbelief* (Rockliff, 1952).

what psycho-analysis is and what it involves. It is difficult to answer this question in an uncontroversial way, since even among analysts themselves there are differences of technique and emphasis, and it is to some extent a matter of personal opinion what are the important points to stress. The following remarks are intended simply for the general guidance of the layman, and are not to be regarded as an 'official' statement of policy.

Treatment by means of psycho-analysis involves a series of interviews, often over a period of years, between patient and analyst. From the evidence of these interviews, it has come to be realized that behaviour is continually influenced by bizarre and irrational phantasies dating back from infancy. As a result of interpretations by the analyst, the patient may come to be aware of these phantasies, and, where they are inappropriate, may cease to be influenced by them.[1] It should be emphasized that not all psychiatrists—i.e. those qualified doctors who have specialized in mental illness—favour psycho-analytic methods of therapy, or even other similar methods, such as those advocated by Jung and Adler. Many prefer to use so-called 'physical' methods, as opposed to 'psychological' ones; they prefer, in other words, to use such things as drugs and shock-therapy rather than extensive use of the personal interview.

Next the question may be raised of the general validity of psycho-analytic theory. Certainly there seems no point in discussing its relevance to religion if, even on purely scientific grounds, it is a mistaken or unprofitable theory. This is a matter, however, which need not detain us. It is not my purpose here either to try to convert the hardened sceptic into accepting a psycho-analytic way of looking at things, or to warn professed converts of the dangers of too uncritical acceptance of psycho-analytic catchwords. I shall assume for purposes of argument that Freud's work has set in motion a train of investigations of fundamental importance, and that the clinical evidence which has come to light requires to be taken seriously. My personal view is that, as far as our understanding of human personality is concerned, psycho-analytically orientated investigations are of incomparably more value than the card-guessing experiments described in the last chapter. By

[1] Mere intellectual awareness, however, is not enough. The patient must 'feel' the situation, or, as has been said, become 'emotionally aware' of it. A key factor in the therapy is the so-called 'transference' situation—the relationship between patient and analyst. The role of the analyst is thought of as that of a substitute-parent; and it has been found that the patient 'transfers' on to him the loves and hatreds of early infancy.

strict scientific standards, admittedly, the evidence in favour of a psycho-analytic viewpoint is far from convincing;[1] but this does not justify the view that research workers in this field are simply following a blind alley.

It may, however, be objected that acceptance of a psycho-analytic viewpoint is incompatible with the behaviourism which was advocated —or at least treated with sympathy—in Chapter 9. This objection is invalid. A behaviourist approach brings home to us that the 'cash-value' of psycho-analytic terms, such as 'the superego', 'the unconscious', 'the libido' and so on, lies in people's behaviour, and in particular in the behaviour of the patient during treatment. But there is nothing in the behaviourism which was advocated in Chapter 9 to tell us what sort of behaviour it is most profitable to study, and it is quite compatible with this version of behaviourism to regard behaviour in a treatment situation as important. Some of us are admittedly made uneasy by the fact that Freud' discoveries, (like those of Jung) are couched in the most uncritical forms of 'ghost-in-machine' terminology; one gets the impression that some analysts believe in para-physical agencies, such as 'the mind' or 'the mental apparatus',[2] operating in para-physical fashion. But it is one thing to say that Freudian theory requires to be purged of 'ghost-in-machine' terminology, and quite another to say that the discoveries made by Freud and his followers are unimportant.

There is in addition the question of whether psycho-analysis—the distinctive label for Freudian theory and methods of cure—is in a better established position than the 'Analytic Psychology' of Jung or the 'Individual Psychology' of Adler. All these systems are alike, of course, in that they involve psychological rather than physical methods of treatment in the sense explained above;[3] but they involve various differences in theory and technique. Much of what is said in this chapter is applicable to all types of therapy. One of my chief reasons for emphasizing psycho-analytic theory is that it is commonly regarded as being the arch-enemy to religious belief, whereas Jungian and Adlerian theory, if suspect at all, are suspect to a much less extent.

We may note in passing that, just as it is illegitimate to invoke Freud

[1] For an interesting and provocative challenge on these grounds, see H. J. Eysenck, *Uses and Abuses of Psychology* (Pelican, 1953), chapter 12.

[2] Thus E. Glover writes, 'Whoever conceives of mind in the structural sense as an *apparatus* or *instrument* is under obligation to concede or at any rate to conceive the existence of mental energy which sets this apparatus in motion' (his italics). From E. Glover, *Freud or Jung* (Allen & Unwin, 1946), p. 52.

[3] See p. 117.

in order to discredit traditional religion, so also it is illegitimate to invoke Jung, as some have done, in support of it. Psychology is in a peculiar position among the sciences in that moral and religious beliefs do, in a sense, form part of its subject-matter. This is not to say that assertions on what we should say about God, how we should live, or how we should treat our fellow men are part of the subject-matter of psychology, any more than they are part of the subject-matter of physics or chemistry. The psychologist does investigate, however, what people have *thought* about such matters and how their behaviour is influenced by their beliefs. Jung is clearly more sympathetic to religious beliefs than Freud. Indeed his sympathies extend to a wide range of religious beliefs, and he tends in general to use what may be called 'language of uplift' where Freud gives the appearance of belittling human nature. For example, one of Jung's books is entitled *Modern Man in Search of a Soul*. In contrast Freud adopts the amazingly perverse procedure of entitling a book on religion *The Future of an Illusion*, and then explaining that he is using 'illusion' in a special sense such that 'X is an illusion' does not necessarily entail 'X is false'. But however much we may agree with Jung's more sympathetic outlook towards religious aspirations, it does not follow that his 'language of uplift' necessarily supplies us with a theory that is better scientifically. In so far as there are genuine theoretical disagreements between Freud and Jung—as opposed to differences of personal temperament—these disagreements can be resolved only by methods appropriate to science.[1]

One final difficulty requires to be mentioned—that of Freud's anti-authoritarianism. Freud was out to shock. His discoveries—at least to my judgment—could have been presented in much less harsh a form. The irrational and conflicting impulses which he has taught us to look for in ourselves and others were operative, not surprisingly, in his case too. He has been described as 'one who called salvation a lie and devised a means of effecting something very like salvation . . ., a moral puritan who described life in terms of sexuality . . ., a loyal Jew who hated Judaism . . ., an intellectual giant, a tireless investigator'.[2] These

---

[1] There are, of course, all degrees of deviation from the original Freudian viewpoint. Even among those who can quite properly be labelled 'psycho-analysts', there are some who are not fully orthodox Freudians, e.g. Melanie Klein, John Bowlby, W. R. D. Fairbairn, and the late Karen Horney. A 'fundamentalist' Freudian viewpoint—acceptance of Freud's original system *in toto*—seems to me hard to defend.

[2] Quoted from *The British Journal of Psychology*, Volume XLVII, Part 2, May 1956. The writer is W. R. D. Fairbairn, in a review of Volume II of Ernest Jones' biography of Freud.

words give us at least some glimmering into the complexities of his character, and suggest the need for an attitude of understanding and tolerance rather than one of suspicion and hostility.

Freud's attacks on traditional religious belief cannot be regarded as serious pieces of scholarship. It follows, from our point of view, that to discover the relevance of psycho-analytic theory to religion it is relatively unprofitable to examine in detail the writings of Freud himself. The procedure which I propose to adopt in this chapter is to formulate in my own words possible sources of conflict between psycho-analytic theory and religion, rather than rely, to any great extent, on the exact words of Freud himself. We can give ourselves, in my opinion, a better appreciation of Freudian theory if we discount his anti-authoritarianism.

For purposes of discussion I propose to group possible sources of conflict between psycho-analytic theory and religion under five main heads. (1) In the first place it might be argued that acceptance of psycho-analytic theory necessarily commits us to being determinists. (2) Secondly, psycho-analytic theory throws interesting light on the origins of our moral beliefs, and, so Freud would claim, on the origins of belief in God. This particular disclosure of origins might seem to suggest that both moral beliefs and belief in God are discredited. (3) Thirdly, psycho-analytic theory tries to explain the emotional significance of particular religious myths and rituals, and it might seem that, if a person's analysis is successful, he would no longer have the need to accept such myths or perform such rituals, which are therefore discredited. (4) Fourthly, it might be argued that the whole moral outlook of psycho-analysts is necessarily anti-religious, that they belittle the ideas of sin and guilt, and, in general, have values different from those of a religious person. (5) Finally, it might be said that psycho-analysis aims at 'the cure of souls' and it is therefore setting up as a substitute for religion.

I

The argument that psycho-analysis necessarily involves belief in determinism, and that belief in free-will is, in Freud's words, 'quite unscientific', has been discussed in Chapter 10, and the question will not be reopened here.

2

The second argument was that psycho-analysis, by revealing the origins of our moral and religious beliefs, makes these beliefs discredited.

Now in a general way it is clearly false to suggest that, once the origins of a belief are revealed, that belief is necessarily false. For example, if someone says, 'My acceptance of Christianity owes its origin to a sermon preached by Canon X last year', he is certainly not giving away information which proves his belief to be mistaken. If the argument is to be valid, therefore, there must presumably be some special reason, peculiar to psycho-analysis, why a disclosure of origins should also be regarded as an attack on validity.

One such special reason seems to be that people in the past have thought of religious and moral ideas as being 'supernaturally imposed'.[1] If therefore it can be shown that they have natural rather than supernatural origins, it would seem that we have less ground for taking them seriously. We can in that case no longer think of conscience as 'the voice of God' or regard our awareness of God or of moral ideas as the direct outcome of a revelation by God.

This argument is one long muddle. The muddle can best be exposed by bringing in the verification principle. If we do so we see at once that the words 'supernaturally imposed' and 'imposed by God' cannot be given the requisite 'cash-value'. We just do not know what psychological findings would enable us to decide whether a belief was 'supernaturally imposed' or 'imposed by God'. As we saw in Chapter 8, the word 'God' cannot function as a causal explanation such as a scientist might wish to invoke. Similarly it is quite uninformative scientifically, if we have no explanation of an occurrence to hand, to invoke the supernatural and say that it must have a 'supernatural' explanation. The assumption that supernaturally imposed beliefs have a special claim on our allegiance is futile for the simple reason that the words 'supernaturally imposed', if not meaningless, are at any rate extremely problematic. There is thus no room for the further argument that beliefs having a 'natural' origin are discredited.

It does not follow, of course, that there is no use for phrases such as 'conscience', 'voice of God within the soul' and so on, provided we are not too literal-minded in our interpretation of such talk. To obey one's

[1] Dr Ernest Jones, writing in *The Observer*, asks whether our moral beliefs 'have a natural or a supernatural origin'.

conscience is to act in accordance with a particular moral conviction, and 'conscience' can be regarded as the faculty by which a person's moral decisions are reached. To say that it is the voice of God should be taken to mean that its demands have a serious claim upon us; it should certainly not be understood as a claim that a para-physical process of 'revelation' has been carried out by a para-physical 'Being'. It is equally meaningless to assert either that this mysterious process did take place or that it did not.

The argument that psycho-analytic theory shows that our religious and moral beliefs have a natural and not a supernatural origin need not therefore be taken seriously. There are, however, more important reasons why belief in God and moral beliefs appear to be discredited as a result of psycho-analytic findings.

Let us take first of all belief in God. A lonely child may have phantasies of imaginary playmates. If he tells us that such playmates are real people, we do not believe him. Freud's claim would be that belief in a human-like God presents something of a parallel. The child has a special motive for wanting an imaginary playmate, and we know from the evidence that in supposing that there actually is such a playmate the child is wrong. Now according to Freud, it is precisely because people have wanted the reassurance of fatherly affection that they have found it necessary to invent God. Belief in God is a neurosis, a relic of childhood. The adult should learn to stand on his own feet, and to face the world as it actually is, cold, hostile, and relentless.[1]

We need to note, however, that there is clearly a difference between believing in the existence of imaginary playmates and believing in God. We know from observational evidence that there are no imaginary playmates; but, unless we are thinking of an altogether human-like god such as some of the ancient Greeks may have believed in, it is not clear whether 'There is a God' is a statement that can be settled as a result of observational evidence at all. This problem (which is to form one of the central themes of Part III of this book) is one which had not even been considered in Freud's day. Even, however, if we try to put ourselves in the position of those who, like Freud, are unaware of the philosophical difficulties in the assertion 'There is a God', it would still not follow that Freud had shown this assertion to be false, let alone used his own

[1] Compare *The Future of an Illusion* (translated by W. D. Robson-Scott, Hogarth, 1928), p. 86. 'Man cannot remain a child for ever; he must venture at last into the hostile world.'

particular clinical findings to do so. It is far from clear that the world is the hostile place which Freud supposes. At best his argument would be 'On the assumption that belief in God is false I can account for the fact that this false belief is widespread'.

If we pass on to the question of our moral beliefs and their origin, further problems arise. Let us take a particular example. A young child, let us say, has aggressive oral phantasies; in phantasy he wants to bite, or even eat up, say, his parents, brothers or sisters.[1] And yet in some part of himself he knows that such phantasies are dangerous. A strong barrier must be set up which prevents these wishes from coming out into the open. (This talk of 'barriers' etc. is, of course, highly metaphorical, but it is the sort of language that is commonly used, and it is not difficult to ignore the misleading aspects of the metaphor.) This barrier takes the form of a strong prohibition—emanating, as Freud would say, from the 'superego'.[2] This prohibition becomes generalized, and in adult life takes the form of a strong resistance to eating *anything* that has been alive. In other words, the person becomes an ardent vegetarian. Another person, let us say, through fear of his primitive aggressive impulses, becomes an ardent pacifist.

Now let us suppose, for purposes of argument, that comparable cases to this are regularly to be found and have been accurately reported. What do they prove? It seems to follow that when we know the origin of a particular belief, we are very much less disposed to take that belief seriously. The person's vegetarianism or his pacifism seems discredited. His convictions may be strongly held; and yet we know that his superego is operating at a primitive or childish level. Prohibitions that were appropriate for early infancy are, as it were, dogging the person's footsteps and preventing him from courses of action that in adult life are appropriate and even desirable. Indeed one of the main purposes of

[1] This example is taken from R. S. Lee, *op. cit.*, pp. 151–2.

[2] The 'superego' is thought of as a sort of monitor who protects the 'ego' from the aggressive impulses emanating from the 'id', the primitive animal part of our nature. These curious personifications are not, I think, an indispensable part of psycho-analytic theory; but many have found such talk illuminating. Compare S. Isaacs, *Social Development in Young Children* (Routledge, 1933), pp. 228–9. It is misleading, however, to equate the technical term 'superego' with the familiar word 'conscience'. 'Conscience' suggests something sacred, whose dictates have a *prima facie* claim as our obedience. The 'superego' should be thought of simply as a biological device (compare J. C. Flügel, *Man, Morals, and Society*, Duckworth, 1945, pp. 259–60); and its dictates, so far from being sacred, may at times be altogether unsatisfactory. Prohibitions which were appropriate in the phantasy-world of the infant may be quite out of place in adult life.

therapy is often said to be the removal of irrational prohibitions so that the person can deal with life's problems realistically.

What the argument does *not* tell us is whether vegetarianism or pacifism are in themselves realistic and sensible answers to particular problems. It is perfectly possible for people to hold correct moral beliefs from bad motives; and, though a knowledge that there are irrational motives leading a person to a particular belief may lead us to view that belief with suspicion, it does not follow that the belief is mistaken. If another person adopts the viewpoint of an ardent militarist, and we somehow learn that he is in effect finding an outlet for some primitive aggressive wishes, this tells us nothing about whether ardent militarism is an appropriate attitude for the present-day world.

If it were found by independent criteria that all those holding a particular moral or religious belief were mentally very sick people, then we should rightly suspect such a belief of being false. There is at least the possibility in principle here of conflict between psycho-analytic theory and religion. But as far as one can tell on the evidence, the church-going population of this country contains all sorts of people, of all degrees of mental health. Even if adequate criteria for being 'neurotic' were laid down, and it was established that there were more neurotic individuals in the church-going population than in the non-church-going population, we should not be justified in supposing church-going to be futile so long as there were even a minority of church-goers whose judgment we respected.

To press home this argument still further, I shall now consider two purely hypothetical examples. These examples are for illustration purposes only, and are not intended to be reports of actual discoveries.

Let us suppose, then, that some research-worker decides to make character-studies of all those, say in Great Britain or elsewhere, who register as conscientious objectors to war. Let us suppose that in a given group of conscientious objectors more neurotic symptoms were displayed than in an otherwise comparable group of conscript soldiers. We need not, of course, concern ourselves with the practical difficulties of establishing such a conclusion, nor, as has been said already, with the question whether such a result is in fact likely. The question which concerns us is, Would such a result serve to discredit the policy of conscientious objection and make us unwilling to take it seriously? The answer, I suggest, is that if there were no conscientious objectors at all who appeared to be acting from rational motives, our views might be influenced; but if even a minority were people whose judgment we respected, no valid conclusions about conscientious objection or about pacifism in general could be drawn.

My second example is admittedly a far-fetched one; but the point which it illustrates is, I think, important. Someone discovers, let us suppose, that all those who were breast-fed as babies regularly profess themselves to be theists, while all those who were bottle-fed regularly profess themselves to be atheists. Even this finding, however, would prove nothing about the relative merits of theism and atheism. It would show only the amazing power of early conditioning, and would indicate that people are not as free to choose their religious beliefs as we might have supposed.

To sum up this section; it would seem that an account in psycho-analytic terms of the origin of our moral beliefs does not show those beliefs to be mistaken, but that there are times when it may make such beliefs suspect. What this amounts to in effect is that even our cherished convictions are liable to error. This, however, is nothing new. As we have seen in Chapter 6, the same conclusion has been reached quite independently of psycho-analysis, and it would seem therefore that psycho-analytic findings merely serve to lend additional emphasis to what we know already.

3

Psycho-analytic theory, as is well known, can contribute to our understanding of religious myth and ritual. To quote examples, it might be said that when Adam is represented in the story of the garden of Eden as being ashamed of his nakedness this represents a phantasy of infantile guilt on sexual matters. Similarly, one of the earliest infantile needs is to take in food. In phantasy this means to the infant an actual taking in of the mother. Now it might be said that light can be thrown on the central Christian rite, the communion service, if we regard it as a *taking in* of Jesus Christ much as the young infant takes in his mother. The whole idea of eating something so as to become like what you have eaten is a very common one among primitive peoples.

Now it might seem as though such treatment of myth and ritual is disparaging. When a person has undergone analysis, it might be thought, he has no need to take seriously myths embodying phantasies about nakedness; they are no longer a problem to him. Similarly he might have no need to re-enact what appear to be infantile feeding situations; the communion service would just not be important for him.

This line of argument seems to suggest in addition that religion is a matter of personal temperament. It might be allowed, perhaps, that even for adults certain religious myths and rituals can provide appropriate answers for their problems, but it would not follow that the same answers are suitable for everyone. The minister of religion thus appears to be offering a patent medicine which he claims is a panacea, whereas the psycho-analyst considers individual needs.

Now many religious people would admit that, within limits, religion is a matter for personal temperament. The exact forms of worship that a person finds appropriate are, on this view, a matter that he can well decide for himself, and a matter on which we can all appropriately be tolerant. But it does not follow that the central demands made, for instance, by Christianity, are demands appropriate only for those of a particular temperament. Religious language such as 'I beseech you, therefore, brethren, by the mercies of God, that ye present your bodies a living sacrifice, holy, acceptable unto God, which is your reasonable service'[1] is intended to be universally binding, and it is clearly quite wrong to say that once a person is cured of his neurosis these demands are no longer applicable. Moreover if people take such demands seriously they may in many cases also see fit to take part in religious ritual which commemorates the 'living sacrifice' of Jesus Christ. The form which the ritual takes may be related to infantile phantasies of eating, but it does not follow that such ritual is necessarily inappropriate for adults.

It is fair to conclude, therefore, that the application of psychoanalytic concepts in the field of myth and ritual does not necessarily establish that any particular myth or piece of ritual is unimportant.

4

We come now to the argument that the moral outlook of psycho-analysts is necessarily anti-religious, that they belittle the ideas of sin and guilt, and in general have values different from those of a religious person.

It may well be the case that some, and perhaps most, psycho-analysts do not take the claims of traditional religion seriously. This, however, is unimportant unless it can be shown that they have special reasons, arising out of psycho-analysis itself, for not doing so.

[1] Romans xii. 1.

Now, as we have argued already in Chapter 6, decisions of policy can be influenced by factual considerations. For example, if we regard it as established that solitary confinement does not induce prisoners to alter their ways, we may be disposed not to advocate the policy of solitary confinement. Now there is no doubt that the factual considerations which psycho-analysts stress have influenced present-day policies in the field of education. We need not here take sides on controversial matters; but it is fair to say that those who take psycho-analytic findings seriously have a tendency, in view of their special knowledge, to take what may be loosely called a 'progressive' view in education. The catchwords include, for instance, 'free expression' and 'security', and the traditional ideas about strict discipline and corporal punishment are viewed with disfavour. A person is regarded as unfortunate if he is able to announce—as some have done in the past—'My father brought me up with a cane in one hand and a Bible in the other'. It can be said, therefore, that there genuinely *is* a conflict between psycho-analysis and this particular variety of 'cane-and-Bible' religion; the standards and viewpoints of the two sides are altogether incompatible. The obvious reply here, on the part of the religious believer, is that 'cane-and-Bible' religion should not be called 'religion' at all, and that those who sympathize with 'progressive' views in education have still a wide range of religious beliefs open to them, many of which are very far removed from beliefs of the 'cane-and-Bible' variety.

It might still be said that there is a special problem in connection with guilt. According to the Christian conception man is a sinner; and it would seem that the analyst, in trying to remove feelings of guilt, is suggesting that these feelings are harmful, and encouraging the patient not to take his shortcomings seriously. This argument, however, is undoubtedly mistaken. Certainly one of the purposes of treatment is to remove guilt that is pathological. A small child, let us say, has wished, perhaps unconsciously, for the death of his younger brother, a hated rival. As things turn out this brother dies. Now to the young child wishes are omnipotent; and it may therefore seem to the child that his own wishes were responsible for killing the brother. Overwhelming feelings of guilt may arise, which have a serious effect on the child's relationships with others later in life. In this case his feelings of guilt are clearly pathological. With an adult knowledge of the facts he will no longer blame himself, and his relations to others may improve. Now on other occasions what the person has done may be something for which he may legitimately blame himself. On such an occasion his guilt is not pathological but rational. Let us suppose, for example, that a person who has taken part in an atom-bomb raid comes in for analysis, and it transpires that he feels extremely guilty about the part which he played in the raid. Now whether we label such guilt pathological or rational depends on our beliefs about the rightness and wrongness of using the atom bomb. In appropriate circumstances such a person could doubtless be helped by an analyst in a number of ways. But the analyst will not, *qua* analyst, take sides on whether it was right or wrong to take part in the raid, nor whether his patient is justified in feeling guilty. The most he can do is to make clear to the patient the patient's own feelings on the matter and free him of irrationalities so that he makes a realistic adult decision. If a decision is realistic, the analyst does not interfere; and if, for instance, the patient decides to spend the rest of his life in a monastery by way or penitence, no analyst would regard it as his job to interfere. When the patient makes a decision on adult grounds, it is not for the analyst to question it.

It may still be said that the notions of sin and guilt are outmoded, and that a religion which lays stress on these notions can no longer be taken seriously in the twentieth century. In earlier times those suffering from disease were assumed to be morally blameworthy,[1] and even until quite recent times so-called 'mental' disease has carried a social stigma. Nowadays, however, on the whole, offending children are put on probation or sent to a child-guidance clinic rather than forced to make retribution;[2] and even in the case of adults the emphasis is on rehabilitation and cure rather than on punishment in the purely retributive sense. The dilemma for the Christian, it would seem—and for the Christian psychologist in particular—is that he cannot both welcome this new attitude as enlightened and also cling to the traditional religious notions of sin and guilt.

If this argument is right, there is no need any longer to take seriously the story of Adam and Eve, or to think of the death of Jesus Christ as supplying 'redemption'.

I would suggest, however, that the apparent conflict arises through misapprehension. It is still part of a reaction against 'cane-and-Bible'

[1] Compare John ix. 2.

[2] Those who still cling to the idea that lawbreakers must at all costs be punished, irrespective of consequences, may sometimes themselves be the victims of irrational prejudice. For further discussion of this point, see K. Friedlander, *The Psycho-Analytical Approach to Juvenile Delinquency* (Kegan Paul, 1947).

religion. It is all too easy to think of a smug nineteenth-century 'religious' person, who is unperturbed by social inequality, and is at all times ready to denounce the sins of others. Harry Graham, in his book *Strained Relations*,[1] has a poem called 'Grandpapa' which brilliantly characterizes this sort of person.

> *If I was late for morning prayers*
> *I saw dire retribution looming,*
> *Though stealthily I crept downstairs,*
> *And knelt, and smelt the study chairs*
> *While Grandpa's voice kept booming,*
> *I knew I should be soundly trounced*
> *After the Blessing was pronounced.*

Now the modern attitude is essentially a reaction against 'Grandpapa' and his kind; and we may wholeheartedly agree that, if this is the sort of association to be attached to the word 'sin', and if the word 'religion' is understood to mean 'religion as practised by Grandpapa', then of course let us abandon all talk of 'sin' and work for the overthrow of 'religion' in general. If God is thought of as a fierce monarch, like Grandpapa but perhaps worse, then it is reasonable to sympathize with Freud and say that the sooner we are rid of such vengeful 'father-figures' the better.

If we turn, however, from this sort of religion to the religion preached by Jesus, it is astonishing to note the change. There were 'religious' people like Grandpapa even in those days; many of the Pharisees were doubtless people of this sort, and perhaps we do not always realize how very respectable and 'religious' they were. It is a 'priest' in the parable of the Good Samaritan who passes by on the other side,[2] and it is the 'religious' people who are told 'The publicans and the harlots go into the kingdom of God before you'.[3] There is denunciation of sin, certainly; but much of it is directed towards those who are self-righteously preoccupied with the sins of others. The message here is, 'He that is without sin among you, let him first cast a stone at her.'[4] There is nothing in all this to suggest that we should not take our own sins and shortcomings seriously; what is stressed is that we are all in the same predicament, and that an attitude of moral superiority to our fellows is misplaced.[5] There is nothing here that an analyst can legitimately

---

[1] Methuen, 1926, p. 9.    [2] Luke x. 31 and 32.    [3] Matthew xxi. 31.
[4] John viii. 7.                                              [5] Romans iii. 22 and 23.

dispute, and indeed it is a message which many analysts might well see fit to accept.

Finally, it may be said that analysts take an irreligious line on sexual matters. The chief point here seems to be that an analysis on Freudian lines necessarily involves paying a large amount of attention to the sexual life of the patient. Rumours therefore fly about that analysts actively encourage patients in a life of sexual incontinence and go so far as to recommend it as a cure for neurosis. It would seem, then, that their standards are quite at variance with those of a religious person.

This argument is based largely on ignorance of what psycho-analysis is attempting to achieve. At the outset it should be noted that it is highly doubtful whether any otherwise responsible analyst has actually encouraged behaviour of that sort. Certainly it would be entirely contrary to the general practice of most analysts. That *stories should arise* of analysts behaving in this way is not surprising. An analyst can quite well appear in that light in the phantasy of his patient, and the patient may genuinely believe his supposition to be right. But nothing that a patient says about his analyst should be accepted uncritically.

In any case the function of psycho-analysis is not to advise people on how to solve their problems. Two of the main purposes are to make the person understand himself better and to free him from irrational prohibitions which prevent him living a satisfactory life. What he does with his life afterwards is no business of the analyst. The analysis is carried out to help the person to 'grow up', and when a person is grown up he must decide life's problems for himself.

Often both patient and analyst may be in full agreement as to what a 'satisfactory life' would be, provided the patient could achieve it. For example a mother may find herself unable, as a result of some child-hood frustration, to love her own daughter. By 'working through' her early phantasies she may find that they cease to influence her. In this case there is no doubt as to the appropriate attitude; it is to give love and affection to the daughter whom earlier she was unable to love. But this is something that the patient must decide, not the analyst. In other cases serious reality-problems may arise—educating children, returning to a husband, and so on. An analyst may be able to give a person insight as to *why* she finds her husband difficult, and thus indirectly alleviate the home situation, but it would never be the business of an analyst to advise or suggest to a patient that she ought to return to her husband.

It may still be argued, however, that implicitly the standards of the analyst are different from those of the orthodox religious person. The right attitude to sexual malpractices, it might be said, is to condemn them. The analyst, by not registering any personal disapproval, is in effect condoning them, and thus inculcating wrong moral standards.

But there is nothing in such an argument to suggest that analysts are people who actually approve of sexual malpractices. That they do not register active disapproval is simply part of their technique. They might well argue that to show disapproval will contribute nothing towards the process of cure, whereas their own techniques may in due course remove the need for them. In the same way an analyst may not show active disapproval if a child in treatment shows a strong wish to break a window. It does not follow that analysts are in general favourably disposed to the breaking of windows.

Certainly the findings of psycho-analysis have influenced ideas on how education on sexual matters should be given, but it is quite mistaken to say that psycho-analysis, as such, involves an immoral attitude towards sex.

## 5

It might be said that psycho-analysis aims at 'the cure of souls' and is therefore setting itself up as a substitute for religion. On this showing the pastoral work of the priest is simply 'quack' psychology. By lucky guesses the priest may achieve a limited amount, but his work has no adequate theoretical basis and he lacks the right sort of training.

This does not seem to me a very sensible view. It is, of course, true that in the present age there is far more specialization than there was a few hundred years previously. In the past it was the rôle of the parish priest to minister to personal needs of every possible kind. Bishop Berkeley, for instance, in advocating tar-water for the citizens of Cloyne, was in effect taking on the rôle of family doctor. Nowadays there is an ever-growing army of specialists—doctors, district nurses, health visitors, probation officers, social workers, N.S.P.C.C. officers, and so on; and to some extent these specialists have taken over jobs that were once done by the parish priest. The psycho-analyst can no doubt be included in this army of specialists, and, in a sense, perhaps, he is doing, more systematically, part of what the parish priest did as best he could.

Most ministers of religion would agree, however, that their central task is to preach the gospel. Anything else that they do—social work, organizing boys' clubs, taking the chair at meetings, and so on—would be regarded by them as incidental. Whether we think that preaching of the gospel is something valuable depends, not surprisingly, on our attitude to the gospel. But it is a great mistake to regard the commands 'Repent ye'[1] and 'Turn unto the Lord your God'[2] as cures for neurosis. They are rather attempts to answer the question 'How ought we to live?', a question that confronts neurotic and healthy people alike.

It may well be that there are important parallels between psychoanalysis and the confessional. Both involve personal interview and the discussion of guilt feelings, and both priest and therapist are in some sense in the rôle of *father*. But there is an all-important difference in that the priest figures as the representative of God, and, as that representative, he is empowered to pronounce forgiveness of sin. The analyst, on the other hand, is simply himself, and he has no right either to pass judgment or to offer forgiveness.

If the parish priest were trying to do the same thing as a psychotherapist, there would be some justification for regarding him as a 'quack'. But apart from a certain amount of overlap, their rôles are very different.

In passing it may be added that the presence of this overlap lends colour to the view that parish priests should receive at least a small amount of training in psychology. This, however, is largely a matter of what is administratively convenient at particular times and places. In the absence of 'preventive' social workers at the present time, there is no doubt that many tasks such as preventing a home from breaking up fall on the parish priest, and, so long as that is so, a knowledge of psychology is likely to help him. But it does not follow that his main rôle in life is that of a social worker.

It might still be argued that the priest and the social worker are using methods which are fundamentally different. The psychiatrically trained social worker will apply special techniques, to a greater or lesser extent of a psycho-analytic kind, while the priest will advocate prayer, worship, and so on. And it may be said that if, for instance, a mother is unable to love her child, as in our earlier example, it is psycho-analytic techniques that will help her, not prayer. Confronted with a body of Christian doctrine which in its general purport drives home to her that she *ought* to love this child, she will feel only the more guilty as a result of prayer and worship, whereas therapy gets to the root of her trouble.

[1] Mark i. 15.    [2] Joel ii. 13.

# The contribution of psycho-analysis

This criticism would be valid, I think, if it is assumed that prayer and worship are aimed at curing neurosis. It is difficult to believe, however, that this is the correct way of regarding prayer. The publican in the parable who says 'God be merciful to me a sinner'[1] is clearly not trying to 'cure' himself of anything in the literal medical sense; he is rather using the language of commitment and dedication. Many people, certainly, regard prayer as a means of self-discipline; but there is nothing in psycho-analytic theory to suggest that, after successful treatment, such self-discipline is unnecessary. In general it may be said that the purpose of psycho-analysis—removal of neurotic phantasies—and the purposes of prayer—commitment and self-dedication—are so different that there can be no question of regarding them as rival methods of achieving the same end.

If someone asks 'Are the findings of psycho-analytic theory incompatible with religious belief?', much depends on what particular religious beliefs the person has in mind. Certainly it would be a mistake in general to suppose that the advent of psycho-analytic theory has had no repercussion on religious ways of thinking. But as far as the central religious notions of repentance, forgiveness, commitment, and dedication are concerned, there is nothing in psycho-analytic theory—any more than in any other factual investigation—to prove or even make plausible the view that such ideas are unimportant, or that a life which gives expression to these ideas is the wrong sort of life to live.

[1] Luke xviii. 13.

# PART THREE

PART THREE

# CHAPTER 13

# *Religious language: Introduction*

The central purpose in Part II of this book was to expose the 'absolute-existence' mistake. To make this mistake is to ask, as a literal, first-order question, what different sorts of entity the universe contains, and whether we are justified in believing in the existence of 'a reality that transcends physical explanation'.[1] Materialism and behaviourism (in the popular sense of these words) involve a negative answer to such questions; psychical research is thought by some to justify an affirmative one. There thus appears to be head-on disagreement. Yet those who disagree at least share the assumption that the question which they are trying to answer is a meaningful one. It is this assumption which I have tried to challenge; and I have argued that the literal materialist and the literal anti-materialist are equally mistaken.

Throughout the argument I have made free use of the verification principle. I have used it, not indeed as a militant logical positivist might have used it, as a means of exposing all sentences as meaningless unless they are empirically verifiable, but rather as a means of making explicit what sort of assertions are being made or what sort of questions are being asked. Even if an assertion cannot be verified or falsified empirically, it can quite well have a legitimate function. I have insisted, however, on the need to know what that function is and what exactly is at stake. 'Absolute-existence' questions have been rejected as meaningless precisely because nothing seems to be at stake and because no indication can conceivably be given of what would constitute a final and adequate solution to them.

It remains, in Part III, to apply the same techniques in investigating the language of religion.

For the most part I shall be concerned with the Christian religion,

[1] Professor Rhine's phrase. Compare p. 106 of this book.

although much of what is said may apply, *mutatis mutandis*, to other religions also.

Religious language is of many different sorts. Much of it is what we shall call in Chapter 16 'the language of parable'; some is simple moral exhortation, some is the language of worship and dedication; some refers to the experiences of the religious believer, and in some cases there is reference to straightforward historical fact. In view of this variety, it is unsatisfactory to ask simply 'What is the function of religious language?' for the only answer can be that it has many functions. What is required is to find out what variety of religious language the questioner has in mind. The argument of this book will be concerned in particular with sentences containing the word 'God'.

My central conclusion is that it is wrong to interpret such sentences in para-physical terms. Just as we cannot legitimately ask whether souls or values exist as para-physical entities in addition to familiar 'physical' entities such as chairs, so we cannot ask whether there exists a para-physical entity called 'God'. Popular controversy has assumed that it makes sense to ask what are the constituents of the universe or what the universe contains, and that the important question is whether a God should or should not be included in the list. A materialist, on this view, is one who says 'No', and a theist one who says 'Yes'. I shall argue that the whole controversy is vitiated by the 'absolute-existence' mistake. It makes no sense to ask whether God is or is not an 'absolute-existent' —one of the contents of the universe—nor whether the universe *contains* a God in the 'absolute' sense. A literal theism is as misguided as a literal materialism.

Some readers may immediately jump to the conclusion that this view involves a fundamental threat to their religion. Let me hasten to reassure them that this is not so. Certain simple-minded ways of talking about God admittedly need to be abandoned; but there is nothing in the argument to suggest that the central truths of Christianity are invalid. What I am urging is in many ways more like a theological technicality than a new set of religious beliefs; and one of my main purposes is to rid religious thinking of what I take to be misapprehensions. Professional theologians will, of course, already be aware of some of the difficulties involved in applying the notion of 'existence' in any literal way to God; and I shall be more than satisfied if they are prepared to treat my central thesis as an attempt to throw further light on these difficulties.

# Religious language: Introduction

For the next two chapters (14 and 15) I propose to write in dialogue form. This will enable me to present two apparently conflicting views side by side for comparison, and to set out argument and counter-argument in an easily recognizable way. I shall try to resolve the apparent conflict between the two participants without asking either to give up anything which he considers important. The spokesman for my own views will be labelled 'Philosopher'; his colleague will be labelled 'Theologian'. 'Philosopher' may be thought of as one who has been influenced by present-day philosophical techniques and is also willing to take the claims of religion seriously. 'Theologian' may be thought of as one who, without being an ardent advocate of these techniques, is none the less prepared to admit that they may have something valuable to contribute.

I shall classify sentences containing the word 'God' into three classes, which I shall label 'simple literal theism', 'qualified literal theism', and 'the language of parable'. The basis of this classification will be explained during the course of the discussion. My general conclusion is that the first two types of sentence have no claim on our allegiance, the language of simple literal theism because it is false, and the language of qualified literal theism because it is meaningless. The language of parable, however, which includes all the important religious assertions about God, such as 'God is light'[1] or 'God is love',[2] has every right to be taken seriously.

In Chapter 16 I shall explain in further detail what I mean by 'the language of parable'. In Chapter 17 I shall discuss the problem of petitionary prayer, and in Chapter 18 I shall try to resolve a number of difficulties that have arisen on the subject of miracles. In Chapter 19 I shall examine a number of different assertions that form part of Christian doctrine, such as those connected with the Incarnation and the Trinity. Such language, it will be suggested, though admittedly meaningless if taken literally, has a perfectly legitimate function if understood as the language of parable. In Chapter 20 I shall make some comments on the historical claims which are part of orthodox Christianity. Chapter 21 will be a summary of the main views put forward in the book.

[1] 1 John i. 5.     [2] 1 John iv. 8.

# CHAPTER 14

## *Sentences containing the word 'God'*

### I. CLEARING THE GROUND

*Theologian:* May we start by trying to clear the ground? I've heard a great deal about modern techniques in philosophy. People tell me that metaphysics is dead, and then other people tell me that it is strongly alive and did not die at all. Some talk about 'logical positivism'; others talk about 'linguistic philosophy'; others still say that neither of these two labels is appropriate. Some say that it all constitutes a basic threat to Christianity; others say that from its very nature it can have no religious significance. The result is that I, and many others, just do not know where we stand. To start with, then, I suggest that you yourself make your own position clear; and I should like, if you are agreeable, to ask you a few questions.

*Philosopher:* Certainly.

*Theologian:* In the first place, are you a logical positivist?

*Philosopher:* No. One of the essential features of logical positivism—at least in my interpretation of the words—is the belief that moral and religious assertions do not require to be taken seriously. I do not myself accept such belief for one moment. If you put some different interpretation on the words 'logical positivist', it is just conceivable that the label would be appropriate in my case, but only in some thoroughly watered-down sense.

*Theologian:* I take it, however, that you would still call yourself an 'empiricist'?

*Philosopher:* No. An 'empiricist', as I understand the term, is one who believes that empirical assertions have some sort of privileged status. I am in no way committed to such an evaluation.

*Theologian:* Do you not share with the logical positivists and other empirically minded philosophers the belief that metaphysics is impossible?

*Philosopher:* If I said 'Yes', I should have to make a large number of important reservations. The trouble here, as with many philosophical questions, is that there are reasons both for saying 'Yes' and for saying 'No'. The metaphysical questions which philosophers are discussing nowadays are not radically different from the metaphysical questions discussed by philosophers of the past. And yet those who said 'Metaphysics is impossible' were, I think, trying to say something important.

*Theologian:* Perhaps you could make your position a little clearer.

*Philosopher:* The only type of metaphysician that I have any quarrel with is the metaphysician who makes the 'absolute-existence' mistake. You know my reasons for saying this already,[1] and I shall not repeat them. All I need say is that I have come to you with no assumptions or presuppositions at all except that 'absolute-existence' assertions are meaningless.

*Theologian:* What is your attitude to the verification principle?

*Philosopher:* I certainly do not wish to claim that all sentences are meaningless if they cannot be verified or falsified by empirical means. But I am willing to use the verification principle as a philosophical tool. In particular I think it is of value in forcing us to distinguish empirical sentences from others, and in exposing sentences which purport to be factually significant when they are in principle unverifiable and unfalsifiable.

*Theologian:* Are you insisting, then, that only empirical sentences can be factually significant?

*Philosopher:* Yes; I want that to be true by definition. In other words I regard with favour the usage in which 'empirical' and 'factually significant' are treated as synonymous terms.

*Theologian:* But by making a linguistic proposal of this sort, are you not begging the important question? The important question, surely, is whether, in addition to empirical facts, there are other facts—metaphysical ones—which cannot be known about by empirical means. Your definition seems to me to beg this question.

*Philosopher:* No. Either to assert or to deny that there are such facts is to make the 'absolute-existence' mistake.

*Theologian:* In other words, if I accept your argument about 'absolute

---

[1] See chapter 4.

existence', I cannot accuse you of begging the question when you say that only empirical assertions are factually significant.

*Philosopher:* Precisely. And my argument about 'absolute existence' is one which I hope you, as a theologian, will be prepared to accept.

*Theologian:* Whether I accept it will depend, I think, on the way in which you apply it to sentences about God. Certainly many people have thought of God as a 'metaphysical entity' in your 'absolute'-sense. That is to say, they would be very surprised if you told them they could not ask whether there existed a God in addition to ordinary empirical objects.

*Philosopher:* A sort of para-empirical or para-physical God, you mean? This is precisely the view which I wish to combat; and I very much hope that you will join me in combating it.

*Theologian:* I must first find out more clearly what you mean. But I certainly have my suspicions that your views—call them 'logical positivism' or what you will—are a serious threat to religious orthodoxy.

*Philosopher:* I shall do my best to convince you that they are not.


2. THE CHALLENGE

*Theologian:* May we take it, then, that there is a challenge to theologians, based primarily on the claim that sentences ascribing existence in what you call the 'absolute' sense are meaningless?

*Philosopher:* Precisely.

*Theologian:* Would you now make clear, then, in what that challenge consists?

*Philosopher:* I should like to start by considering a number of different uses of the word 'exist'. Before I start on my main argument, however, may I dispose of a philosophical technicality which may otherwise confuse our argument?

*Theologian:* Please do.

*Philosopher:* Let us consider, then, the four following assertions— (*a*) Does X exist? (*b*) Is X a real existent? (*c*) Does there exist an X? (*d*) Is there an X? Now I do not think these four assertions are equivalent; and for purposes of argument I want us to concentrate on (*c*) and (*d*). In other words I want us to leave 'Does God exist?' and 'Is God a real existent?' and concentrate on 'Does there exist a God?' and 'Is there a God?' My reasons for adopting this policy are these. (i) In 'Does God exist?' the word 'God' is functioning as a proper name, and the notion

of 'existence' as applied to proper names is at best a problematic affair.[1]
(ii) 'Is God a real existent?' involves the use of the word 'real', which in
many ways is so different from the word 'exist' that we are likely to run
into serious difficulty if we confuse the two.[2] Are you agreeable, then,
that we should concentrate on 'Does there exist a God?' and 'Is there
a God?' rather than on the other two expressions.

*Theologian:* Certainly.

*Philosopher:* Then I will embark on my main argument. I should like us
now to consider the following assertions—(*a*) Are there any prime numbers between fifteen and twenty-five? (*b*) Are there any duties which
are absolutely overriding? (*c*) Are there any dogs with pink spots? All
these questions I should like to label 'existential' questions. (*a*) is a
mathematical existential question. The right answer is that there are
three such prime numbers, viz. seventeen, nineteen, and twenty-three.
(*b*) is a moral existential question. Let us suppose—it does not affect
the argument if you disagree—that the duty not to take life is overriding.
(*c*) is an empirical existential question. Let us suppose that there are
three dogs with pink spots, Fido, Rufus, and the dog at the farm. There
are no doubt other possible questions which begin with the words 'Are
there . . .' and 'Is there . . .' and are logically different from these; but
these three varieties of existential question are all that we need consider
for purposes of argument.

Now if someone says that there are only *two* prime numbers between
fifteen and twenty-five, viz. seventeen and nineteen, we can reply 'What
about twenty-three?' If someone says that there are *no* duties which are
absolutely overriding, we can say, 'What about the duty not to take life?'
If someone says there are *two* dogs with pink spots, Rufus and the dog
at the farm, we can say, 'What about Fido?' In all cases the suggestion
would be that *something has been left out*.

Of course if a person believes that there are only two prime numbers
between fifteen and twenty-five, we cannot say 'No, you have left out
Fido'. Similarly if scientists are engaged in investigating empirical
questions, we cannot say to them 'No, you have left out duties.' Anyone
who said this would be putting the word 'Fido' or the word 'duties' into
the wrong list.

[1] 'Homer never existed' is not simply an assertion about Homer.

[2] The main function of the word 'real' seems to be to guarantee genuineness
in some way. The form of this guarantee varies with the context. Thus 'A real
dog' suggests 'not a stuffed one', 'a real oasis' suggests 'not a mirage'. Compare
J. L. Austin, 'Other Minds' (*Aristotelian Society*, Supplementary Volume xx
for 1946) p. 159.

The challenge of modern philosophy to theology, I would say, is this. Modern philosophy forces us to ask the question, To what list does the word 'God' belong?

It is assumed by many self-professed theists that the atheist has *left something out*, that 'God' refers to an extra entity which should have been included in some list but has been left out. To this assumption, I would reply, 'To which list?'

You will agree, presumably, that 'Is there a God?' is not comparable with 'Are there any prime numbers between fifteen and twenty-five?' In other words, whatever answer is given to the latter question you would not wish to say, 'But what about God?'

*Theologian:* Clearly 'God' is not a number-word like 'nineteen', and cannot therefore be included in a list of numbers.

*Philosopher:* Similarly, I take it, you would agree that the word 'God' cannot be included in a list of duties?

*Theologian:* I agree.

*Philosopher:* The problem, then, is that of trying to place 'There is a God' in the right frame of reference. I am not of course claiming that 'mathematical', 'moral', and 'empirical' is an exhaustive list of such frames of reference. But if anyone claims that 'There is a God' belongs to some other frame of reference—not mathematical, not moral, and not empirical—it is up to him to say what sort of frame of reference it is and by what methods arguments within that frame of reference are conducted. I think you will agree with me that in the case of 'There is a God', it is the empirical frame of reference which requires to be considered.

*Theologian:* But might not there be a God in the sense of some non-empirical, super-sensible reality?

*Philosopher:* This, surely, is to say that there exists a God in some 'absolute' sense, independently of any frame of reference at all. The use of the word 'exist' in such a context—or lack of context—is illegitimate and unintelligible.

*Theologian:* I think it will be best if I do not challenge you over your views about 'absolute-existence' until you have made your position plainer.

*Philosopher:* The difficulty, as I see it, is this. If you wish to assert the truth of 'There exists a God', either you are using 'exist' in an 'absolute' sense and therefore talking unintelligibly, or you must allow that it is an *empirical* existential assertion, in which case you must be willing to treat it like any other empirical assertion. I shall try to show you that the latter choice gives rise to difficulties no less than the former.

*Theologian:* Can I take it that your argument applies also to other sentences containing the word 'God', such as 'God is love'?

*Philosopher:* Sentences containing the word 'God' are by no means a homogeneous group. But I agree that the same sort of problem can helpfully be asked not only of 'There is a God' but of other types of theological assertion also. The central question which I want to raise is whether sentences containing the word 'God' are or are not to be regarded as empirical.

### 3. TYPES OF THEISTIC LANGUAGE

*Theologian:* What would your own answer be to this question?

*Philosopher:* I should say that some sentences containing the word 'God' are empirical and some are not.

*Theologian:* Since you say that sentences containing the word 'God' are not a homogeneous group, could you give me some details of the way in which you think they should be classified?

*Philosopher:* Any philosophical classification is useful only within limits; and I should like to say at the start that my suggestions here are of course not intended as the one and only correct way of classifying sentences containing the word 'God'. With this reservation, I should like to make a distinction between three sorts of theological language, which we may label the language of 'simple literal theism', the language of 'qualified literal theism', and 'the language of parable'. Let me now set out my position without attempting to justify it. I believe that the first two types of language have no special claim on our allegiance—simple literal theism because it is false, qualified literal theism because it is meaningless. The third, the language of parable, is certainly meaningful; whether a particular parable is true or false is a matter for personal religious conviction. The important religious assertions, such as 'God is light'[1] and 'God is love'[2] are the language of parable. There are two things which I want to achieve in the rest of our discussion. The first is the negative one of convincing you that the language of qualified literal theism is meaningless (I shall assume that you do not want to dispute that the language of simple literal theism is false); the second is to convince you that, though in all strictness nothing can be said of God, we may

[1] 1 John i. 5.     [2] 1 John iv. 8.

none the less break our silence by telling appropriate parables, and that 'silence qualified by parables' represents a view not very different from your own.

### 4. SIMPLE LITERAL THEISM

For examples of the language of simple literal theism I cannot do better than turn to Homer and Virgil. The gods depicted in Homer and Virgil are anthropomorphic gods; they appear in the guise of human beings. In particular they are, at least at times, visible and tangible. Thus Ares (Mars) actually takes part in the fighting before Troy, and is wounded;[1] and when Venus later appears to Aeneas, reference is specifically made to her neck, hair, and feet.[2] The gods of Greece and Rome did, of course, have more than human powers; they could disappear at will; they could pass rapidly through space. But my central point is this; their presence or absence allows of empirical verification, just like the presence or absence of a human being in a particular place at a particular time.

*Theologian:* But surely Virgil for certain (and perhaps also the writer or writers of the *Iliad*) did not in fact believe in the literal existence of such beings?

*Philosopher:* Perhaps not. But that does not affect my argument. My point is simply that, if you take the stories in Homer and Virgil literally, you are speaking the language of simple literal theism. The language of simple literal theism involves empirically verifiable assertions about visible and tangible gods. How far particular people or races believed in visible and tangible gods need not concern us.

*Theologian:* You are saying no more, then, than that such language is in fact false.

*Philosopher:* Yes. Or rather I am assuming it to be false, since I take it that you will have no wish to disagree. I need hardly say that if good evidence of visible and tangible god-like figures taking part in human affairs were produced, you and I would be forced to take note of it; but I presume this is not a contingency that we need take seriously.

*Theologian:* No.

*Philosopher:* I should like to add that there is nothing *philosophically* objectionable about the language of simple literal theism. If we use it, we are not making the 'absolute-existence' mistake, nor are we being

---

[1] *Iliad* v. 846–52.          [2] Virgil, *Aeneid* I, 402–4.

misled by would-be empirical assertions that are in fact bogus. The language of simple literal theism admits of straightforward empirical verification or falsification, and, even though false, is certainly meaningful.

### 5. QUALIFIED LITERAL THEISM

*Theologian:* But surely, even among primitive peoples, belief in a visible and tangible god is not all that common?

*Philosopher:* Once again I think we can leave on one side any historical question of that sort. My distinction between simple literal theism and qualified literal theism can still stand even if simple literal theists were very few.

*Theologian:* What, then, are we to understand by 'qualified literal theism'?

*Philosopher:* Let me cite what may be taken as a standard case: 'This event was due to the activity of a god, but not a visible or tangible god.' I want to convince you that this form of words is meaningless.

*Theologian:* Would the distinction between simple literal theism and qualified literal theism have made sense to primitive man?

*Philosopher:* I do not suppose it would. But I still suggest that the distinction is crucial. Let us take the following account of primitive thinking—'If the wind blows, it is because some being more or less human, though of course superhuman, is blowing with his cheeks. If a tree is struck by lightning, it is because someone has thrown his battle-axe at it'.[1] Now at first sight it seems as though the person who is blowing or who is throwing his battle-axe is thought of as visible and tangible. If this is the claim, it allows of straightforward empirical verification and falsification. But suppose no such visible and tangible being is discovered. In that case it is possible to preserve the 'theistic' explanation by qualifying it. 'A god did it', we might say, 'but he ran away and we cannot see him'.[2] Even this may still be simple literal theism, if it is assumed that, somewhere, somehow, the god will be found to be visible and tangible after all. But if enough qualifications are added, there comes a stage when we have passed over to the language of qualified literal theism. In particular, this stage is reached if we say, 'Yes, a god did it, but not a visible or tangible god.'

[1] From Gilbert Murray, *Five Stages of Greek Religion* (Thinkers' Library, 1935), p. 23.
[2] Compare Gilbert Murray, *op. cit.*, p. 26. 'The real (god), tremendous, infallible, is somewhere far away, hidden in clouds perhaps, on the summit of some inaccessible mountain. If the mountain is once climbed, the god will move to the upper sky'.

*Theologian:* What is your objection to this form of words?

*Philosopher:* It is one of those pseudo-hypotheses which masquerades as a genuine one, but is found on examination to be unverifiable and unfalsifiable. Where there cannot in principle be verification or falsification, we cannot of course conclude, *ipso facto*, that an assertion is meaningless; but where that assertion *purports to give factual information*, we have every right to suspect it. What we are in effect saying is, This is an empirical assertion, and yet it is inconceivable that any empirical test should indicate its truth or falsity; it is an empirical assertion which has no empirical 'cash-value'. I appeal to you, and to all thinking people; is it not futile to pretend to subscribe to assertions of this kind?

### 6.  QUALIFIED LITERAL THEISM (continued). DIVINE INTERVENTION

*Theologian:* Yes, I do see that there is a genuine difficulty here. But has this difficulty any relevance to present-day beliefs? We have spoken, so far, of people who believed in gods—many different gods. Yet nowadays we do not believe in gods—we believe in God. This is something very different from the primitive variety of theism which we have so far considered.

*Philosopher:* The difference between 'gods' and 'God' is certainly an interesting one, since 'God' is usually (though not always) a proper name, whereas talk of 'gods' involves a reference to members of the class 'god'. But this difference does not affect my argument. Whether we use the word 'God' as a proper name—the name of the one and only god—or whether we speak of one or more members of the class 'god', there is still the danger that we may be misled by the language of qualified literal theism. Let me give an example. At a discussion group early in the Second World War, I was told that the escape of the British army at Dunkirk was due to the direct intervention of God. If questioned, the clergyman who made this claim would of course have said that God was invisible. He was clearly not under the impression that some visible and tangible Mars-like figure could have been observed deliberately foiling the plans of the German army. On the other hand, he was certainly not making an assertion like 'Wasn't it providential!' or even like

> *There's a divinity that shapes our ends*
> *Rough-hew them how we will.*

He undoubtedly believed that in some quite literal sense God had intervened. The word 'God' was intended by him to function as a straightforward proper name, and the sentence as a whole to refer in a literal way to activity on the part of the person named.

Now the difficulty with 'God intervened at Dunkirk' is that, if understood literally, it clearly purports to be factually significant, and yet it admits of no verification or falsification by observational means. If we agree that the word 'God' indicates something invisible and intangible, there are just no criteria for deciding whether God intervened; and in the absence of such criteria it is as pointless to assert that he did intervene as to assert that he did not. A person who was told to inspect the facts and see if God had intervened would just not know what to look for; and even if he had microscopes, telescopes, X-ray cameras, and all the resources of modern science at his disposal he would still be none the wiser. 'God intervened at Dunkirk' is thus objectionable on linguistic grounds. It purports to be factually significant, and yet no account can be given of its 'cash-value'.

*Theologian:* Presumably a person who denies that God intervened at Dunkirk might just be talking the language of simple literal theism, in which case his assertion, even if false, would at least be meaningful.

*Philosopher:* One would need to inquire very closely as to what such a person had in mind. Indeed I do not see how one can pronounce 'God intervened at Dunkirk' to be true, false, or meaningless without knowing the sort of way in which it is said.

*Theologian:* But are you not claiming that it is meaningless?

*Philosopher:* It is meaningless if understood as the language of qualified literal theism. There are perhaps other ways of understanding it; but I would remind you once again that it is *literal* theism only which is the object of my attack.

## 7. 'THEORETICAL CONSTRUCTS'

*Theologian:* There is a possible answer to your view which I think should be considered, though as a theologian I do not subscribe to it myself.

*Philosopher:* What is it?

*Theologian:* It is that the word 'God', though not the name of any visible or tangible entity, is none the less playing a legitimate part in empirical assertions since it stands for a 'theoretical construct'. As examples of what I mean by 'theoretical constructs' let us take terms such as 'magnetic field', 'superego', 'the unconscious'. Magnetic fields, super-egos, and unconsciouses are none of them visible or tangible, and yet we can legitimately believe in their existence on empirical grounds. Might not the term 'God' be comparable?

*Philosopher:* I find it hard to take this view seriously. I suppose one *could* use the word 'God' in some such way, but I am sure it would not be a sense acceptable to you as a theologian. Let us try to work out a parallel. Suppose we take the case of 'the unconscious'. A person, let us say, makes the sort of slip of the tongue that Freud was interested in; when he was trying to say 'The honourable member for Central Hull' he inadvertently says 'The honourable member for Central Hell'.[1] To explain this behaviour we invent a theoretical construct—the unconscious. There are forces, we say, emanating from his unconscious, which make him act in this inappropriate way. Freud admittedly speaks sometimes as though the unconscious was an extra entity in addition to familiar ones; but for purposes of argument let us assume that he is wrong, and that the words 'the unconscious' stand for what you call a 'theoretical construct'. This construct serves to link together this particular slip of the tongue with other parts of the person's behaviour, e.g. his irrational failure to co-operate with the honourable member in question. What you are saying, then, is that we might believe in the existence of God in much the same way as some of us believe in the existence of the unconscious. Neither is a visible or tangible object, but their presence has to be postulated to explain the results which we are able to see and touch. Is this your argument?

*Theologian:* Yes.

*Philosopher:* We must see how the parallel would work. Let me take another example so as to indicate the difference between an inde-pendently discoverable entity and a theoretical construct. If I come home and find my spoons missing, a possible explanation is that a burglar has stolen them. If in addition I see some footprints on the flower-bed outside the kitchen window, the burglar hypothesis becomes all the more probable. Now the burglar is an independently discoverable entity in addition to the spoons and the flower-bed; and if I actually catch him, this is an independently discoverable event, quite separate from the finding of missing spoons or footprints on the flower-bed. In

[1] S. Freud, *Introductory Lectures on Psycho-Analysis* (Allen & Unwin, 1922), p. 25.

the case of the unconscious, however, there is nothing comparable to actually catching the burglar. There is a legitimate sense of 'explain' in which both the slips of the tongue and the failure to co-operate with the honourable member can be said to be 'explained' by the activity of the unconscious. The words 'the unconscious' function, that is, as an explanatory concept as a result of which these two separate events can be brought under the same general law. But the activity of the unconscious does not explain either of the events in the same sense of 'explain' as that in which the activity of the burglar explains the missing spoons. The unconscious is not an independently discoverable entity at all, and while 'There are hostile feelings in his unconscious' can be given 'cash-value' in terms of his slips of the tongue, his failure to co-operate with the honourable member etc., 'There has been a burglar' cannot be given 'cash-value' in terms of 'The spoons are missing', 'There are footprints on the flower-beds', or any conjunction of similar assertions.

You can say, if you like, that it is *as though there were* an entity operating to produce the slips of the tongue; but in that case you need to make clear that such an entity is in principle not discoverable by independent criteria.

How, then, would a parallel in the case of 'God' operate? It is not, of course, very clear what precisely would count as evidence for the activity of God; but it would presumably count as relevant evidence if people were continually discovering a series of opportune events—answers to prayer, satisfactory outcomes to problems, and so on. Could we not believe that the activity of God explains such occurrences in the way in which the activity of the unconscious explains the slips of the tongue? The 'cash-value' of 'There is a God' would thus lie in the answered prayers etc., but God himself would never be an object of experience any more than the unconscious is an object of experience. This is not, of course, because God and the unconscious are particularly elusive—like the Loch Ness Monster; but because the word 'God' and the words 'the unconscious' do not stand for anything of which one could conceivably have experience; one could as well hope to experience an 'if.' Your argument would be that we might believe in the existence of such a God, even though 'God' was only a theoretical construct, not an independently discoverable entity.

*Theologian:* Even if it is not *my* argument, I should be interested to hear your reply to it.

*Philosopher:* I can only say that it is not for me to stop anyone from using the word 'God' in any way that he chooses, provided he makes clear what he means. But I am quite sure that this is not the way in which people ordinarily think of God. If we order our discourse differently we can dispense with theoretical constructs in a way which is impossible in the case of words for people and things. If we had no word 'chair' (or some equivalent word or other sign), we should be seriously handicapped when it came to talking of chairs; but the existence of the unconscious is a matter for verbal decision in a way in which the existence of chairs is not.[1] Does anyone seriously want to say that the existence of God is a matter for verbal decision? The ordinary person regards God as the explanation of answered prayers not in the sense in which the unconscious is the explanation of slips of the tongue, but in the sense in which the burglar is the explanation of the missing spoons. Answered prayers are *evidence*, it would be said, for the existence of God, much as footprints in the flower-beds are evidence for the existence of a burglar. And if the word 'God' is thought of as referring to an independently discoverable entity, my original objection still holds. It makes no sense to speak of an independently discoverable entity unless we are prepared to say what results would constitute its discovery.[2]

*Theologian:* Yes, I see your point.

### 8. THEISM WITHOUT TEARS

*Philosopher:* May we then pass on to another possible answer to my problem—an answer which I am sure both of us would reject without hesitation? This answer I propose to label 'theism without tears'.

*Theologian:* That sounds disparaging.

*Philosopher:* It is intended to be. I do not in fact know of anyone who holds it, and I certainly do not suggest that you yourself would wish to hold it. But it is one which conceivably might arise in the present-day

---

[1] Compare p. 38.

[2] The same problem arises if we examine the so-called 'teleological' argument for the existence of God—the argument in which it is said that the beauty and orderliness in nature suggest an all-wise designer. If the existence of an all-wise designer is supposed to 'explain' the orderliness in the same way in which the presence of a burglar explains missing spoons, we need to ask, once again, by what independent criteria the presence of this all-wise designer could be detected. In the absence of any situation comparable to actually seeing the burglar, we are simply misleading ourselves in invoking such an independently discoverable designer. We are saying, in effect, in the same breath, both that he is independently discoverable and that there are no criteria for discovering him.

philosophical climate, and is therefore worth mentioning, even though I am in no doubt that it should be dismissed.

*Theologian:* What does this 'theism without tears' involve?

*Philosopher:* It might be labelled an 'emotive' view of sentences containing the word 'God'. You remember how some philosophers have taken an 'emotive' view of moral terms such as 'good' and 'right'.[1] To say that an act is good, on the emotive view, is to express a favourable emotion towards it. In that case it follows that there is a perfectly good use for moral assertions even though they are neither empirical generalizations nor recondite statements about some non-empirical state of affairs. Now the suggestion which I am considering is that the same principle might apply to theological assertions as to moral ones—that they are neither empirically verifiable nor descriptive of something recondite and non-empirical, but that they none the less can be legitimately used. Thus 'There is a God' might be taken as a sort of poetic exclamation of optimism about the world in general; and some theological assertions might be fully assimilated to straightforward moral exhortations. Thus 'All men are children of God' would be taken as equivalent to 'All men ought to treat one another as brothers'. On this interpretation anyone who looks on life with optimism or who believes in human brotherhood would have the right to call himself a theist.

*Theologian:* What are your reasons for rejecting this view?

*Philosopher:* In the first place the word 'theist' is being used in a completely new sense, and the connection with any form of theism of the past would be extremely flimsy. Such a 'theist' would do better to say 'Abandon belief in God and believe what I advocate instead', rather than pretend fatuously that the views which he advocates are anything like those of traditional theism.

*Theologian:* I agree.

*Philosopher:* Moreover I suspect that the motive behind his policy is a disreputable one. He is in effect using a verbal dodge so as to avoid calling himself an 'atheist'—a label which he presumably finds distasteful. By means of this dodge he is able to pose as a theist without being one.[2] It is as though he said 'I want to associate myself with the

---

[1] See p. 49.

[2] A similar comment was made by Freud about allegedly religious 'believers'. 'Philosophers stretch the meaning of words until they retain scarcely anything of their original sense; by calling "God" some vague abstraction which they have created for themselves they pose . . . as believers before the world.' From *The Future of an Illusion* (translated by W. D. Robson-Scott, Hogarth, 1928), p. 57.

Christian tradition. I cannot use their language as it stands, so I will place a new interpretation on it, which can conveniently be forgotten when I talk with orthodox Christians'. Indeed his implicit argument seems to be, 'I WILL say that I believe in God; I am therefore going to invent a new sense of the word "God" so that I may reasonably continue to do so'. I call it a 'theism without tears', not because it demands no moral effort—indeed the moral effort which it calls for may well be very great—but because no tears need in that case be shed over the problem of 'cash-value'. Theological language is simply interpreted in such a way that the problem of 'cash-value' is avoided.

*Theologian:* And at the cost, I should say, of not being theological language at all.

*Philosopher:* I agree.

*Theologian:* I am quite prepared to allow that the 'theism-without-tears' view cannot meet your difficulty any more than did the expedient of treating the word 'God' as a theoretical construct.


### 9. MYSTICISM AND THE SENSE OF THE NUMINOUS

*Philosopher:* There is one more answer to my problem which I think we ought to consider, though again I do not think that it is an answer which you, as a theologian, would wish to give.

*Theologian:* What answer is that?

*Philosopher:* It is the attempt to give 'cash-value' to sentences containing the word 'God' by appealing to the experiences of the mystic and to the feeling, which many people claim to have experienced, that God is somehow present even though he is invisible. This general feeling I propose, following Otto,[1] to label a 'sense of the numinous'. Now I mentioned earlier, you remember, that in the language of qualified literal theism the word 'God' is supposed to stand for something invisible and intangible.

*Theologian:* I remember well.

*Philosopher:* Someone therefore may say to me, 'Why pick on vision and touch? Not only are there other senses, but there may quite well be non-sensuous means of experiencing God'. An argument might therefore be developed suggesting that sentences about God can be 'cashed' in terms of the experiences of the believer, even though these are not necessarily visual or tactual experiences, and indeed may not

---

[1] See R. Otto, *The Idea of the Holy* (Oxford, 1923).

even depend on any sense-organ at all. Thus, when it is said in a well-known hymn,

> *What if thy form we cannot see*
> *We know and feel that thou art here,*[1]

the writer is relying on what he 'feels' rather than on what he can touch or see. Similarly when St. Paul says that at some stage we shall see God 'face to face',[2] we must assume that this is not to be thought of as seeing by means of the sense-organs at all.

*Theologian:* 'There is a God' in that case seems to mean the same as 'Mystics—or believers in general—have experiences of the numinous'. To me this does not sound at all convincing.

*Philosopher:* There is, of course, a side issue here which perhaps should be mentioned in case it provides an extra stumbling block. As you probably know, some philosophers have favoured the view known as 'phenomenalism', in which, for example, 'There is a table in the room' is taken to mean the same as 'If anyone were to go into the room he would have certain experiences'. I do not say they are right; but it is inadequate to reply 'That is certainly *not* what I mean when I say "There is a table in the room".' Similarly, it is not enough to object to regarding 'There is a God' as equivalent to 'Believers have experiences of the numinous' merely because we object to the phenomenalist programme in general.

*Theologian:* No, I see that.

*Philosopher:* I am not, of course, in any way disparaging the insights which mystics and religious believers through the ages have given us. Much of what they say can be treated as the language of parable—a type of language which we have not so far discussed. The question which I want to raise now is whether you would be willing to allow that 'There is a God' can be taken as equivalent to 'Believers have experiences of the numinous'. I must say that such a view seems to me profoundly unsatisfactory.

*Theologian:* And to me, too. What are your reasons?

*Philosopher:* The most important reason, I think, is that I do not regard it as a legitimate step to pass from 'I have a feeling of something' to 'There really is something there'. Let us consider the problem, so well beloved of philosophers, of whether the chair in front of me is a

---

[1] From 'At even ere the sun was set', H. Twells (1823–1900).
[2] I Corinthians xiii. 12.

real one and not a hallucination. When I say that it is real, I mean, in this context, that it can be relied on to *do* the things we expect of a chair. If it is a real chair it will support my weight and not just vanish into thin air; other people besides myself can touch and see it. But if I have a vague feeling of the numinous, what exactly is meant by saying that something is 'really there'? Certainly one might mean that other people might have an experience of the numinous in similar circumstances; but the words 'really there' suggest in particular that the object in question is tangible and can *do* things. To say 'Something is really there but most of the criteria for being "really there" are not satisfied' is clearly futile; and if you do not accept my criteria for being 'really there' you are using the words in some new and unexplained sense. Moreover when people invoke the experiences of the mystic in religious discussion, they normally assume that such experiences are evidence for the existence of God not in the sense in which slips of the tongue etc. are evidence for the existence of the unconscious,[1] but in the sense in which missing spoons and footprints in the flower-beds are evidence for the existence of a burglar. In that case God is still being thought of as an independently discoverable entity. My original difficulty, therefore, still holds, and I wish to know by what criteria one tells whether this independently discoverable entity is present. My general conclusion is that, whatever value we place on the experiences of the mystic, it is no answer to this particular difficulty to say that the 'cash-value' of sentences containing the word 'God' lies in mystical experience or the sense of the numinous.

*Theologian:* I agree with you. May I now suggest that we temporarily adjourn our discussion? I am certainly clear where your challenge lies, and I should like to think about it further. When we meet again I hope to say something constructive.

*Philosopher:* Certainly.

---

[1] For this argument, see pp. 150–1.

# CHAPTER 15

---

# *The way of silence*

## I. GOD AS INFINITE AND TRANSCENDENT

*Theologian:* I have been reflecting since our last discussion on the difficulty which you have raised. Your problem, in effect, seems to be this—that many assertions containing the word 'God' cannot be given appropriate 'cash-value'. People talk as though the existence of God were something which could be discovered empirically, without saying what empirical evidence is relevant. Such procedure is clearly self-defeating.

*Philosopher:* Precisely.

*Theologian:* Now it seems to me that there is a very important point which your argument has overlooked. What you say may hold in the case of simple-minded views of God; but you have failed to take sufficient note of what is said about God by theologians. Theologians apply to God such words as 'infinite' and 'transcendent'. I do not suggest, of course, that these words can be taken exactly at their face value; but the use of such language brings out clearly, I think, that the word 'God', as used by theologians, is not an ordinary class-word like 'chair' or an ordinary proper name like 'Jones'.[1] The conjunction 'chairs and tables' is familiar enough; but, as a theologian, I should be very unhappy to say that 'God and finite things' is the same sort of conjunction as 'chairs and tables'.

[1] For further discussion of this point, see articles by J. N. Findlay and G. E. Hughes in *New Essays in Philosophical Theology*, edited by A. G. N. Flew and A. C. MacIntyre (S.C.M. Press, 1955). Compare also Anselm's phrase 'than which greater cannot be thought'. The so-called 'ontological' argument for the existence of God, as formulated by Anselm and others, is in effect an attempt to call attention to some of the peculiarities in the concept 'God'.

Since this chapter was written a further important contribution to the subject has been made by I. M. Crombie in his essay, 'Possibility of Theological Statements', published in *Faith and Logic* (ed. Basil Mitchell, Allen & Unwin, 1957).

*Philosopher:* This seems to me a very important matter.

*Theologian:* As a theologian I believe that God is a mystery. And if God is a mystery, there is no justification for lamenting that sentences containing the word 'God' cannot be given appropriate 'cash-value'. Indeed I should be seriously worried if such 'cash-value' *were* possible, since any mystery about God would then have disappeared. If a sentence purporting to be about God were 'cashable', then by definition that sentence would not be about an infinite or transcendent Being. Here, I suggest, lies a further objection to the view which we discussed in our earlier talk—that sentences containing the word 'God' could be given 'cash-value' in terms of the experiences of the believer.[1] If this were so, we should certainly no longer be justified in thinking of God as an infinite or transcendent Being. He would simply be one object of experience among others.

*Philosopher:* I should like to take you up over your key terms—'mysterious', 'infinite', and 'transcendent'. A mystery, surely, is something which we do not understand but which is capable in principle of being understood. We can apply the word to anything that baffles us. If Mr X was murdered in Birmingham it may be a complete mystery how his body was found half an hour later in a disused house in London. Or it may be a complete mystery how the dog could have entered the sitting-room, when half an hour earlier he was seen in the garden, and all the house-doors were locked in the meantime. But nothing can be a mystery unless we know what would count as a solution of that mystery; and if you say that God is a mystery you must make clear just what it is that we do not know about him.

*Theologian:* When I say that God is mysterious you must not understand me literally. I do not mean that he is mysterious in the way in which a sinister character in a detective-story is mysterious. I mean only that God is not an object of ordinary knowledge.

*Philosopher:* Again, what about your use of 'infinite' and 'transcendent'? I know in mathematics what an infinite series is, but I am not clear what could possibly be meant by applying the same word to 'God'. Similarly 'transcendent' suggests some sort of spatial relationship; 'transcendere' in Latin meant to over-step or pass beyond. I cannot see what could be meant by applying this spatial metaphor to God. Is it not as unintelligible to say that God is infinite or transcendent as to say that he intervened at Dunkirk?

[1] See pp. 154–5.

# The way of silence

*Theologian:* When I say 'God is infinite' or 'God is transcendent' I am not saying anything comparable to 'Smith is tall'. I am saying, rather, that it makes no sense to say of 'God' the sort of things we say of other proper names. 'God' is unique among proper names, or, if you prefer, should not be classed as a proper name at all.

## 2. DEFINITIONAL JOKERS

*Philosopher:* But does this meet my difficulty? I ask you for 'cash-value' for sentences about God, and you reply '"God" is a special word which does not allow of "cash-value" of the usual kind.' Is not this simply a verbal dodge?

*Theologian:* By what right do you exclude the possibility of an entity such as that to which the word 'God' is assumed to refer?

*Philosopher:* I am not excluding the possibility of anything. There may be all sorts of things in the universe of which neither you nor I have any knowledge at all. But if you are making an empirical assertion in saying that there is a God, I want to know the 'cash-value' of these words. If you cannot tell me, you are talking unintelligibly.

*Theologian:* Surely my answer here is plain? Just as I was not using 'mysterious', 'infinite', and 'transcendent' in any literal straightforward sense, so, when I say 'There is a God', I am not using 'there is' in any literal straightforward sense. I do not mean anything comparable to 'There are no fairies', 'There used to be dodos', or 'There are plenty of lions'.

*Philosopher:* I am very glad to have secured this admission. But I am forced to say that in that case I have no idea whatsoever of what you *do* mean. If 'there is' is not being used in its familiar, empirical frame of reference, you must be using it in some 'absolute' sense. Do you not accept my view that the notion of 'absolute existence' is unintelligible?

*Theologian:* I feel that it is a point on which you should be challenged. I am still not clear why an infinite Being should not exist in some 'absolute' sense. I agree that in that case we cannot treat 'God and finite things' as a conjunction like 'Fido and the dog at the farm'; but by your attack on 'absolute existence' you seem to me to be trying to rule out something which you have no business to rule out. Who are you to say how we should or should not use the word 'exist'?

*Philosopher:* Far be it from me to stop you from using the word 'exist' in any way you like. But if you do, it is incumbent on you to explain what you mean.

*Theologian:* Suppose I reply by saying that I do not know what I mean?

*Philosopher:* Are you suggesting that, though you personally do not, some other theologian does? In that case, please let me continue the argument with a theologian who does. Or are you saying that, though no one knows what 'There is a God' means, you are none the less willing to profess belief in it. That, surely, is irresponsible.[1]

*Theologian:* I agree that the notion of 'existence' may not be applicable in its normal sense when applied to God. But how can you rule out the possibility of the existence of God in some extended sense of 'exist'? If you do, are you not simply taking tricks by means of a definitional joker?[2] All you are saying is 'God cannot exist, because I am not going to use the word "exist" in that way.'

*Philosopher:* Tell me; if God is as you say, what do you suggest can be known of God?

*Theologian:* I am not saying that anything can be known of God. When we say of God that He is like a father or like a judge, theologians agree that this is true only by analogy. Some have said that we should proceed by negation rather than affirmation when talking of God.[3] It is as though we said 'He is like a father', and then denied it because the words were inadequate.

*Philosopher:* Is it not odd that words taken from our ordinary experience, like 'father' and 'judge', are admitted to be inadequate when applied to God, yet the word 'exist', which also derives from ordinary experience, is assumed to be adequate?

*Theologian:* All right. Let us agree that the word 'exist' is inadequate too. But I still say that by refusing to use it you are denying something important, and that in making this denial you are taking tricks by means of a definitional joker.

*Philosopher:* I agree that I have no right to take tricks if you mean by that making assertions of any kind about the nature of things. But I am not doing that. I am simply keeping silent. You, on the other hand, are professing to believe in the existence—in some unexplained sense of 'existence'—of an infinite Being—in some unexplained sense of 'infinite' and some unexplained sense of 'Being'—about whom you

[1] 'Philosopher' owes the argument in this paragraph to Mr B. A. O. Williams.
[2] Compare chapter 4, p. 37.
[3] For example, Scotus Erigena in his *De Divisione Naturae*, Book I, section 14.

want to talk by means of negative assertions. Can you really claim that your position is in any way better than mine?

*Theologian:* So long as you limit yourself to saying nothing I have no quarrel. What I suspected you were doing was to rule out God by definition, and then speak as though this was sufficient to show that religious belief was discredited. If this is not your intention I am much reassured.

*Philosopher:* If I have succeeded in allaying your suspicions I am very glad. I should like to add further that, in my opinion, no manipulation of definitional jokers can justifiably turn a believer into an unbeliever.


### 3. SILENCE QUALIFIED BY PARABLES

*Theologian:* Despite your reassurances, I am not fully satisfied.

*Philosopher:* How can I satisfy you further?

*Theologian:* If you regard it as fair, I should like to challenge you as to your own religious beliefs. You have just this moment agreed that manipulation of definitional jokers cannot turn a person into an unbeliever; yet if anyone makes an assertion which purports to be about God you pull him up and say that he is talking unintelligibly. If you are not a believer, I should like to know on what grounds; if you *are* a believer, I am even more curious to know what you believe in.

*Philosopher:* Taking sides on a religious issue is not, of course, part of philosophy in the narrow, technical sense. None the less, since you ask for my view, I am prepared to give it. I *am* a believer.

*Theologian:* There is nothing, then, in modern knowledge, which in your opinion makes belief impossible?

*Philosopher:* No.

*Theologian:* But belief in what? If you say you believe in God, what sort of a God? You cannot, on your own showing, say that God exists in some 'absolute' sense, nor that he exists in the sense of being an entity that can be known empirically. What, then, do you take to be the difference between a believer and an unbeliever?

*Philosopher:* The difference lies in the sort of parable that they tell. A believer, for our purposes, may be regarded as one who accepts what I call the 'theistic' parable—the parable of a loving father who has called us all to be like him and to become his children. As a technical philosopher it is not for me to say whether this parable is the right one to live by; but as a plain man I am in no doubt that it is. My general message, on the religious side, could be summed up in the words 'silence qualified by parables'.[1]

*Theologian:* Does not this involve some shift from your original position? After all, there is nothing specifically *religious* about your original demand for silence, since this demand arises simply from linguistic considerations—from considerations of what it makes sense to say. How then do you pass from a prosaic demand for silence to what is clearly a religious position—a position where you call not just for silence but for what appears to be a specifically religious silence?

*Philosopher:* This step is legitimate, provided only that one accepts the theistic parable. A person who insists on linguistic grounds that sentences containing the word 'God' cannot be understood literally is not committed to accepting the theistic parable; but he is not committed to rejecting it either. If he accepts it, as I do, he can no longer adopt what you call a 'prosaic' silence; he must accept what I call 'the way of silence' —a phrase which I have deliberately chosen on account of its religious overtones, and its affinities with traditional religious thinking.[2]

*Theologian:* There are many points about the language of parable on which I should like to question you further. For the moment, however, may I remind you of something that you said at the start of our discussion—namely that the view of 'silence qualified by parables' is not radically different from what I believe myself? I am still not clear why you should say this; indeed I cannot see how your position can be compatible with orthodox Christianity at all.

*Philosopher:* With some unsophisticated beliefs of relatively simple-minded Christians I agree that it is incompatible. I cannot, for instance, share the view that the word 'God' stands for an extra 'para-physical' entity in addition to ordinary 'physical' ones. Whether the majority of religious people do or do not think of God in this way I do not know.[3]

[1] Compare Scotus Erigena: 'When it is said that God *wills, loves, cares for, sees, hears*, and the like, we must suppose that his ineffable essence and goodness are being conveyed to us in human terms, lest our true and devoted Christian faith should so far be silent about the Creator of all things as not to dare to say anything of him at all.' (From *De Divisione Naturae*, Book I, chapter 73.)

[2] For a further account of these affinities, see H. D. Lewis, 'The Cognitive Factor in Religious Experience' (*Aristotelian Society*, Supplementary Volume XXIX for 1955). Of particular interest is an Indian text found by Professor Lewis in the writings of the commentator Samkara. This text, in Professor Lewis's words, 'tells of a pupil who pleads with his teacher to expound to him the nature of the Absolute Self understood religiously as Brahman. To each request the teacher turns a deaf ear until at last he answers the insistent "Teach me, Sir," with the words "I am teaching you but you do not follow, the Self is silence".'

[3] For a discussion of this point, see C. C. J. Webb, *Problems in the Relations of God and Man* (Nisbet, 1911), pp. 144–8.

But if they do, I am certainly in disagreement with them. I should gladly give support to any campaign directed to removing from religious practice any language suggestive of this mistake, and in particular what I call the language of 'qualified literal theism'. As far as the theologians are concerned, on the other hand, I am not at all clear that my views are unorthodox at all.

*Theologian:* But surely you claim to base your views on a so-called 'revolution in philosophy' which has taken place in the last fifty years? I do not wish to make light use of the label 'logical positivism'; but are not your views essentially the product of the logical positivist era and its aftermath? The traditional theologians believed in metaphysics in what you would call the 'old and bad' sense. You have abandoned all that. Surely your views *must* be unorthodox compared with those of theologians tainted, as you would say, by traditional metaphysics?

*Philosopher:* I believe great harm can be done by over-stressing the novelty of my views. There are many theologians—perhaps Scotus Erigena in particular[1]—whose views have obvious connections with those which I am offering. And as for all this talk of metaphysics being dead, how misleading it is! Since the logical positivist era traditional metaphysical problems have been continually found to re-emerge in a new guise.[2] All the points which I have been making about the use of word 'exist' can with full propriety be labelled 'metaphysical' or even 'ontological'. Modern developments show up these questions in something of a new light; but it seems to me that the similarities with the past need to be stressed at least as much as the differences.

*Theologian:* Yet I still suspect that there is some fundamental difference between us.

*Philosopher:* Let us look again at our respective views. God, to you, is a mystery; to me even the word 'mystery' has an empirical taint, and is misleading. You say 'I do not know' and try to talk; I say 'I do not know' and remain silent. You admit that your talk is not literal; I qualify my silence by telling parables. Is there really all that difference between us?

*Theologian:* But I claim that what I say is objectively true—true, albeit by analogy, of the actual world. You, it seems, do not.

*Philosopher:* Precisely. You say your talk is true by analogy of the actual world; I say that mine is literally true in the world of parable.

*Theologian:* But do you not want to say that your parables are true in the sense of having objective validity?

[1] See p. 162, note 1.    [2] Compare pp. 30–1.

*Philosopher:* What does 'objective validity' mean? This is the sort of language that we use when speaking of veridical perceptions in contrast with illusions and hallucinations. Such talk is inapplicable in the case of God. I will have none of it.

*Theologian:* But might not your parables be objectively valid in some extended sense of these words. You cannot limit people's use of them. That is the offence of trying to take tricks by means of a definitional joker.

*Philosopher:* It makes no difference. If you insist I am willing to shift my ground and allow that parable-language can be 'true' or 'objectively valid' and can refer to what has 'real existence'. But the concession is of no help to either of us, since the words 'true' etc. are now being used in an extended sense, and what constitutes 'objective validity' in this new sense neither of us can possibly say. I began by saying that we cannot ask if a particular parable is objectively valid. If I shift my ground in the way that you suggest I am saying instead that we can ask this question all right but can have no idea of what constitutes the answer. I do not see that the change has any great significance.

*Theologian:* I agree that it has not.

*Philosopher:* Have I convinced you, then, that the difference between us is not as great as you may have supposed?

*Theologian:* You have.

*Philosopher:* In that case I will now try to say something more on the language of parable.

\*     \*     \*

At this point let us leave the participants. Through the arguments of 'Philosopher' I have attempted to establish in the last two chapters (1) that the language of qualified literal theism must be regarded as meaningless, and (2) that the formula of 'silence qualified by parables' can legitimately be used as the basis of a religious system.

# CHAPTER 16

## The language of parable

This chapter will be divided into four main sections. In the first I shall call attention to a number of features that are characteristic of parables, and try to show how these features are characteristic of theistic language also. In the second I shall discuss what arguments can be used in support of one parable rather than another. In the third I shall comment on the difference between the language of parable and the language of qualified literal theism. In the fourth I shall attempt to throw light on what is involved when people disagree in their choice of parables and when a person changes from one set of parables to another. I cannot claim that my use of the word 'parable' coincides fully with its use in normal speech. But I know of no other existing word which would serve my purpose better; and, if I were to coin a completely fresh word, more, I think, would be lost than gained.[1]

[1] Professor R. B. Braithwaite (*An Empiricist's View of the Nature of Religious Belief*, Cambridge, 1955) uses the word 'story' and allows that the words 'parable', 'fairy-story' 'allegory', 'fable', 'tale', and 'myth' would also serve his purpose. Detailed examination of Braithwaite's views would be out of place here; but since there is at least a superficial resemblance between them and the views expressed in this book, a few comments may perhaps be made. It seems to me in general that Braithwaite's views are presented in too harsh a form, and for this reason are likely to leave many Christians dissatisfied. In particular his admission that his stories are comparable to 'fairy-stories' and 'fables' does not seem to me to do justice to the need (stressed in the present book) for *silence*. His stories are 'mere' stories, whereas here I am offering a doctrine not of 'mere' parables but rather of silence qualified by parables. Moreover we are told that it is 'an empirical psychological fact' (p. 27) that people are helped in their behaviour by these stories, even, apparently, though 'the story associated with the behaviour policy is not believed' (p. 27). One may query in passing how Braithwaite knows this. It follows, however, whether he is right or wrong, that his 'stories' would have to be given up if entertaining them was found to be of no special help towards living what he calls an 'agapeistic' life, i.e. a life of love. The 'way of silence', on the other hand, is not dependent for its validity on the results of any such psychological survey. Thirdly it seems to me that Braithwaite sets too much store by the rather provocative label 'empiricist'. My reasons for rejecting this label are given on p. 45. Despite these points of difference, however, I am in full agreement with Braithwaite over the difficulty in regarding sentences containing the word 'God' as straightforward literal truth.

I

In the standard sense of 'parable' there are three characteristics of a parable to which I wish to call attention. (*a*) In the first place the question of its literal truth or falsity is unimportant. In other words it does not matter in the least if the characters in the parable were or were not actual historical figures. (*b*) Parables contain, for the most part, assertions that are empirical; and we know perfectly well what states of affairs would constitute the 'cash-value' of these assertions. (*c*) Thirdly, and most important, parables convey a message.

Let us illustrate with an example. We are told in the gospels[1] of a man who planted a vineyard and let it out to husbandmen. He later sent a servant to the husbandmen, who was beaten and sent away empty. Another servant was stoned. Finally the owner of the vineyard sent his son; but the son, too, was killed and sent out of the vineyard.

(*a*) The first point is obvious. No one is interested in the question of whether the characters in the parable were real people. No historian would be justified in wondering when the characters in the parable lived or where the particular vineyard was located.

(*b*) Secondly, this parable, like any other parable, contains assertions that are empirically verifiable and falsifiable. For example, it contains the assertion 'They took him and killed him and cast him out of the vineyard' (verse 8). This is comparable to any empirical assertion made in a work of fiction. Even though the context is fictional, there is no difficulty whatever in knowing what is meant, and there is no question of our being misled by language which cannot be given appropriate 'cash-value'.

(*c*) Thirdly, this parable has a message. It is not just a bare record of events, whether fictional or otherwise, nor does it relate to a handful of husbandmen of unknown origin. It relates rather to a series of historical events—the growth of the prophetic movement, the coming of Jesus himself, and the rejection of him both by his contemporaries and by those who came later, including ourselves. It invites us to view these events in a particular way; it gives us a new 'slant' on them, a new insight into what was happening. If we take the parable seriously, then the crucifixion of Jesus was not just a sordid incident in the history of a persecuted race; it was not just the death of a tiresome preacher who

[1] Mark xii. 1–12.

# The language of parable

came into conflict with the authorities. It was rather the story of one of whom it was said: 'He came unto his own, and his own received him not. But as many as received him, to them gave he power to become the sons of God'.[1] Those who accept this parable are necessarily committed to a completely new way of life.

These three characteristics of a parable are characteristic of theistic language also. For illustration purposes let us consider the account of creation, as given in the opening words of the book of Genesis—'In the beginning God created the heaven and the earth'.[2]

(a) Just as it is unimportant if the characters in a parable were real people, so it is unimportant, I suggest, whether this account of the creation is literally true. To call attention to timeless truths it is a legitimate device to make use of a quasi-historical story; and whenever this device is used, questions of historical accuracy have no special relevance or importance.[3]

There is a difference between the parable of the husbandmen and the Genesis account of creation in that it is at least *false* that the husbandmen were real people, whereas a literal doctrine of creation should be regarded not as false but as meaningless. Literal talk of 'creation by God' is meaningless for the same reason that 'God intervened at Dunkirk' is meaningless. It allows of no 'cash-value'; we do not know what sort of occurrence would count as 'creation by God', nor what sort of scientific instruments would serve for detecting such an occurrence. Moreover, in the absence of any timing-device such as the movement of the sun or the movement of the human pulse, it is hard to see how any literal sense can be placed on the words 'in the beginning'.[4]

Despite this difference, however, we can say that the two narratives are alike in the sense that there is implicit agreement in both cases to ignore questions of literal truth and falsity.[5]

[1] John i. 11 and 12.  [2] Genesis i. 1.
[3] Compare Rousseau's doctrine of a 'social contract'. Some have supposed that, *as a matter of history*, our ancestors banded together and agreed to adopt the rule of law. The importance of the 'social contract' theory, however, lies not in its historical accuracy (which is highly questionable), but in its attempt to convey the idea that all of us, here and now, are under implicit contract to obey the law. For further discussion, and comparison with the Genesis story, see J. D. Mabbott, *The State and the Citizen* (Hutchinson, 1947), chapter 2.
[4] Compare Kant, *Critique of Pure Reason*, First Antinomy.
[5] For further treatment of the Genesis story in the light of recent philosophy, see the discussion on 'Creation' by Professor A. G. N. Flew and Professor D. M. Mackinnon (*New Essays in Philosophical Theology*, edited by Flew and A. C. MacIntyre, S.C.M. Press, 1955), pp. 170–86.

(*b*) Like the parable of the husbandmen the Genesis account of creation contains assertions which, within the context of the parable, allow of empirical verification and falsification. The events described in this account can quite easily be given 'cash-value' in terms of familiar experience. We know exactly what it is like for a craftsman who is both powerful and loving to create something; and we can quite well imagine a new object occupying a hitherto empty space.[1] The literal meaning of the words used is thus perfectly clear; and no one who speaks in this way can be criticized on the grounds that he is indulging in any form of verbal mystification. In contrast, when we are told that 'Thoughtful people want to be reasonably well assured that the revelation of Christ and the holiness of his spirit are *really one with ultimate transcendent reality*'[2] (my italics), we may suspect that the writer is indulging in what Berkeley would call 'an useless and unintelligible jargon'. Talk of creation can be given 'cash-value'; talk of things being 'really one with ultimate transcendent reality' cannot.

(*c*) Just as the parable of the husbandmen gives us a new 'slant', a new orientation, so also the doctrine of creation, if we take it seriously, forces us to look at the world in a new way. We are forced to recognize that every event is part of God's purpose. Those who make this recognition would claim that they see God not only in the beauties of nature, but in all the trivial routine happenings of ordinary day-to-day life. 'The earth is full of thy riches' says the psalmist.[3] 'The world is charged with the grandeur of God' says Hopkins.[4] We can seek God, says Keble, in 'the trivial round, the common task'.[5] According to Francis Thompson,

> *The drift of pinions would we hearken,*
> *Beats at our own day-shuttered doors*[6]

---

[1] Berkeley (*Third Dialogue between Hylas and Philonous*) suggests that when we consider the creation we may legitimately think of 'a parcel of plants or vegetables of all sorts, produced by an invisible power, in a desert where nobody was present'. He adds, 'In this naked conception of things, divested of words, there will not be found any notion of what you call the *actuality of absolute existence*. You may indeed raise a dust with those terms, and so lengthen our dispute to no purpose. But I entreat you calmly to look into your own thoughts, and then tell me if they are not an useless and unintelligible jargon.' We need not share Berkeley's view on the literal truth of the Genesis narrative; but the passage quoted serves admirably to emphasize his refusal to acquiesce in any form of verbal mystification.

[2] From G. L. Prestige, *God in Patristic Thought* (Heinemann, 1936), Introduction, p. xv.

[3] Psalm civ. 24.      [4] G. M. Hopkins, *God's Grandeur*.

[5] J. Keble, From 'New Every Morning' (*Songs of Praise*, no. 31).

[6] F. Thompson, *The Kingdom of God*.

and, according to a recently discovered papyrus in Egypt, Jesus is reported to have said, 'Raise the stone and there thou shalt find me; cleave the wood and there am I'.[1] I need not multiply instances. They are to be found not only in the Bible but in religious literature of all ages.[2]

Not only does the doctrine of creation give us a new orientation. The orientation is such that our whole way of life is affected. To a Christian, of course, the doctrine of creation does not stand on its own. He believes, too, that 'The word was made flesh',[3] and that 'God so loved the world that he gave his only begotten Son, that whosoever believeth in him should not perish but have everlasting life.[4] If we take these doctrines seriously, and if the loving father of the parable is assumed to be all-good and all-wise, it follows that we have a paramount duty to do his will. God gave himself without limit; it is our duty to do the same. As St. Paul puts the matter, 'I beseech you, therefore, brethren, by the mercies of God, that ye present your bodies a living sacrifice, holy, acceptable unto God, which is your reasonable service.'[5]

I have tried to indicate in this section the points of similarity between parable-language—in its ordinarily accepted sense—and the language of Christian theism. In both cases literal truth or falsity is unimportant; both sorts of language make use of familiar everyday illustrations, such as fathers, sons, husbandmen, and creation; and both sorts of language carry a message which we are invited to take seriously. In what follows, therefore, I propose to describe any language having these characteristics as 'the language of parable'.

On this showing the doctrines of creation, original sin, atonement, and resurrection can all be classified as the language of parable; and the doctrinal controversies of the early Church can be regarded as the search for the most suitable parable.

The doctrine of creation by an all-loving God I shall refer to as the 'theistic parable'. We have already seen[6] how talk of the 'existence' of God is misleading, in that it suggests that God is in some way an extra entity in addition to familiar ones. I suggest that, in place of the question 'Do you believe in the existence of God?', we should substitute, 'Do you accept the theistic parable?'

[1] Quoted in *The Bedside Book* (Gollancz, 1940), p. 801.
[2] For further quotations the reader is referred in particular to two recent anthologies compiled by Victor Gollancz, *A Year of Grace* (Gollancz, 1950), and *From Darkness to Light* (Gollancz, 1956).
[3] John i. 14.    [4] John iii. 16.    [5] Romans xii. 1.    [6] Chapter 15.

2

In this section I shall discuss what sort of arguments can be used in support of one parable rather than another.

The crucial question here is whether parables can be said to have 'objective validity'. If they can, the further question arises of how this 'objective validity' is determined.

This problem has already been discussed in Chapter 15. The suggestion on the part of 'Theologian' was that the theistic parable might be true, not literally but by analogy, of the actual world. There is some analogy, on this showing, between the empirical realities described in the parable and some other 'reality', which cannot be discovered empirically, but whose existence cannot just be ruled out by definition. The difficulty here is that words such as 'exist', 'real', 'true', 'objectively valid' etc. are taken from familiar experience no less than are words such as 'father' and 'judge' which are agreed to be inadequate when we speak of God. Even if we concede—as 'Philosopher' finally does for purposes of argument—that some extended sense of 'exist', 'real', 'true', and 'objectively valid' is legitimate, this involves no major change of viewpoint. Instead of saying that it makes no sense to ask whether the theistic parable is objectively valid, we are saying that the question makes sense but that we have no idea of what constitutes the answer. If there is a change at all, it is from saying nothing to saying 'I do not know'. In neither case is there any radical departure from the 'way of silence'.

The same type of argument is applicable in the case of moral assertions. Many philosophers, as we saw in Chapter 5, are hesitant to say that moral assertions can be 'objectively' true or false. If we grant, however, that they can, in some extended use of 'objectively true', we are no nearer to discovering an objectively true answer to a particular moral problem. Most of us would want to say, for instance, that cannibalism is wrong; but, however strong our conviction, there is no question of our being able to discover some 'objective reality' which proves us to be right. If 'There is something objectively grounded in the nature of things which *makes* cannibalism wrong' is meaningful at all, the 'something' in question must be completely unknown. The demand for objectivity, whether in the case of the theistic parable or in the case of moral assertions, must be met by the way of silence.

# The language of parable

This is not to say, of course, that choice of parable is a matter merely of personal preference. If I choose the theistic parable and you do not, the situation is not comparable to one in which I express a preference for cider and you express a preference for beer. In exactly the same way, if I say that cannibalism is wrong, I am not simply expressing a personal preference different from that of the cannibal. Though the demand for objectivity must be met by 'the way of silence', it can still be claimed that one moral belief is right and another wrong, and that one parable is better than another.

In what follows I shall speak of parables as 'good', 'appropriate', 'important', 'plausible', and so on, rather than use the problematic phrase 'objectively valid'.[1] Even this procedure, however, may give rise to misunderstanding, since the person who refuses to speak of 'objective validity' appears, at least at first glance, to be taking away something of importance. It should be emphasized, therefore, that the 'way of silence', so far from taking away something important, deprives us only of commonplace concepts, such as 'existence' and 'objective validity', which cannot be literally applicable in the case of God.[2]

Whether a particular parable is a good one is a matter in the last resort for personal conviction rather than rational argument. In this respect choice of parable is entirely comparable to a moral choice. It is misleading, in both cases, to say that no reasons at all can be given in support of or against a particular view; but in neither case can argument settle the matter conclusively.

Our choice of parable can be influenced by considerations of empirical fact. No assertion or group of assertions made by the astronomer or the geologist can be taken as equivalent to the assertion, 'In the beginning God created the heaven and the earth'; but empirical findings can make a parable appear either relevant and plausible or inappropriate. Thus it might seem that the existence of evil makes it difficult to continue holding the theistic parable,[3] or that difficulties arise as a result of

---

[1] There is no special objection, I suggest, to saying that a particular parable is 'true', since 'true' can be regarded as a general word of commendation applicable to many different types of assertion (compare p. 43). But since, to some, 'true' suggests 'true of some objective reality', I have thought it best not to refer to parables as 'true' and 'false'.

[2] Compare Diogenes Laertius, *Life of Epicurus*, Book X, 23. 'It is not profane to deny the gods of the common people, but it is profane to apply to the gods the notions of the common people.' (Quoted by Francis Bacon, Essay XVI, *Of Atheism*. Bacon himself says at the start of Essay XVII, 'It were better to have no opinion of God at all, than such an opinion as is unworthy of Him.')

[3] Compare p. 178, note 3.

Copernicus' system of astronomy and Darwin's theory of evolution.[1] If it were established on scientific grounds that no acts at all were freely chosen, then the parable of Adam and Eve in the garden of Eden, in which man falls through his own free choice, would be inappropriate. If it were established on historical grounds that Jesus was fallible on matters of importance, it would be all the more difficult to accept any parable which says that he is the incarnate son of God.[2] I am not attempting here to discuss whether the Christian parables should or should not be regarded as vulnerable on these grounds. My purpose is simply to indicate that factual considerations can quite well be relevant to our choice of parable.

Finally we need to consider the relation between parables and moral beliefs. The situation here seems to me to be one of complex interaction. Acceptance of a particular parable, as we saw,[3] may commit us to particular moral beliefs. Alternatively, if we are sure independently of a particular moral belief, then we may use this certainty to help us in our choice of parable. Thus acceptance of the parable that God gave himself without limit commits us to the view that we too should give ourselves without limit. If we did not recognize the need to give without limit, acceptance of the Christian parables could legitimately lead us to such recognition. Alternatively if we are sure independently that giving without limit is desirable, we may be led to view with favour parables which make this demand upon us, and to view with disfavour parables which point in the opposite direction. Again, while it would be logically consistent to argue from the parable 'The Lord is a man or war'[4] that wars are desirable, those who are sure independently that war is not something to be glorified will necessarily regard such a parable with disfavour. Similarly, Swinburne's Hertha rejects on moral grounds the idea of a God who can be angry:

> *In the darkening and whitening*
> *Abysses adored*
> *With dayspring and lightning*
> *For lamp and for sword*
> *God thunders in heaven, and his angels are red with*
> *the wrath of the Lord.*

The implicit argument is that *because* the idea of God thundering in heaven is an immoral one, such a parable must be rejected. Objection

[1] These two theories are discussed briefly in chapter 20, p. 209, footnote.
[2] Compare the argument in chapter 20.
[3] p. 53.
[4] Exodus xv. 3.

might also be raised on moral grounds to the Christian parables of original sin, atonement, and hell. Whether or not we regard such an objection as justified,[1] the principle still holds that parables can in general be open to attack on moral grounds. How far, in fact, people choose a particular parable because it makes sense of their existing moral beliefs, and how far they choose moral beliefs as a result of having accepted a particular parable I do not know.[2] Both types of choice, I suggest, can be logically justified.

Acceptance of a set of parables, like acceptance of a set of moral beliefs, is a matter for individual decision. There is no expertise and there are no technical advisers who know the answers. Even if an individual decides at some point to leave the decision to his church or to some other authority, the decision to trust that authority is still his own personal one.

## 3

In this section I shall discuss the problem of distinguishing the language of parable from the language of qualified literal theism.

The difficulty here is that a large amount depends on the way in which the words in question are said. Certain assertions lend themselves readily to being interpreted as the language of parable, certain others seem obviously to be qualified literal theism; but there are many which cannot be classified unequivocally as one or the other. In these cases

---

[1] The problem here seems to me to be largely one of formulation. I agree that language which suggests that the anger of God had to be appeased by the sacrifice of an innocent victim is an affront to our moral convictions, and that it is a further affront to suggest that God takes a sadistic pleasure in watching the torments of the damned. But theologians would agree, I think, that such language is a totally misleading caricature of what Christians are required to believe. The doctrine of atonement, as I understand it, tells us that we are all fit for hell but for the infinite love of God. The word 'hell' should, I think, be understood as a state of separation from God. The question of how we should envisage hell can be answered only by the way of silence. Some may object on moral grounds to the vivid pictorial imagery which has been used by both Jesus himself and by subsequent thinkers, e.g. the 'everlasting fire prepared for the devil and his angels' (Matthew xxv. 41); but, whatever our views on this pictorial imagery, the central message of the parable—that our pride and selfishness cannot be shrugged off as unimportant—remains unaffected. To underestimate the importance of the parable of hell seems to me very dangerous.

[2] A person, for instance, might come to be a Quaker because of an existing moral belief that the method of war (which many Quakers oppose) was wrong. Alternatively, having accepted independently the Quaker parable that there is a spark of the divine in all men, he might come to realize as a result that the method of war was one which he ought not to accept.

we can judge only by the way in which the words are said and by the general attitude of the person saying them. To quote some examples, 'God is light'[1] and 'God is love'[2] can be taken with no difficulty as the language of parable. 'Is' here apparently means 'is identical with'; and to say that God is identical with an entity such as light or identical with the noun of the verb 'to love' is clearly not literal use of language. In the case of 'God intervened at Dunkirk' the matter is again clear. These words—at least in most contexts—carry the unmistakable stamp of literalness. If someone tells us, however, that 'God made the world', it is not clear without consideration of the context whether the speaker is expressing belief in the parable of creation or whether he literally believes in a para-physical activity of 'making something' carried out by a para-physical agency. We all know that the assertion 'God made the country and man made the town' is a witticism, and we should be seriously uneasy if someone said this in a tone of voice indicative that he did not realize that it was a witticism at all. In the same way we have every right to be uneasy when the words 'God made the world' are used in such a way that the speaker appears to regard them as literal. There can be all degrees of uneasiness, from extreme uneasiness in the case of e.g. 'God intervened at Dunkirk' to complete absence of uneasiness, as in the case of 'God is light' or 'God is love'. We are dependent in the last resort on the general 'feel' of the sentence in question.

Two possible pointers may be mentioned, but they are not infallible. The first is the use of language somewhat removed from our everyday experience; the second is the use of language about God which would never be used of ordinary people. It is easier, it seems to me, to regard 'In the beginning God created the heaven and the earth'[3] as parable-language for the very reason that it is not the language of everyday life. In that respect it has a rather different 'feel' from 'God made the world' which seems prosaic and trivial in comparison, and therefore lends itself more readily to being interpreted literally. Again we should never say of an ordinary person that he 'is light' or 'is love', whereas we can easily say of an ordinary person that he 'intervened' somewhere. The first pointer, however, clearly does not take us far; and the second can at times mislead us. Thus I have heard it said of a devoted clergyman whose work had received no official recognition, 'But God will give him a cabinet position in the next world'. Such talk caused me no uneasiness

[1] 1 John i. 5.     [2] 1 John iv. 8.     [3] Genesis, i. 1.

whatsoever, despite the fact that giving away a cabinet position is a specifically human activity; it was perfectly clear from the way in which the speaker said the words that he was not seriously thinking of a literal heaven in which God distributed positions in the cabinet as rewards. The same words said by someone else in a different context might have seemed all too painfully the language of qualified literal theism.

A further complication needs to be mentioned here. An assertion which appears at first glance to be a literal factual one may be found after examination to have the status of a parable. There is a saying, for instance, that 'God always answers prayer, but sometimes the answer is "No".' At first glance this appears to be a literal factual assertion—an account of what happens if one prays. Many would no doubt interpret it as such. But what, in that case, do we say if time after time the answer continues to be 'No'? Some would say that the assertion has been falsified, and that the prayers have gone unanswered. Many, however, would insist on saying, 'The answer is still "No".' To say this is not necessarily a disreputable subterfuge. It is, in effect, to turn the original assertion into a parable, to express willingness to accept the theistic parable whatever the empirical facts.[1] A comparable situation arises with other parables, e.g. parables for understanding the course of history. Assertions which look *prima facie* as though they can be verified or falsified by historical evidence are found on examination to be attempts to supply a special 'slant' on the course of history. Some versions of Marxism, for instance, involve assertions of this kind.[2] The borderline between literal assertion and parable is thus by no means a clearly marked one.

In the case of sentences containing the word 'God', however, enough has been said, I hope, to indicate the general 'feel' of literal assertions as compared with the language of parable, and to enable the reader to classify at any rate the clear-cut cases one way or the other.

[1] R. M. Hare (in *New Essays in Philosophical Theology*, edited by A. G. N. Flew and A. C. MacIntyre, S.C.M. Press, 1955), pp. 99–103, cites the example of a lunatic who is convinced that all dons want to murder him. It transpires that *nothing* will convince him that this is not so. Since his assertion has thus become unfalsifiable it is no longer a straightforward empirical one. Hare labels it a 'blik', and suggests that belief in God is a kind of 'blik', though of course a far more valuable one.

[2] Compare T. D. Weldon, *States and Morals* (London, 1946), especially his discussion of international capitalist solidarity on p. 161.

4

Finally it remains to consider what is involved when people disagree in their choice of parables, and when a person changes from one set of parables to another.

Now it is commonly supposed that those who believe in God have in their possession some factual knowledge which is not available to unbelievers. It has been one of the main purposes of this book to argue that such a view is mistaken. The word 'God' cannot be thought of as the name of an extra para-physical entity, since the notion of a paraphysical entity makes no sense. However important the insights of the religious believer and the mystic, we cannot claim that they are the possessors of extra factual information which the unbeliever lacks. Two people may have access to exactly the same factual information, may feel the same joys and sorrows, may be confronted with the same good fortunes or disasters, and yet may tell different and conflicting parables. It is not that one person is better informed on his facts than the other; it is rather that they see the same facts, as it were, through different spectacles.

The matter has been put very strikingly by Browning in *Bishop Blougram's Apology*. The bishop admits that his professed beliefs do not admit of certainty, but neither would he have certainty, he says, if he became an unbeliever.

> *All we have gained then by our unbelief*
> *Is a life of doubt diversified by faith*
> *For one of faith diversified by doubt:*
> *We called the chess-board white,—we call it black.*

On the one hand we can cite all the many evils that surround us—promising lives cut short by accidents, the agonies of cancer and other diseases, and natural disasters such as floods and earthquakes; on the other hand we can call attention to men's supreme achievements in the world of art and literature—Beethoven's Fifth Symphony, for instance, or some passages in Shakespeare. It is not that those who accept the theistic parable have overlooked the evils, nor that those who reject it have overlooked the things that are valuable. The question is rather whether the achievements of a Beethoven or of a Shakespeare are touches of glory in a universe where all is vanity, or whether disease and natural disaster are in some way the disfigurements of a world made by a God of love. The analogy of the chess-board serves to bring out that the believer is not necessarily someone who has access to factual information which other people lack.

Disagreement over choice of parables is, as we have seen, less like disagreement over a factual question and more like disagreement over a moral question. As with moral beliefs, so with parables, people are entitled to assert, whatever the difficulties of rational justification, that their answer is the right one; they are entitled to believe that the person who gives a different answer may be missing something of supreme importance. Again, as with moral beliefs, so with parables, a person who changes his views undergoes what we would normally call a 'conversion' or 'change of heart'. Acceptance of the Christian parables is said to involve 'rebirth'[1] and 'eternal life'.[2] This is something very different from acquiring new factual knowledge or even new intellectual insight of some other kind.

A story is told of a well-known theologian who, after addressing a large meeting, was invited to meet some of his audience informally at their canteen. Discussing the address, one of his new hosts said, 'Yes, it's all very well. But personally I don't believe in God'. The preacher proceeded with all his brilliance of scholarship to produce a series of well-established 'arguments for the existence of God'. His logic, so the story goes, was irresistible, and at the end his host nodded calmly and said, 'Yes, I see. Now I believe in God.' It is small wonder that the eminent theologian was horrified. To make the verbal pronouncement 'I believe in God' is something very different from being converted, and whatever the theologian had achieved he had certainly not achieved conversion.

Acceptance of the theistic parable commits us to action. There may, of course, be people who profess to believe a particular parable but fail to act in accordance with their profession. Applications of the theistic parable to particular occasions are not always easy; but if we are sure that the theistic parable commits us to a particular moral policy—e.g. to condemnation of apartheid or refusal to use the hydrogen bomb—then we are likely to say that those who disagree with us on such matters do not really take the theistic parable seriously. They profess to accept the theistic parable, we might say, but they do not genuinely accept its implications. Conversely there may be those who make no explicit profession of faith, or who, like Abou Ben Adhem, make no reference to God in their professions of faith, but whose actions are none the less

[1] John iii. 3.  [2] John x. 28.

entirely in accordance with the theistic parable. Our argument serves
to bring out that it makes no sense to speak of conversion to a new set
of parables if there is mere verbal assent unaccompanied by appropriate
action. Those who say 'Lord, Lord' are not necessarily those that go into
the kingdom of heaven.[1]

Our whole discussion will serve, too, to indicate how very misleading
and unsatisfactory the label 'atheist' can be.[2] Self-professed atheists
may be doing no more than denying that a venerable figure with a beard
is to be found beyond the clouds. If that is how the word 'atheist' is to
be understood, then few of us are anything but atheists. The word
'atheist' serves, of course, as an exciting label, and some may be
influenced in their choice of it by the desire to be shocking, just as many
call themselves 'theists' without having worked out the implications of
their belief. What is quite clear is that it is foolish to condemn a self-
professed atheist or regard him as missing something important in life
until we know what his attitude to life really is. We can discover this
attitude if we know what parables he tells. If it is said that an atheist
is one who does not accept any parable at all, my comment would be
this. All of us alike are confronted with the question how we ought
to live; and, whatever way of life we choose, we can be said to be
implicitly accepting one set of parables or another. If the parable which
we accept is not that of the loving father, it is likely to be that of a
purposeless world, indifferent or actively hostile to man's highest
endeavours. Such a parable cannot be shown to be wrong. But to live
in accordance with it involves a commitment no less than does living in
accordance with the theistic parable.[3] The self-professed atheist or
agnostic may not explicitly have made such a commitment; but all living

---

[1] Matthew vii. 21.

[2] The label 'agnostic' presents rather different problems. As commonly used
it indicates an unbeliever, one who, in the absence of knowledge, *rejects* religious
belief. But we need to remember the high degree of 'agnosticism' involved in
the 'way of silence'.

[3] This argument is specially relevant, I think, to those who say that the
existence of evil makes the theistic parable untenable. Those who accept the
theistic parable are forced to say that earthquakes, famines, painful diseases, and
other apparent evils are not evil *sub specie aeternitatis* but are all parts of God's
plan; and since this seems hard to accept, it might be thought that rejection of
the theistic parable is an easy and obvious way of avoiding any problem. Rejection, however, no less than acceptance, involves a crucial decision as to how
life should be lived. What is more, acceptance, particularly when it is accompanied by 'the way of silence', does not commit us to the claim that we can
*understand* why there should be evil; our choice is between the ignorance of
belief and the ignorance of unbelief. I see no good reason for regarding the
ignorance of unbelief as the more satisfactory position of the two.

involves implicit acceptance of one parable or another. It follows, in our present use of the word 'parable', that the question is not whether to tell parables but what parables to tell.

This is a matter for personal conviction. There is no easy or obvious answer.

★     ★     ★

The main conclusions of the last three chapters may now be summarized. 1. The language of simple literal theism is false. 2. The language of qualified literal theism is meaningless; no sense can be attached to the phrase 'divine intervention' if taken literally. 3. The appropriate religious policy is one of silence qualified by parables. 4. Instead of 'Do you believe in the existence of God?' we should substitute, 'Do you accept the theistic parable?' This rids us of the temptation to think of God as an 'extra entity'. 5. The questions whether there is such an entity and whether the theistic parable is objectively true can be met only by 'the way of silence'. 6. There is no linguistic difficulty over parable-assertions comparable with the difficulty involved in assertions which use the language of qualified literal theism. 7. Parable-assertions are not equivalent either to factual or moral assertions, but factual and moral considerations can influence our choice of parable. 8. Acceptance of the theistic parable involves conversion and a change of outlook.

# CHAPTER 17

# God and prayer

It has been thought in the past that there is a basic conflict between 'science' and 'religion' over the question whether God answers prayer. Many have supposed that the religious person who argues for the efficacy of prayer—or at any rate of petitionary prayer—is vainly trying to defend the impossible, since in the modern world it is scientific understanding rather than prayer which produces results. Thus prayers are no substitute for penicillin, and prayers will not mend a damaged motor car or a broken wireless set. Others, however, have stressed the need for caution on the part of the scientist. Sweeping claims, they would say, about what can or cannot happen are inappropriate; the appropriate attitude is one of caution and humility. Both arguments seem to me to be important in their way; but neither, I suggest, does justice to the full complexity of the problem.

I shall argue in this chapter that some modification of the traditional Christian attitude to prayer is unavoidable. I shall not, however, be making any claim as to what can or cannot happen. My main plea is simply for further reflection on the meaning of words. The argument in the first part of the chapter will be that the words 'God answers prayer', if taken at their face value, are the language of qualified literal theism, and must therefore be rejected as meaningless. In the second part I shall suggest that the language of qualified literal theism should be replaced by the language of commitment and dedication.

I

For the moment I shall be concerned only with what is called 'petitionary' prayer—the making of *petitions* to God, as a result of which it is hoped that He will arrange the course of nature in accordance with the requests of the person praying. The following are examples—prayers for recovery from sickness, prayers for rain in time of drought, and prayers for victory in war. In all these cases there appears to be the hope that, by means of the agency of God, the prayers will produce the required effect.

Some may wish to draw a distinction between prayers offered in a genuinely deserving cause and prayers which seem like attempts to use the power of God for our own selfish ends. It would then be said that God may sometimes answer the first sort of prayer, but that we cannot be surprised if he does not answer the second. Since prayers for a change of weather are frequently of the second sort, we must not, on this view, be surprised if such prayers have no effect. Prayers for recovery from sickness, on the other hand, may quite well be answered, it would be said, provided they are offered to God with genuine humility. I do not dispute the importance of this distinction in some contexts; but for present purposes it need not concern us. All such prayers, whether selfish or otherwise, have in common the attempt to influence the course of nature through the medium of divine activity; and it is this attempt in general which I am concerned to discuss.

If 'God answers prayer' is understood literally—and it is difficult to interpret the words in any other way—it is apparently similar to 'Jones answers when you talk to him at meals', and both appear to admit in principle of being answered by empirical means. It might seem, therefore, that the only problem to be solved is that of assessing the evidence. This, however, is not the case. For purposes of discussion I propose to break up 'God answers prayer' into two constituent assertions, namely, (*a*) 'Prayers sometimes produce results', and (*b*) 'These results are caused by God'. (If 'God answers prayer' is true, both these assertions must be true also.) I shall argue that, whatever view we take over (*a*), (*b*) must be rejected as meaningless.

Although the main argument of this chapter concerns (*b*), a few comments will be made first of all on (*a*).

'Prayers sometimes produce results' is a genuine empirical assertion. There is no short cut to determining its truth or falsity; the only possible procedure is to examine all available evidence. Although such examination is outside the scope of this book, a number of methodo-logical points deserve mention. In particular we need to insist that, since the problem is an empirical one, it can be settled only by empirical methods. This being so, there is no objection in principle to that characteristically empirical device, a controlled experiment with statistics. An example of such an experiment would be a comparison of the recovery rate in two wings of a hospital, in one of which only ordinary methods of treatment were used, in the other of which these methods were supplemented by prayer. Some people have treated with scorn the idea that the efficacy of petitionary prayer could be tested in this way. Thus it has been said that if we perform such an experiment we are being irreverent and are 'tempting God'.[1] One of the necessary preconditions if prayers are to be answered, it would be said, is genuine humility and readiness to submit to the will of God. Since in a controlled experiment these conditions are almost certain to be absent, no conclusions could be drawn if the experiment had a negative result. This argument, however, though it might serve to account for this or that series of negative results, is not an objection against statistical methods as such. If by some means it were possible to discover prayers offered in genuine humility, these would be the prayers to include in the statistics. I am not saying, of course, that such experiments are free from practical difficulties. To ensure that prayer alone was the operative variable would be extremely difficult, to say the least. I am saying only that, for an empirical question, the statistical approach is correct in principle, and usually offers the best chance of obtaining accurate information.

This is in effect agreed by those defenders of petitionary prayer who say that countless men and women through the ages have found that prayers were answered. This claim is itself, after all, an appeal to statistics of a kind; it is different from a statistical table only in being less precise and in failing to give comparable figures for *un*answered prayers.

It is worth noting, too, that, since the matter is an empirical one, it needs to be referred not to the individual conscience but to the appropriate scientific investigator. Thus experiments studying the effect of prayers on the weather would be part of meteorology, and experiments studying the effect of prayers on recovery from sickness would be part of medicine, psychology, or sociology.

We need not, of course, regard it as a foregone conclusion that all statistical investigations on the effectiveness of prayer would necessarily give negative results. As far as I know, meteorologists normally assume that prayers are not among the operative factors in producing particular weather conditions, and orthodox British doctors do not regard prayer as a serious alternative to other methods of treatment. To assert

[1] My source for this argument is C. S. Lewis.

uncompromisingly, however, that prayers *never* produce results seems to me unwarranted. We should in that case be committed to saying that all cases of so-called 'faith-healing' (where results are sometimes said to be brought about by prayer) are bogus or erroneously reported; and although this is possible, it would be rash to regard it as the obvious truth. The phenomena connected with hypnotism, and, in particular, the events that happen in the so-called 'transference'-situation in psycho-therapy—the relationship of the patient to his therapist—suggest the need for caution; all sorts of factors may be operating of which at present we know very little. Moreover, even if it is agreed that in twentieth-century Britain prayers do not normally appear to influence the course of nature, it is a large step to generalize from this evidence to the whole of humanity.[1]

As far as the argument of this book is concerned, taking sides is unnecessary, and I have not attempted to do so. My concern has been to point out that the matter is an empirical one, and that a thoroughgoing use of empirical methods is the only honest course.

Our central argument concerns the claim that, when prayers produce results, these results are *caused by God*—the claim, in other words, that it is *God* who answers the prayers.

Let us assume for purposes of argument that prayers for rain have been followed by rain a sufficiently large number of times to make us suspect a connection. (It does not matter, for this purpose, whether or not this assumption is regarded as a likely one.) It is still not clear that the evidence justifies the conclusion that the rain was caused by God.

'This rain was caused by God' suggests activity on the part of an 'extra entity'. We need not recapitulate in detail the arguments of Chapter 14 which show the 'extra-entity' view of God to be mistaken. All that will be said here is this. Even those who say that God does literally answer prayer agree that the word 'God' is not the name of something visible or tangible; and it must also be agreed that the word 'God' is not the name of a theoretical construct like 'superego' or 'the unconscious'. In 'God answers prayer', as in 'God intervened at Dunkirk', we have an apparently empirical assertion, and yet no

---

[1] This argument, however, should not be pressed too far. Any negative generalization, e.g. 'There are no fairies', can be treated as vulnerable on the grounds that the evidence is inadequate. Most of us, however, are satisfied that there are no fairies on the relatively small amount of evidence available to us; and while the claim 'Prayers never produce results' can rightly be met with the query, 'Have you sufficient evidence?', it should not be met with the triumphant, 'Ah! but you haven't examined the whole universe!'

criteria which enable that assertion to be verified or falsified. As has been shown already, if we claim that this assertion is true, we are misleading ourselves with words.

The most the evidence would establish is that by some unknown means prayers were affecting the weather. It adds nothing to say that the changes in the weather were 'due to the activity of God'.

According to the 'way of silence' all such talk is inappropriate. If we qualify our silence it must be with the language of parable. Those who accept the theistic parable can quite well say, like Browning's *Abt Vogler*, 'Here is the finger of God'; indeed they will see the working of God in everything; but they are not obliged to believe in a sort of para-physical activity by a para-physical entity. Whether such activity ever occurs is either a meaningless question or else a totally unanswerable one. Only the most naïve person would believe that God literally has fingers. According to the 'way of silence' it is equally naïve to suppose that we can apply to God the literal notion of 'activity'.

Now the great difficulty with much prayer-language is that it tends to encourage precisely this mistake. All too frequently the language appears to be that of qualified literal theism. The suggestion is that contact is being made with the person, God, of whom sentences in the language of qualified literal theism purport to be true. God is thus thought of as a 'para-physical' Being, and it is supposed that in reply to people's petitions, he will take 'para-physical' action—action of an 'immaterial' kind not detectable by scientific instruments. Moreover when children are told 'Talk to Jesus as you would to your best friend',[1] such language again suggests a 'para-physical' person who has the power (in an entirely literal sense) of doing things, and we have every right to be uneasy.

Those who believe on empirical grounds that prayers produce results are logically justified in using prayer as a technique for producing these results. But it is no more than a technique. The suggestion that God is, in a literal sense, the cause of the results is to ascribe to God notions that are quite inappropriate. If it is then suggested that God is the cause of the results (or even their part-cause) in some extended use of 'cause', this suggestion can be met only by the 'way of silence'.

Our conclusion is that 'God answers prayer', if interpreted as the language of qualified literal theism, must be regarded as meaningless.

[1] This instruction is in fact given to adolescents at certain Christian holiday camps.

# God and prayer

## 2

It remains to consider the consequences of this view for religious practice.

It is, of course, completely outside the scope of this book to argue on general grounds as to what religious practices, if any, are desirable. But if our main argument is right, it follows that one particular religious practice—namely, the use of petitionary prayer when the language is understood in a straightforward literal way—requires to be abandoned. If 'God sends rain in answer to prayer' is a pointless form of words, then 'O God, please send some rain' is pointless also. These words could legitimately be used as a formula for producing rain by those who believe on empirical grounds that the formula is effective; but as an address to a person they are essential features of the mistake which we have been attacking throughout Part III of this book—namely the belief that the word 'God' stands for a para-physical entity who *does* things (in a quite literal sense of 'does') on request. Prayer-language which embodies this mistake I shall refer to as 'pseudo-causal' prayer-language. The intention behind such prayer-language is to cause results, but the causation is not of the genuine sort, since the causal agent is supposed to be a 'para-physical entity'—a supposition which has been shown to be meaningless.

There are, of course, other forms of prayer-language which are not vulnerable in this way. Those, for instance, who say the words 'Thy will be done' are not trying to produce a result by means of a para-physical agency; they are making an act of submission. As will be seen in a moment, the language by means of which we make acts of submission is very different from pseudo-causal prayer-language.

'Thy will be done' constitutes what may be called 'performatory' prayer-language. To make this point clear a few words should be said in connection with so-called 'performatory' language in general.[1] In ordinary speech, when we say 'I agree' or 'I undertake', the purpose of these words is not to convey information about ourselves; in saying the words we are actually *giving* the agreement or the undertaking. In the same way the very utterance of the words 'Thy will be done' is itself an expression of acknowledgement. When performatory language is being used, the word 'hereby' frequently serves to make the meaning plainer.

[1] The notion of 'performatory' language owes its origin to Professor J. L. Austin. See especially his article, 'Other Minds' (*Aristotelian Society*, Supplementary Volume xx for 1946), p. 173.

Thus to say 'I declare the meeting closed' is to say 'I *hereby* declare the meeting closed'. Similarly 'Thy will be done' requires to be understood as 'I hereby acknowledge the need to do according to thy will'.

A distinction therefore needs to be made between two varieties of prayer-language, 'pseudo-causal' prayer-language and 'performatory' prayer-language. A standard case of the former is 'O God, please send some rain'; a standard case of the latter is 'Thy will be done'. According to the argument of this book, any prayer-language of the former sort requires to be abandoned.

I am not, of course, saying that the first of these expressions should be abandoned because the request is an *unworthy* one, whereas the request in the second case is more deserving. The point is rather that 'Thy will be done' is not a request at all. In using these words (and similar ones) we are committing and dedicating ourselves, not trying to persuade an unknown agency to influence the course of nature.

I shall not attempt to specify in detail how much prayer-language is open to the charge of being 'pseudo-causal' and how much can be regarded as 'performatory'. But the distinction between the two will, I hope, provide a touchstone by means of which all prayer-language can be judged. Any prayer-language which appears at first glance to be 'pseudo-casual' can then be either reinterpreted or abandoned.

Let us try to elucidate the principle further. The first point which requires to be emphasized is this. We need not be troubled if acts of dedication and commitment involve the use of parable-language, provided, of course, that this parable-language is recognized for what it is. One of the parables which plays a central part in Christian thinking is that of human relations. Not only is God thought of as a loving father; the Christian himself is told to *love* God. Addresses to God as a person are not necessarily, therefore, to be excluded, provided we are not just being simple-minded about them. Thus the words 'Thy will be done'—an address to a 'person' who is assumed to have a 'will'—are perfectly justified provided we are not misled into taking them literally, and provided we regard the parable of human relationships as a good one.

The next point is this. Much prayer-language does not fall readily on to one side of the dividing-line or the other. There are all sorts of doubtful intermediate cases. This point can be made clear by consideration of examples. The words 'God be merciful to me a sinner'[1] could conceivably be taken as an attempt to influence an unknown agency into

---

[1] Luke xviii. 13.

giving merciful treatment; but it seems to me that they can more readily
be classed as performatory prayer-language. They must in that case be
regarded as constituting an acknowledgement of the theistic parable in
general and of human shortcomings in particular. In other words, they
are more like 'Thy will be done' than they are like, 'O God, please send
some rain'. On the other hand, 'Defend us from all perils and dangers
of this night'[1] can more readily be taken as a request for protection than
as an acknowledgement which says (using parable-language) that we are
in the hands of a loving God. It follows that, if these words are to be
retained at all, it is necessary to place a somewhat forced interpretation
on them. As a third example, let us take the prayer from the communion
service, 'Almighty God, unto whom all hearts be open, all desires
known, and from whom no secrets are hid; Cleanse the thoughts of our
hearts . . .'[2] It is not at first glance obvious to which group this prayer
belongs. I do not doubt that many have taken it as a request to an
unknown agency to perform a para-physical operation of cleansing; but
I have no hesitation in suggesting that it ought to be interpreted as
performatory prayer-language. It is as though we said, 'I hereby
acknowledge the theistic parable, the parable of one who sees all our
inmost thoughts, and I hereby acknowledge my shortcomings and the
need for cleansing.'

These examples will, I hope, give some indication of the way in which
the general principle requires to be applied. Detailed application of the
principle, however, is a matter which each religious group must work
out for itself; and no attempt has been made, except for purposes of
example, to suggest which individual prayers can or cannot be retained.
The general principle is that all prayers which are comparable to 'O God,
please send some rain' require to be abandoned, while those comparable
to 'Thy will be done' are not exposed to the same difficulty.

One final point deserves mention. Although advocating the abandonment of 'pseudo-causal' prayer-language, I am neither accepting nor
rejecting the view that prayer-language can have a causal influence on
the person using it. According to this claim, particular acts of
'performatory' prayer may sometimes help a person to lead a more
adequate kind of life; and even literal petitionary prayers may sometimes have an influence on character. (Thus a person who uttered the
words 'O God, make me humble', intending them as a request, might

---

[1] Evening Prayer, 3rd Collect.
[2] Holy Communion, Collect for Purity.

on this view find himself becoming more humble simply as a result of what he had said.) Whether prayer-language does in fact have this effect is an empirical matter, and one on which for present purposes it is unnecessary to take sides. It should be stressed, however, that 'performatory' prayer-language can quite well be regarded as valuable irrespective of its effects on the character of those who say it, and that 'pseudo-causal' prayer-language must be regarded as a muddle irrespective of any beneficial effects which may accidentally accrue.[1]

*     *     *

The conclusions of this chapter are, in effect, three. (*a*) The assertion 'God answers prayer', if interpreted literally, is the language of qualified literal theism, and therefore requires to be abandoned. (*b*) 'Pseudo-causal' prayer-language is vulnerable in a similar way. (*c*) 'Performatory' prayer-language is not discredited. My general plea is for the replacement of literal petitionary prayers by 'performatory' prayers—that is, by the language of commitment and dedication.

---

[1] The claim that prayer 'is merely auto-suggestion' is one of those provocative slogans which cannot be discussed until its meaning is more fully elucidated. Those who make this claim are, in my opinion, right in so far as they are unwilling to consider para-physical action by para-physical agencies, but wrong if they are implying that the value of 'performatory' prayer-language lies in its psychological consequences. The more the difficulty over 'pseudo-causal' prayer language is appreciated, of course, the less likely is it that these beneficial consequences will follow.

# CHAPTER 18

## *Miracles*

It has often been supposed that modern science forces us to reject all miracle-stories as false. My purpose in the present chapter is to examine whether this conclusion is justified.

I shall argue that it is not. If an event is sufficiently well attested, no one is entitled to argue that it could not have happened.

No attempt will be made to discuss whether particular events, such as the so-called 'miracles' described in the gospels, did or did not take place. The question which I shall try to answer is whether modern science compels us to believe that they did not. Whether they are credible on other grounds will not be discussed here.[1]

Before starting the main argument, it is necessary to clear up some ambiguities in the word 'miracle'. By derivation 'miracle' means simply 'wonderful event'. This usage, however, need not concern us, since it does not involve any controversy. No one has the right to deny that wonderful events—events which are remarkable, and which surprise us—happen from time to time. We should be surprised, for instance, if we discovered a trout that had been born with two heads; but this phenomenon is not unknown. Controversy arises only when the word 'miracle' is given the special meaning assigned to it by philosophers and theologians, namely an event which is an exception to known laws of nature. Thus, according to known laws of nature, the human body gradually decomposes after death; and any instance of a body *not* decomposing, as is reported of the body of Jesus, would be classed as a miracle in this special sense. The appearance of a trout with two heads, on the other hand, would not be a miracle, since it admits of a straight-forward biological explanation. A third sense of the word 'miracle' also

[1] For a brief discussion of this point, see p. 212.

needs to be mentioned, the sense in which it is defined as 'an interference with Nature by supernatural power'.[1] This phrase suggests not only an exception to known laws, but a deliberate suspension of those laws by some sort of 'Being' outside nature. This definition will be examined in a moment.

It is sometimes asked if the so-called miracles described in the gospel story 'were really miracles'. If 'miracle' means simply 'wonderful event' this question makes no sense; but it is perfectly intelligible to ask if the events described were miracles in the sense of being exceptions to the laws of nature as we know them. Thus if we suppose that the so-called 'miracles of healing' described in the gospels were brought about by suggestion on the part of Jesus, and that those who were cured were responding to suggestion in much the same way as patients under hypnosis are known to respond to suggestion, then these events were not 'miracles' in the special sense. Miracles in the special sense involve exceptions to a known law.

Before we embark on our main discussion, a few words should be said about C. S. Lewis's definition of a miracle as 'an interference with Nature by supernatural power'. Professor Lewis claims to be offering a defence of miracles, but his very definition of 'miracle' seems to me to send us off on a completely wrong track. If 'miracle' is used in his sense, there is no means of telling whether any event is a miracle or not; the word 'miracle' is serving no useful purpose. Some might say that an event would count as 'an interference with Nature by supernatural power' if it happened opportunely or unexpectedly or if it involved some exception to natural laws. But clearly none of these criteria constitute the actual 'cash-value' of 'caused by supernatural power'. 'Caused by a supernatural power' is not intended to mean the same as 'happening opportunely' etc., and it can no more be 'unpacked' into 'happening opportunely' etc. than 'There is a burglar' can be 'unpacked' into 'The spoons are missing', 'There are footprints on the flower-beds' etc.[2] Moreover if an event appears to be inexplicable, it adds nothing to say 'Therefore we must account for it by postulating the activity of supernatural power'. Such a would-be 'explanation' is vacuous and tells us nothing. In the absence of criteria for recognizing such activity, we are misleading ourselves with the language of qualified literal theism. We may conclude, therefore, that to define a miracle as 'an

[1] See C. S. Lewis, *Miracles* (Geoffrey Bles, 1947), p. 15.
[2] Compare the argument on pp. 150–2.

interference with Nature by supernatural power' results only in confusion.[1]

It may still be said that God, being all-powerful, is able to overrule existing natural laws when he chooses, and that we have no right to set limits to God's power. To say this, however, is not only to be guilty of using the language of qualified literal theism; it is also to be misled by what is meant by 'laws of nature'. The word 'law' is in many ways misleading.[2] It suggests that God lined up all the atoms and said to them, 'You behave in this way, or else. . . !' This implies a parallelism between 'laws' of nature and 'laws' of a country which certainly does not hold. A very powerful monarch can hold the laws of his country in suspension when he chooses; to speak of God doing this to the laws of nature is sheer confusion.

Let us now pass on to considering the arguments which suggest that acceptance of a scientific world-outlook forces us to reject the miraculous. It seems to me that there are three main arguments, all of them philosophically interesting, but none of them justifying the conclusion that particular events did not happen.

(*a*) Since the notion of 'supernatural interference' involves a vacuous explanation, there is a good case for saying that the word 'miracle' (in the sense of a supernatural interference with natural laws) should be excluded from our vocabulary altogether. This is not just a verbal quibble. It is a matter of principle for the scientist that vacuous explanations must be avoided; to bring in the supernatural is just such a vacuous explanation.

The crucial point, however, is this. Even if we rule out the miraculous by definition, it does not follow that the *so-called* 'miracles' of the gospel-story, or any other alleged 'miracles', did not occur. It follows only that such events, if they did occur, should not be labelled 'miracles'. To determine whether a particular event did or did not occur the scientist (and the historian) are dependent the whole time on empirical evidence. If an event is well attested, then the occurrence of that event is something which cannot be disputed. If the occurrence does not fit in with existing ideas, then these existing ideas require to be modified. To

---

[1] For an exposure of similar confusion, see P. Nowell-Smith's article entitled Miracles' in *New Essays in Philosophical Theology*, edited by A. G. N. Flew and A. C. MacIntyre (S.C.M. Press, 1955).
[2] I owe the argument which follows to Mr. T. D. Weldon.

argue that an event *could not* have happened cuts very little ice if the evidence shows that it *did* happen.[1]

The argument which we have considered states an important scientific principle—namely that vacuous explanations should be avoided; but from its very nature it cannot help us in assessing whether any particular surprising event took place.

(*b*) A second argument against miracles arises from consideration of the model of the enclosed billiard-table.[2] It is one of the rules implicit in this model that there cannot be interference from outside. A billiard-ball moves only when struck by another billiard-ball, and it is assumed that in the total system there can be no loss of energy. In that case it would seem to follow that the widow's cruse could not have been refilled with oil, as described in the book of Kings,[3] unless the oil *came from somewhere*. It is inconceivable that Jesus could have been born of a virgin unless we suppose that *something* happened to make fertilization possible. Similarly it is inconceivable that after his death his body vanished completely; we are forced to assume that the elements comprising it were converted into something else.

This argument seems to me of very considerable philosophical interest.[4] None the less it will not serve to discredit the stories in question or any others. Once again it is a question of examining the evidence. If the evidence is adequate in a particular case, then any preconceived notions we may have as to what is or is not possible must be abandoned. In effect, if we insist that the model of the enclosed billiard-table must be retained at all costs, then our only choice is to bolster it up with some *ad hoc* additions. We might assume, for instance, that some force, hitherto only 'potential', became operative in the virgin's womb, or that some 'potential energy' became released when Jesus' body ceased to be visible or tangible. Such hypotheses are useless unless they are independently verifiable, but they are the only way of combining belief in

---

[1] I was told the following story recently by a laundryman. He had been accused, in fact wrongly, by a hotel-manager of failing to return some sheets to the hotel after laundering. The hotel-manager had said that the sheets must be at the laundry, since they were not at the hotel. The laundryman replied, 'I dare say they *must*, but they *aren't*.' Similarly, if a miracle is sufficiently well-attested, a scientifically minded observer might feel like commenting 'I dare say it *couldn't* have happened, but it *did*.'

[2] For an account of this model, see pp. 71–4.

[3] 1 Kings xvii. 14–16.

[4] I am inclined to think that philosophers in general (with the notable exception of Kant) have failed to take the implications of the model of the enclosed billiard-table sufficiently seriously.

the events in question with acceptance of the model of the enclosed billiard-table.

(*c*) It may still be said that the very idea of a miracle, at least in the sense of something inexplicable by known scientific law, is an affront to the scientific conscience. A scientist can quite well say, 'This looks like an exception to the law as it is now formulated'; but, on the present view, he should add at once, 'I must try to formulate the law more adequately'. To decide that a particular event is totally inexplicable is therefore incompatible with the scientific outlook; whatever happens, the scientist must *look for* explanations.

This is no doubt an important point of scientific principle. But whatever the scientist's hopes and aspirations, there is nothing absurd in supposing that there are some events which cannot satisfactorily be brought under any law at all. It is perfectly conceivable that the so-called 'miraculous' stories in the gospels were of this sort. In such cases a scientist may legitimately wish to investigate further, or, in the case of past events, may legitimately wish that further investigation with modern equipment were possible; but such investigations would not necessarily result in the formulation of any general law in terms of which the events could be explained.

It may still be said that the people who reported the miracles described in the Bible lived in a pre-scientific age, and that present-day knowledge of natural laws makes many of the events described, if not impossible, at least extremely improbable.

It is outside the scope of this chapter to become involved in problems of assessing historical evidence, reliability of witnesses, and such matters. But in so far as the problem is one of scientific principle, it requires discussion. The main point is this. Accounts of events to which there are parallels are in general more easy to credit than accounts of events whose occurrence would be unique. If an event seems totally unparalleled, and appears to run counter to all reasonable expectations, then the amount of reliable evidence needed to justify belief in that event would, in general, be very high. It is for this reason that some have supposed that the miracles of healing described in the gospel stories are more likely to have taken place than the so-called 'nature' miracles such as the stilling of the storm. In the former case modern psychiatry suggests at least the possibility of some parallel; the latter case, if it genuinely occurred, defies all attempts at explanation.

Many Christians, however, would argue that, since the miraculous events described in the gospel story are unique, the search for parallels is misguided. They might agree that these events were improbable in the sense of being exceptions to otherwise well-established laws; but they would insist, none the less, that these events (or some of them) did in fact take place as described. The only way in which this view can be called in question is by challenging the adequacy of the evidence. In that case, however, each miracle-story must be considered on its merits and in relation to our assessment of the gospel narrative as a whole. There is no justification for saying that science demands unconditional rejection of all of them.

*     *     *

I have attempted in this chapter to remove certain ambiguities in the word 'miracle', and I have indicated the difficulty involved in regarding a miracle as 'an interference with Nature by supernatural power' (C. S. Lewis's phrase). I have examined three alleged 'arguments against miracles'—the argument that miracles must be ruled out by definition, the argument that miracles are incompatible with the model of the enclosed billiard-table, and the argument that science requires us to believe that all events can be brought under natural laws. My conclusion is that these arguments, though interesting, do not give us grounds for asserting that this or that historical event did not happen.

# CHAPTER 19

# Some problems in Christian doctrine

I shall argue in this chapter that much doctrinal language, though meaningless if taken literally, can still be regarded as true and important if understood as the language of parable.

In the first section I shall comment on the distinction which has often been drawn between 'natural' and 'revealed' truth. In the second I shall try to indicate what is involved in acceptance or rejection of the doctrine of the incarnation. In the third I shall do the same in connection with the doctrines of original sin, grace, and resurrection. I shall suggest that the question at issue throughout is that of choosing the appropriate parable.

It is, of course, nothing new to say that doctrinal language is the language of parable; but the change of outlook induced by recent philosophy makes it all the more urgent that the parable-like character of such language should be emphasized.

## I. NATURAL AND REVEALED TRUTH

According to St Thomas the doctrine of the Trinity and the doctrine that the world had a beginning in time can be known only by revelation.[1] The contrast which we meet here and elsewhere appears to be between so-called 'natural' truths—truths which can be known by the unaided human reason—and 'revealed' truths—truths which can be known only as the result of an act of revelation on the part of God.

Now it is very easy, it seems to me, in discussing the notion of 'revelation', to relapse into the language of qualified literal theism. There is, of course, a perfectly legitimate use of the word 'revelation' in ordinary speech. We say of a particular discovery that it was an

[1] *Summa Theologica I*, Q. 32, Art. 1, and Q. 46, Art. 2.

'absolute revelation'. Thus it may be an absolute revelation to hear how beautiful a certain piece of music may sound when played by a particular artist; it may be an absolute revelation to learn how altogether unselfish a particular friend can be at a time of crisis. Indeed any piece of profound insight can be referred to as a 'revelation'. But this is not the sort of revelation which seems to be suggested by much theological language. Theological language frequently suggests that particular truths are the result of revelation in the sense of being undiscoverable by natural reason and discoverable only as the result of some intervention on the part of God.

Once again we need to ask, By what criteria do we tell if such intervention took place? That a Christian thinker should suddenly have a flash of insight or should suddenly find himself able to formulate a new and illuminating parable is perfectly intelligible. Moreover, if we accept the theistic parable we can regard any and every piece of insight as given by God. But we cannot say that one piece of insight was due to divine intervention and another was not, unless we are prepared to state the criteria for recognizing divine intervention. As we have argued already, if the words 'divine intervention' are taken literally, no criteria can possibly be given. There is danger, therefore, when we contrast 'natural' with 'revealed' truth, of our saying, in effect, 'There is a difference between A and B but there are no criteria for judging how they are different.'

To make matters more difficult, the truths which are commonly supposed to be 'revealed', e.g. the doctrine of the Trinity and the doctrine that the world had a beginning in time, are precisely those which on strict logical positivist principles would appear to be meaningless! As we shall see later in the chapter, the doctrine of the Trinity cannot simply be dismissed in the way a militant logical positivist would wish to dismiss it. But we certainly cannot claim that this doctrine requires to be accepted, obscurities and all, simply *because* it is revealed truth. If the notion of 'revelation' itself gives rise to difficulties, it is no use appealing to revelation to overcome difficulties in other doctrines; and even if acts of faith are sometimes meritorious, there is no special merit in professing to subscribe to a verbal formula whose meaning we do not understand.

If we speak of 'revelation' at all, our words must be understood as the language of parable. Those who accept the theistic parable are likely also to accept the further parable that God has revealed himself during the course of history. This does not mean that the Hebrew prophets and other religious thinkers were literally 'inspired'—that is, breathed upon—by some para-physical agency. A pseudo-causal theory of inspiration—a theory which invites the use of scientific measuring devices in an attempt to detect the cause of the inspiration—is unintelligible, since one could not even indicate what one was looking for. To say of the Hebrew prophets and others whose writings form our Bible that they were 'inspired' or that they were the recipients of God's revelation is to commend their insight. A revealed truth is a *special* truth—one which, in parable language, forms a special part of God's revelation. Thus official Christianity recognizes the doctrine of the Trinity as a revealed truth, but not the theory of evolution or the doctrine of the divine right of kings.

I am not here taking sides on the question of what truths, if any, should count as 'revealed' and thus be given a privileged status. I am concerned only to point out the difficulties in the notion of 'revealed truth' if these words are understood literally, and to suggest a possible meaning which could be attached to them if they are understood as the language of parable.

## 2. THE INCARNATION

In examining the incarnation from the special viewpoint of this book our first need is to draw a distinction between historical language and doctrinal language. An example of the former would be, 'Jesus was the son of Mary', an example of the latter, 'Jesus was the son of God'. The truth or falsity of historical assertions is determined empirically. There may be difficulties in practice in deciding whether a particular historical assertion is true or false, but there is no difficulty whatever in deciding what that assertion means. Sentences of the form 'X was the son of Y' present, for our purposes, no special problem. In the case of 'X was the son of God', however, the matter is very different. As with other religious assertions, many of us have been all too ready to align ourselves on one side or the other without adequate reflection on what it is that the disagreement is about.

Confronted with the assertion 'X was the son of God' (whoever X may be), we can justifiably raise the question, What evidence would settle the matter? If the truth or falsity of 'X was the son of God', like the truth or falsity of 'X was the son of Mary', is an empirical matter, there must be some empirical tests for discovering the answer; yet if we ask ourselves what empirical tests, it seems quite impossible to say. It is clear, on reflection, that no psychological or medical examination of a person would reveal whether or not that person was the son of God.

It might be objected that criteria for determining whether a person is the son of God can be found in the way in which he lives, and that all his actions and behaviour supply relevant evidence. This, however, would be evidence only in the sense that missing spoons and footprints in the flower-beds are evidence that there has been a burglar. We cannot suppose that the 'cash-value' of 'X was the son of God' is merely that X performed the actions in question or adopted that particular way of life; and it seems very unconvincing to try to 'unpack' 'X was the son of God' into a group of empirical assertions about X's behaviour. At any rate, if we make the identification we are using the words 'was the son of God' in an extremely peculiar way.

There is danger, too, that we may unwittingly adopt what, by analogy with other mistakes which I have tried to expose in this book, may be called a 'para-physical' theory of the incarnation.[1] According to this view the incarnation involved not only certain historical events—events of a 'physical' kind—but also some recondite 'non-physical' or 'para-physical' events. Our outlook can very easily be influenced by 'ghost-in-machine' ways of thinking.[2] To put the matter very crudely, one is tempted to suppose that, if the doctrine of the incarnation is true, the same ghost which occupied God the father came also to occupy Jesus. On this view the point to be decided is whether this 'occupation' did in fact take place, whether the ghost did in fact come (in 6 B.C. or whenever the date was) and take possession of Jesus' body; and though the events, being 'para-physical', would be undetectable by scientific instruments, it is assumed that the question at issue is a genuinely factual one, exactly comparable, in that respect, to 'Jesus was the son of Mary'.

It would, of course, have been perfectly possible, on this view, that the ghost should have entered Socrates, the Buddha, or Mohammed. That it did not do so is taken to be a straightforward matter of historical fact.

---

[1] I am not accusing any competent theologian of having made the mistakes which I am about to criticize; but I am deliberately using provocative language as an attempt to challenge what I believe to be muddled thinking on the subject of the incarnation. How far a 'para-physical' theory is a temptation to others I cannot be sure, but I know that I myself have been misled by it.

[2] For an explanation of the phrase 'ghost-in-the-machine', see p. 80.

To dispose of the para-physical theory of the incarnation, we need only ask what are the criteria for recognizing if para-physical events have taken place. Since clearly no criteria can be given, to talk of such events is simply to mislead ourselves with words.

'Jesus was the son of God' requires to be understood as the language of parable. Just as the word 'father' is not strictly applicable to God, so the word 'son' is not strictly applicable to Jesus. But if the parable of the husbandmen is taken as an important key for understanding the course of history, it is legitimate to think of Jesus not only as having taught this parable but as having actually fulfilled it in his own life. There need be no factual disagreement between those who accept the parable of the incarnation and those who do not; but those who accept it are claiming, among other things, that the agreed historical facts require to be understood in a special way.

In accordance with the general policy of this book, I am not taking sides on the question of whether acceptance is appropriate; I am simply trying to make explicit what it is that one is being invited to accept.

Many different parables have, of course, been put forward as an attempt to interpret the significance of the life of Jesus. What parables were suggested can be learned by studying the doctrinal controversies of the early Church. Thus, according to the formulae adopted in the Nicene creed, Jesus was said to be 'begotten not made, being of one substance with the father', and it was said that the Holy Ghost 'proceedeth from the father and the son'. It is wrong, I suggest, to claim, as an extreme logical positivist might wish to claim, that these doctrines are all meaningless. What is required, for their understanding, is a detailed consideration of what words such as 'person' and 'substance'[1] conveyed to early Christian thinkers, and an examination of what are

---

[1] A very puzzling doctrine involving the notion of 'substance' is that of transubstantiation. The claim that the bread and wine at the communion service become the body and blood of Christ certainly appears at first glance to be factually significant. Yet if we look for criteria for telling if this change has taken place, there do not seem to be any. Indeed we are particularly told that the chemical properties of the bread and wine do not change, and it follows therefore that no application of chemical tests would be relevant. That being so, however, it is very hard to see what claim is being made, at any rate if the doctrine is understood literally. One is tempted to recommend that the doctrine of transubstantiation should be understood as the language of parable. In that case, what is required is a detailed historical investigation which would make explicit the purpose of the parable and the reasons for using the Aristotelian notions of 'substance' and 'accident' in its formulation. Whether the parable should be regarded as *important* is, of course, another matter.

the consequences, both for religious practice and for life in general, of preferring one formula to another.

As far as the twentieth-century thinker is concerned there are a number of different possible choices. For purposes of discussion I have classified these choices under five headings, which may be labelled (*a*) fundamentalist trinitarianism, (*b*) non-fundamentalist trinitarianism, (*c*) unitarianism, (*d*) a-historical mysticism, and (*e*) rejection. No special finality is claimed for this classification; but it serves to make explicit a number of issues which a twentieth-century thinker can justifiably regard as 'live' ones. It has been drawn up in such a way that everyone must find himself committed to one of the views in question.

(*a*) A fundamentalist trinitarian is one who accepts the whole of the Bible as revealed truth. The label 'fundamentalist' has somewhat 'blurred edges'; but the main feature of this approach is its total acceptance of all that is written in the Bible. Since the doctrine of the Trinity has biblical authority,[1] a fundamentalist view must necessarily be trinitarian, and in general it comes fairly close to the main body of Christian orthodoxy.

(*b*) A non-fundamentalist trinitarianism involves acceptance in principle of the parable of the Trinity, or at any rate the willingness to take seriously the attempts of the early Church to find an adequate formula. Thus Jesus Christ is accepted as one to be worshipped, and recitation of the creeds is usually regarded as an important feature in religious practice.

(*c*) The unitarian view attaches less importance to the parable of the incarnation and other such formulae. Jesus is accepted as lord and master, but not necessarily as an object of worship; and, though his teaching in general demands allegiance, he is not to be thought of as necessarily infallible.

(*d*) By a-historical mysticism I mean a view which is prepared to accept a Christ-figure as an object of worship, who finds his inspiration in the parable of the word becoming flesh, but is not necessarily prepared to attach any special significance to the historical Jesus. As an expression of this view I cannot do better than cite the words of the Hindu philosopher, Sri Aurobindo.[2] 'Such controversies' he writes 'as

[1] Matthew xxviii. 19.
[2] Quoted by Victor Gollancz, in *From Darkness to Light* (Gollancz, 1950), pp. 20–1.

the one which has raged in Europe over the historicity of Christ would seem to a spiritually-minded Indian largely a waste of time. . . . What does it matter in the end whether a Jesus, son of the carpenter Joseph, was actually born in Nazareth or Bethlehem, lived and taught and was done to death on a real or trumped-up charge of sedition, so long as we can know by spiritual experience the inner Christ, live uplifted in the light of His teaching and escape from the yoke of the natural law by that atonement of man with God of which the crucifixion is the symbol.' This view should not, I think, be regarded simply as the passing comment of an outsider belonging to another continent. Even in the western world, a number of thinkers have at least had some tendency towards a-historical mysticism. Schweitzer, for instance, seems to come very near it when he writes, 'It is not Jesus as historically known, but Jesus as spiritually arisen within men, who is significant for our time and can help it.'[1] I would even suggest that the writer of the fourth gospel (though his intentions clearly cannot be deduced with any certainty) was more concerned with the Jesus of mysticism than with the Jesus of history. My personal impression from reading this gospel is that very often the narrative is no more than a peg, so to speak, on which the writer hangs his own personal convictions. The characters in the fourth gospel are not really the historical Jesus and his con-temporaries; they are the Jesus of mysticism and ourselves. The words which are attributed to them—for instance 'He that believeth in me, though he were dead yet shall he live',[2] 'Whereas I was blind, now I see',[3] 'Now we believe, not because of thy saying: for we have heard him ourselves'[4]—seem like a record of what the Christian set of parables mean or could mean in the life of Christians rather than a literal account of actual historical events.

By 'a-historical mysticism', then, I mean any extremist view along these lines. (How far the writer of the fourth gospel was an extremist in this sense is necessarily a matter of speculation.) Those who adopt this view can quite legitimately make use of traditional Christian formulae, such as 'The unsearchable riches of Christ',[5] or

> *Jesu, the very thought of thee*
> *With sweetness fills the breast,*[6]

but in using them they are not necessarily committing themselves to

[1] *The Quest of the Historical Jesus* (London, 1952), p. 399.
[2] John xi. 25.      [3] John ix. 25.      [4] John iv. 42.
[5] Ephesians iii. 8.      [6] *Songs of Praise*, no. 547.

belief in a historical Jesus. Whether there actually was such a person as the carpenter of Nazareth is left an open question, or at any rate the answer to it is regarded as unimportant.

(*e*) Finally there is the possibility of complete or near-complete rejection of the Christian message. On this view there is no reason why Jesus should not be regarded as a wise teacher whose maxims can in general be followed. But no particular authority is ascribed to him and no special importance is attached to the parable of the loving father who sent his son to die on the cross.

Some further comments will be made in Chapter 20 on the problem of decision. For the moment I am concerned only to give some account of what the issues are. The problem seems to me to be essentially one of choosing the right parable. Acceptance of the parables of the incarnation and the Trinity does not involve belief in some para-physical events or states of affairs not detectable by ordinary empirical means. It involves something more like a moral decision—a decision that Jesus Christ is to be treated as an object of worship. The problem is thus not one of trying to discover correct factual information; the question for decision is whether or not to make an act of personal commitment.

### 3. ORIGINAL SIN, GRACE, RESURRECTION

According to the doctrine of *original sin*, 'all men are equally sinners in the sight of God'.[1] This assertion should not be regarded as a generalization about human nature capable of being verified or falsified by psychological tests. A psychologist might well make a generalization such as 'All men have aggressive impulses'. In saying this he is not saying anything very precise, since there are no detailed criteria for recognising an aggressive impulse; but we know in a general way what is meant, and there is no doubt how such an assertion could be falsified. 'All men are equally sinners in the sight of God', on the other hand, is not falsifiable at all. It is rather a parable about man's present state and forms part of a wider system of parables. Admittedly factual considerations have given rise to the parable. It is a fact that people act in particular ways—ways which on moral grounds are thought to be wrong. If it were not the case that men 'loved darkness rather than light',[2] the parable would have no importance. But it is quite possible

[1] This formulation of the doctrine is taken from R. Niebuhr, *The Nature and Destiny of Man* (Nisbet, 1941), p. 233.
[2] John iii. 19.

to agree that men act in certain anti-social ways, and to decide on moral grounds that such actions are wrong, without being committed to the view that all men are equally sinners in the sight of God. The parable of original sin is part of the general Christian nexus of parables; and although if the facts had been different, if men had not acted aggressively and so on, this parable would not have arisen, it does not follow that it is equivalent to a series of literal factual assertions.

An even greater difficulty over literalness arises in connection with the doctrine of *grace*. When people pray, for instance, that God will 'send down . . . the healthful spirit of (his) grace',[1] such language readily suggests a sort of para-physical activity by a powerful para-physical agency. One is thus tempted to think of the doctrine of grace as a piece of rather recondite bio-physics, as though the word 'grace' stood for a sort of para-physical energy whose operation constituted the explanation of changes in a converted person's behaviour.

No one, of course, disputes that as a result of conversion to the Christian parables people's behaviour may change in all sorts of ways. What I am protesting against is the use of the word 'grace' as the name of an entity not recognizable by any independent tests, but brought in as a piece of pseudo-science to explain such changes.

To speak of 'grace' is to speak the language of parable. An important member of the group of Christian parables is the parable of God as a judge. Some may say that this parable has been overworked, and that its distasteful aspects—where the judge is thought of as perhaps narrow-minded or vindictive—have been given too much prominence. But the important point, I think, in this parable is the sort of defence which we, as prisoners, can hope to put up. An accused person may in many cases wish to call attention to his good character and stress that he does not deserve the rigours of the law. In this trial, however, such defence has no place. We do not ask the judge to 'weigh our merits'.[2] Whatever we achieve will certainly fall short of the perfection required of us, and it is a question of being dependent on the mercy of the judge. If he takes his stand on the letter of the law there can be no acquittal. According to the parable, however, we are not under 'law' but under 'grace'.[3] Acquittal is possible, but this acquittal stems from the mercy of the judge, not from anything that we ourselves have achieved.

The doctrine of grace thus plays an important part in the Christian

[1] Morning Prayer, Prayer for the Clergy and People.
[2] Holy Communion, Prayer of Oblation.
[3] Ephesians ii. 8. Compare Romans v. 12–15.

parables, and its validity can be discussed within the context of such parables. On the other hand the findings of the scientific investigator— the physiologist or psychologist, for instance—do not need the word 'grace' as an explanatory concept. To condemn them for leaving it out would be like condemning a producer of *Macbeth* for leaving out Polonius. Indeed they would be even more at fault if they brought it in. Producers of *Hamlet* can discuss how much of Polonius's part should be cut, and, even if they disagree, they will at least be, so to speak, on the same 'wave-length' as each other; but if, whenever a producer of *Hamlet* argued with a producer of *Macbeth*, they failed to realize to which play a particular character belonged, their argument would be an extremely curious one. Once we see to what 'play', so to speak, the word 'grace' belongs, we have a much better chance of avoiding confusion.

Finally some comments require to be made on the Christian doctrine of *resurrection*.

It is widely assumed that all assertions on the theme of life after death are factually significant and require to be understood literally. There are difficulties, however, over attaching a meaning to many apparently literal assertions; and even if we agree that the general claim 'People have experiences after death' is literally meaningful, the Christian doctrine of 'resurrection' should be regarded as the language of parable.

Many thinkers have spoken of 'the immortality of the soul'. A central difficulty in this formula is that it suggests 'ghost-in-machine' ways of thinking.[1] The body, we know, disintegrates at death; and it might seem that what is being asked is whether the ghost occupying the body disintegrates also—an apparently straightforward question of fact. Yet if the problem is a factual one at all, it certainly cannot be settled by watching the behaviour of things called 'souls'. We should not know what to look for; it seems quite impossible to say how 'The soul is immortal' could be given 'cash-value'. In the same way theories of transmigration and reincarnation must *prima facie* be regarded as meaningless. When Malvolio says that, according to Pythagoras, 'The soul of our grandam might haply inhabit a bird',[2] we may legitimately ask how these words can be given 'cash-value' and by what criteria we are supposed to decide whether 'the soul of our grandam' was present.

There is a similar difficulty over the words 'I shall survive death'. This difficulty can be indicated by drawing a contrast between 'I shall

---

[1] Compare pp. 80 and 89.　　　　[2] *Twelfth Night*, Act iv, scene 2.

survive death' and 'I shall survive this battle'. In the latter case at least part of what is meant is that *my body* will continue to function after the battle. In the former case no claim, apparently, is being made about my body; and the result is to leave very unclear just what it is which is supposed to survive. Moreover, if there is to be genuine survival, it is essential that the person who survives should be the same person as he was before death; yet in normal usage one of the main criteria of whether X and Y are the same person is bodily continuity. A case of mistaken identity is a case where it is thought there was bodily continuity when in fact there was not. In the absence of bodily continuity, it is not clear in what sense the person who survives can be 'the same person' as he was before death.

According to the same principle one may legitimately be uneasy when it is claimed e.g. that the Virgin Mary appeared to certain people at a particular time and place. In the absence of bodily continuity, it is not clear what possible criteria there could be for saying that the apparition 'really was' the Virgin Mary.

This general difficulty, however, does not seem to me insuperable. We have indicated already[1] that ghost-in-machine language, however misleading at times, cannot simply be dismissed on all occasions as a foolish blunder. In particular our awareness of the space occupied by our own bodies gives the impression of something 'ghostly' inside us; and it is perfectly meaningful, whether or not it is true, to claim that such awareness lasts even after death. Moreover bodily continuity is not the sole criterion of whether the words 'same person' are appropriate. A further criterion is that of continuity of memory. We should not hesitate to say of someone that he was the same person as the Mr X whom we knew before his death if there was continuity of experience and memory between that person and Mr X. If in fact people have experiences after death, it is perfectly possible that such continuity should occur.

There is, of course, the problem of giving 'cash-value' to all assertions, of whatever kind, which relate to other people's experiences;[2] but this is not a problem connected specifically with survival or immortality. It seems to me that there is a good case for regarding 'People have experiences after death' as a literal, factually significant assertion, capable in principle of being verified or falsified by experience. The only difficulty, in that case, is that, until we die, there is no means of

[1] pp. 82 and 86.    [2] Compare pp. 113–14.

discovering the true answer.[1] Speculation, of course, is possible. It might be argued, for instance, that according to neurology awareness of the space occupied by our bodies (and of spatial relationships in general) is possible only when the brain is functioning normally, and that after death, when the brain disintegrates, no such awareness will be possible.[2]

Whatever the value of this sort of speculation, I do not think the answer has any relevance to the beliefs of orthodox Christianity. The official Christian doctrine is that of resurrection. The words of Professor J. V. Langmead Casserley seems to me particularly relevant here. Professor Casserley disputes whether 'a part of man, called his "mind", has within it some inherent property which gives it the power to survive the dissolution of the body'. 'The problem for the Christian' he says 'is whether God can and will revive mortal man, and lift him above time and make him a partaker of eternal life.'[3] It may be said, of course, that resurrection will mean nothing to us unless we survive and have experiences of being made one with God. But it does not seem to me necessary that there should occur experiences in any literal sense of the word. The words 'occur' and 'experiences' are appropriate on earth; we have no reason for supposing that they are appropriate in heaven! If we are asked what will happen after death, our only answer can be silence; either the question is unintelligible or we have no idea of the answer.

This silence is then qualified by the parable of resurrection. We know exactly what it is like for a body to rise out of the grave and to become assimilated to another body. The parable is of God enabling man to rise from the grave and become one with the risen Christ. To use these terms from human experience (which are agreed to be inadequate and misleading) is the only alternative to complete silence.

Besides accepting the parable of the resurrection, many Christians also claim to believe, as a literal historical truth, that Jesus did in fact

---

[1] If people have no experiences after death, it will never, of course, be possible for us to know this. But I do not think this point raises any major philosophical problem.

[2] This argument has been used by J. O. Wisdom in 'The Concept of Phantom-Body' (*Actes du XIème congrès international de philosophie*, Volume VII for 1953). It is said that Nelson regarded his awareness of a phantom-arm (where his actual arm was missing) as evidence for the immortality of the soul! It is interesting that Dr Wisdom argues in precisely the opposite way. There seems to me no doubt that awareness of a 'phantom-body' has influenced people's thinking on the subject of immortality.

[3] *The Retreat from Christianity in the Modern World* (Longmans, 1952), p. 24.

rise from the dead. His body, on this view, did not 'see corruption' in the tomb in the way that other bodies do.

Now we have seen from Chapter 18 that there is no justification for blandly asserting that this event could not have happened. If someone then asks whether it is sensible to believe that it actually did happen, the matter is one for individual decision. All sorts of considerations are relevant, not only the historical evidence, but also one's general attitude to the Christian parables as a whole. All that need be said here is that it is not just manifestly unreasonable or stupid to believe that such an event occurred; and if it did occur, then clearly it has an importance unique in the history of the world. 'Christ being raised from the dead dieth no more; death hath no more dominion over him'[1] is of course the language of parable. To many, however, it is not only the language of parable; it is a parable which received literal fulfilment in a historical event.

The purpose of this chapter has been to offer a further working out of the difference between parable and literal truth. There are many parts of Christian doctrine which, if understood literally, would have to be abandoned as meaningless. Once we realize that they are the language of parable, the charge that they are meaningless no longer holds, and the way is clear for a decision as to how their challenge is to be answered.

[1] Romans vi. 9.

# CHAPTER 20

## *Some historical problems*

Some readers may be disappointed that this book should come to an end at the very place where the important decisions begin. As has been made clear, however, it has not been my task to convert the reader to any particular set of parables, but rather to make explicit what he is required to decide about and what arguments are relevant to his decision.

It has, I hope, been made plain that parable-assertions from their very nature do not admit of being vindicated or discredited like scientific generalizations or mathematical reasoning. If anyone claims that he has a demonstrative proof that Christianity (or any other religion) is discredited, we can be sure without examining his argument that the claim cannot be made good. This is not to say that no arguments can be given at all as to why one set of parables should be preferred to another; still less is it to say that, in the absence of demonstrative proof, one set of parables is as good as another. I am saying only that those who hope that the 'wise man' or philosopher can supply a set of infallible answers are doomed to disappointment.

In so far as there can be argument about choice of parables, what is required is to set the parables of the different religions side by side for comparison. It is then possible to stress particular features of one system of parables which might be thought to render it superior to other systems. If someone does not acknowledge this superiority, what is called for is not further argument but conversion and a change of heart.

No such detailed comparison will be attempted in this book. If some-one says, Why should I not be a Buddhist, a Mohammedan, a communist, or a humanist, rather than a Christian?, the only answer is,

## Some historical problems

Examine what parables are involved and decide for yourself.[1] Nor do I propose to take up in detail long-standing points of controversy such as whether the existence of evil makes the theistic parable impossible, or whether the theories of Copernicus and Darwin are a genuine threat to Christianity. I do not myself regard arguments of this sort as sufficient to discredit the Christian parables,[2] but this is not to say that those who think differently are necessarily guilty of any absurdity or fallacious reasoning.

The problem which I want to raise in this chapter concerns the relevance of the *historical* evidence to the acceptance of Christianity. Even if it is agreed that Christianity is not necessarily in conflict with the outlook of the physical and biological sciences, there is still the possibility of conflict over matters of history.

Five possible answers were suggested in the last chapter to the challenge presented to us by the coming of Jesus. These answers were (a) fundamentalist trinitarianism, (b) non-fundamentalist trinitarianism, (c) unitarianism, (d) a-historical mysticism, and (e) rejection. Since views (a) and (b) involve historical claims, anyone professing to hold either is forced to take the historical evidence into account.

I shall suggest in this chapter that the historical evidence makes (a) impossible, and that there are certain difficulties in (b) which at least require to be taken seriously. My general conclusion, however, is that the historical evidence does not enable us to rule out (b), (c), (d), or (e) unconditionally.

There are all sorts of different methods open to the historian. He may study documents and inscriptions; he may use the findings of geology and archaeology; recent knowledge on the subject of radio-activity may

[1] Communism, in its modern form, is at least something *very like* a religious system. It has its own set of parables, involving a particular way of viewing the course of history, and a fairly clearly defined political programme. For further discussion, see *Christian Faith and Communist Faith* (edited by D. M. Mackinnon, Macmillan, 1953). The humanist does not explicitly profess belief in any set of parables, but, as we saw on pp. 178–9, the very act of living involves implicit acceptance of one set of parables or another.

[2] In the case of the findings of Copernicus and Darwin, one of the main lines of argument is to call attention to the appalling wastefulness of nature; it is suggested that if the arrival of man—and the coming of Jesus Christ in particular—marks the climax of God's purpose, this end could have been achieved without a long and painful process of evolution and without the creation of countless uninhabited stars countless millions of miles apart. But I do not think we are justified in judging this matter by ordinary human standards of what is wasteful.

With regard to the presence of evil in the world, I have already indicated (p. 178, footnote) why its existence does not seem to me to justify us in regarding the theistic parable as a mere absurdity or blunder.

help him with his dating, and so on. All these methods are alike, however, in that they are empirical; and where empirical evidence is convincing we are being guilty of dishonesty if we ignore it.

Before referring specifically to the parable of the incarnation, let us briefly examine the impact of these historical methods on biblical interpretation in general.

In taking the Bible literally, the fundamentalist is forced to believe that the world was created in six days some few thousand years before the present time,[1] and that the appearance of Adam followed soon afterwards. This is incompatible with the facts of astronomy, geology, and biology, which must be taken as established. Astronomy and geology show that any reckoning in terms of a few thousand years is totally inadequate, and biology has made clear that there was animal life on this planet millions of years before the evolution of man. It can, of course, be argued that in the phrase 'six days' the word 'day' should not be taken literally; but in general attempts to 'square' the Genesis story with modern scientific knowledge cannot be regarded as convincing. In claiming that the opening chapters of the book of Genesis are scientifically accurate the fundamentalist seems to me to be unequivocally wrong.

Further changes in outlook appear necessary as a result of other pieces of historical criticism. There are good grounds for supposing, for instance, that the Psalms were not all written by David, that the fourth gospel was not written by John the apostle, that the epistle to the Hebrews was not written by St Paul, and so on. Perhaps not all claims of this sort can be regarded as conclusively established; and if a person insists on keeping to the more traditional and fundamentalist views, it is hard to prove him wrong. But there is strong weight of evidence against him.

What is at stake in this controversy, however, is not really how far the more modernist or the more traditional views are right. There seems rather to be a major difference of attitude towards biblical criticism, and the question is in effect whether there should be such a thing as biblical criticism at all, or whether the whole idea of treating the Bible in that way is somehow wrong. There can be no doubt, to my mind, that those who accept the need for critical inquiry are in the right; and if this is so, both conservative and modernist biblical scholars should at least be

[1] Archbishop Usher's date for the creation is 4004 B.C.; but we are presumably not expected to take this exact date too seriously.

willing to share the same methods. If the modernists are wrong, what is required is not to abandon biblical criticism, but to produce abler and better biblical criticism which shows how and where they are wrong.

It should be stressed that even if fundamentalism is shown to be mistaken, it does not follow that the Bible, as a source of religious truth, is discredited. Those who accept the Christian nexus of parables cannot but regard the writings which unfold these parables as being of supreme importance. It is possible to accept the central message of the Bible without regarding every single passage as having to be taken as the final revelation of historical, moral, and religious truth.

Besides these difficulties in (*a*)—the fundamentalist view—there are also possible difficulties in (*b*). A non-fundamentalist need not be troubled if passages in the Old Testament are shown not to be historically accurate, if problems of authorship in both Old and New Testaments are matters of debate, and so on. But he asserts uncompromisingly that the historical Jesus was a real person, and that the gospel narratives have some fairly high degree of historical reliability. Not only is it possible in principle that further historical research might do something towards discrediting these claims; it is also possible that acceptance of the parable of the incarnation should be shown, as a result of existing historical evidence, to involve considerable difficulty and discomfort.

Arguments on this matter are made more complicated by the fact that it is not entirely clear what historical evidence would be needed to render this discomfort too acute to be tolerable. For instance, many who accept the parable of the incarnation may be quite untroubled by the fact that Jesus was fallible in points of detail—that he mistakenly attributed a particular psalm to David,[1] for instance, or believed in the literal truth of the story of Jonah.[2] On the other hand, if it were shown beyond all possible doubt that no such person as Jesus ever existed, or that he had committed some particularly horrible murder, then, whatever value the parable of the incarnation might have as an eternal truth, belief in historical Christianity would clearly be impossible. Orthodox Christians would, of course, take their stand on the belief that no such conclusive evidence will in fact ever be forthcoming. What is not altogether clear is how much evidence of fallibility on the part of the historical Jesus is necessary to discredit the parable of the incarnation, and how much reliability the gospels must be believed to have before the claims of this parable can legitimately be given a hearing. No precise

[1] Mark xii. 36.    [2] Matthew xii. 40.

ruling can be given in answer to such demands; it can only be said that we know in a general way what sort of historical findings would serve to make the parable of the incarnation progressively more convincing or progressively less so.

The difficulties confronting orthodoxy as a result of historical evidence seem to me to be twofold. First, there are difficulties connected with the miracle-stories; secondly, there are difficulties over certain sayings which the gospels attribute to Jesus. For purposes of argument let us limit ourselves to consideration of the synoptic gospels, since the fourth gospel is agreed to raise special problems.

In a sense the crucial issue—as it has been for many years—is still that of miracles. Nothing that has been said in this book can serve to remove the difficulty. We may agree, certainly, that no one has any right to assert that particular events did not happen. This, however, does not alter the fact that many of the events recorded in the gospels sound desperately unplausible. The virgin-birth, the story of the wise men and the star, the stilling of the storm, the walking on the water, the feeding of the multitude—these and many other events perhaps *could* have happened, but it strains our credulity to the utmost to believe that they *did* happen. There are other stories—the sending of devils into swine, for instance, and the withering of the fig-tree—which are not only unplausible but pointless and perhaps even morally degrading. It is not unreasonable to say that people have a duty to accept a particular parable, to view the world in a particular way and act accordingly; but it is very hard to suppose that people have a duty to accept a particular piece of historical evidence as authentic, particularly when such acceptance goes against their better judgment.

Of course we can always say that this or that story is legendary or the result of misunderstanding. Perhaps Jesus was really born at Nazareth; perhaps he really walked *by* the sea, not *on* it; perhaps the feeding of the multitude and the withering of the fig-tree were pieces of teaching, not accounts of things that he actually did. But the more we are reduced to this sort of device, the more disreputable the whole procedure becomes. The right to regard an occasional passage as a corruption or misunderstanding is one thing; the right to expurgate passages en bloc whenever it suits us is another. If we reject the miracles of healing along with the other miracles, then the 'real' Jesus behind the stories certainly becomes an extremely elusive figure. What is more, such cavalier procedure forces us to ignore completely the author's intentions. In the gospel of Mark, for instance, it seems clear that the miracles are intended to be a central part of the story; and if we discount the author's intentions we are *ipso facto* treating him as an unreliable authority. It seems that we are forced either to believe in stories which sound extremely unplausible or else to admit that the historical Jesus is someone about whom very little is known.

When we consider some of the sayings attributed to him, the difficulties increase. He used what certainly appears to be the language of qualified literal theism; he seems to have believed in petitionary prayer,[1] in a literal hell,[2] and in possession by devils.[3] His mission, he says, was only 'unto the lost sheep of the house of Israel';[4] he may have thought that God had forsaken him on the cross;[5] and, if Schweitzer is right, remarks such as 'Ye shall not have gone over the cities of Israel till the Son of Man be come'[6] and 'This generation shall not pass till all these things be done'[7] were intended absolutely literally.[8]

Once again, as with the miracles, we can start 'explaining away' awkward passages. The belief that a particular sort of devil 'can come forth by nothing but by prayer and fasting'[9] may be a 'later addition'; the cry 'My God, my God, why hast thou forsaken me?'[10] may not have been a cry of disillusionment, and so on. But if the parable of the incarnation can be retained only at the cost of manœuvres of this sort, then the more such manœuvres are necessary, the less convincing the parable becomes.

As a result of these historical considerations it seems to me that we must rule out completely any 'fundamentalist' view about Jesus himself. We cannot regard him as infallible on every point of detail, and some may wish to say that, as historical narratives, the gospels are far from

[1] Matthew vii. 11.    [2] Matthew viii. 12.    [3] Mark ix. 29.
[4] Matthew xv. 24.    [5] Mark xv. 34.    [6] Matthew x. 23.
[7] Mark xiii. 30.
[8] See Albert Schweitzer, *The Quest for the Historical Jesus* (Black, 1952). Also, for a brief account, *My Life and Thought* (Allen & Unwin, 1933), pp. 51–4. Similar problems arise as a result of the critical work of R. Bultmann (see especially his *New Testament and Mythology*, chapter I of *Kerugma and Myth*, edited by H. W. Bartsch, S.P.C.K., 1953). Bultmann insists (p. 9), that 'we cannot save the Kerugma by selecting some of its features and subtracting others'. He also makes a plea (p. 9) for 'absolute clarity and ruthless honesty'. Those who take the arguments of Schweitzer and Bultmann seriously are likely to turn more readily to an a-historical view of Jesus (view (*d*) in our terminology) rather than to the orthodox historical one, view (*b*). Moreover unitarianism (view (*c*)) becomes somewhat uncomfortable, since if Jesus was as much deceived as Schweitzer and Bultmann in effect make out, the case for regarding him as a great teacher is correspondingly weakened. How far Schweitzer and Bultmann would themselves wish to depart from view (*b*) is a matter of some obscurity.      [9] Mark ix. 29.      [10] Mark xv. 34.

trustworthy. In the case of non-fundamentalist views—in particular view (*b*), which involves certain definite historical claims—no such assurance seems to me possible. Many would say that, even if some of the miracles reported in the gospels are false, there still emerges a clearly recognizable personality. If in fact he had unusual powers of healing, then so much the more credible does the gospel story become. Nor is it surprising, they would add, that Jesus should use the thought-forms of his time and speak of God, prayer, and hell in the same way as his contemporaries. The limitations of the historical Jesus do not, on this view, preclude us from worshipping him, nor do they make it impossible for us to regard his coming as the fulfilment of the parable of the incarnation.

My conclusion is that there is no incontrovertible argument which enables us to rule out (*b*), (*c*), (*d*), or (*e*). There is a possible case for saying that the historical evidence makes (*b*) uncomfortable, but it is a case which does not seem to me to be overwhelming.

# CHAPTER 21

## *Summary and conclusions*

We are at the end of our task. It remains to gather threads and offer certain suggestions by way of conclusion.

We made it our starting-point to ask three questions—questions which we assumed might be asked by an inquiring layman in connection with the claims of religion at the present day. These questions were (1) Has science disproved the existence of God? (2) Is there a conflict between science and religion? (3) Is it reasonable for a person living in the twentieth century to accept some form of Christian orthodoxy?

At the risk of over-simplification I shall start by offering straight answers to these three questions. Explanations and qualifications will be added in a moment. My conclusions are (1) No important assertion containing the word 'God' is discredited as a result of the progress of science. (2) There is no need for any permanent conflict between science and religion. (3) Some versions of Christianity, e.g. so-called 'fundamentalist' views, which ascribe literal truth to the story of Adam and Eve, and total infallibility to the historical Jesus, must be ruled out; but other versions of Christianity can be defended.

(1) It has widely been assumed that the great enemies of Christian theism are the allegedly 'scientific' systems of materialism, behaviourism, and determinism. According to this formulation of the problem, everyone agrees that there is such a thing as *matter*. What is required is to find out if there is also a God, whether men have souls as well as their material bodies, and whether they have free-will, as a result of which they are independent of the ordinary laws of physical motion.

All that can ever happen, however, on this formulation of the problem is a bandying about of assertion and counter-assertion, with no solution and no conceivable way of achieving one. 'We do not need to assume a God', 'You have no right to say there is *no* God'—these are the sort of battle-cries that arise. Both parties claim the victory, and yet the other side obstinately refuses to lie down. The important move is a realization that *there is something wrong with the way in which the problem has been formulated*.

This realization is not simply a product of the twentieth century. Among philosophers, Berkeley and Kant in particular have been out to destroy this kind of formulation; and many theologians of the past have appreciated that 'God and the world' is not a straightforward conjunction like 'chairs and tables'. It cannot therefore be claimed that the logical positivism of the twentieth century has supplied an approach to religious problems that is altogether new. What can be claimed—and what I wish to claim in this book—is that the serious challenge to our thinking on the subject of religion comes not from materialism, behaviourism, or determinism, but from the general line of approach and the general techniques which are the outcome of logical positivism. This is the challenge which I have tried to take up.

In Part II I have used these techniques to examine what the claims of materialism, behaviourism, and determinism really amount to. My suggested answers were that materialism, if understood as the literal belief that 'nothing exists except matter' is a meaningless theory; if understood as the commendation of a particular scientific model, the model of the enclosed billiard-table, it is a legitimate theory within its own limits. It cannot, however, be regarded as an account of 'what really exists', since the final outcome of the logical positivist attack on metaphysics was taken to be the realization that questions about 'what really exists' in such a context are meaningless. It follows, therefore, that materialism has no special claim on our allegiance.

There is, of course, a further sense of the word 'materialism' in which it means the placing of a high value on material goods—food, clothes, housing etc.; but a decision on that question is a moral decision, and has no reference to the findings of science.

Behaviourism can similarly be regarded as a meaningless theory if it is regarded as the assertion that *souls have no real existence*. If it is simply regarded, however, as a ruling that the word 'soul' serves no useful purpose for the experimental psychologist or physiologist, it is a convenient methodological rule.

Determinism is more hydra-like than the other two. Its different 'heads' involve a variety of different problems. Here, too, however, there is a case for saying that 'No actions are freely chosen' is either meaningless, or else an indication that the words 'freely chosen' serve no purpose in some contexts. At most, scientific findings might make us less ready than we otherwise should be to hold people morally responsible; but this is in no way a fundamental attack on any central religious belief.

If materialism, behaviourism, and determinism are not the enemies which some have supposed, then it is quite unnecessary to invoke findings in the field of psychical research in the attempt to prove them wrong. Psychical research may or may not be a fruitful field for experimentalists; but even if it does turn out to be fruitful, it has no special importance as a prop for religion; it would simply become a branch of ordinary psychology.

Psycho-analysis provides all sorts of information that could be relevant and interesting for students of religion; but it cannot be said that there is anything in psycho-analysis which makes the basic religious claims impossible to accept.

In Part III I have tried to come to grips with the question of what exactly is the purpose and function of assertions containing the word 'God'. This is a question which requires to be settled before we can hope to have any profitable discussion of their truth or falsity.

It was suggested that sentences containing the word 'God' could be classified as the language of *simple literal theism*, the language of *qualified literal theism*, and the language of *parable*. Assertions in the language of simple literal theism are agreed to be false; assertions in the language of qualified literal theism must be regarded as meaningless. The reason for saying this is that they purport to give factual information and yet do not admit of being given 'cash-value' in the requisite manner. If 'God' is regarded as standing for what is altogether incomprehensible, then literal assertions necessarily make no sense, and we must either say that we know nothing whatever about God, or else refuse to say anything at all. In either case the only possibility open to us is to speak the language of parable. 'God is love',[1] 'God is light',[2] 'In the beginning God created the heaven and the earth'[3] are all examples of the language of parable. The events *in the parable*, e.g. the activity of a person creating something, allow of straightforward 'cash-value', but the 'objective validity' of such a parable is either a meaningless phrase or constitutes something totally unknown. In either case religious belief needs to be tempered with a high degree of agnosticism. To accept the theistic parable is to commit ourselves to a particular way of life, and

[1] 1 John i. 5.    [2] 1 John iv. 8.    [3] Genesis i. 1.

choice of parable can legitimately be regarded as a matter of supreme importance.

Once it is realized that such theistic language is the language of parable, difficulties in connection with verification and 'cash-value' can be met. Such language does not purport to give straightforward factual information, and therefore cannot be condemned for failing to do so. On the contrary a positive account can be given of its function in terms of the language of parable. A number of assertions of church doctrine, including, for instance, 'Jesus was the incarnate Son of God', though meaningless if understood literally, have a legitimate function if understood as the language of parable. There are other assertions, particularly those relating to divine intervention, such as 'God intervened at Dunkirk', which cannot but be regarded as literal, and, in the absence of criteria for determining their truth or falsity, must therefore be rejected as meaningless. Failure to appreciate this particular problem has led to some rather futile and unnecessary argument on the subject of petitionary prayer and miracles. These literal assertions, such as 'God intervened at Dunkirk', require to be abandoned; but the loss cannot be regarded as a serious one. As was said at the start of this chapter, no important assertion containing the word 'God' is discredited.

(2) On the general question of a conflict between science and religion, there is a central part of the problem which we can safely claim to have settled once for all. This claim is not the presumptuous one that it sounds, for the matter is one of logical necessity, and it would be muddled thinking to claim anything less. Religious language is of many different kinds; there is the language of parable, the language of moral exhortation, the language of worship, and so on. Only if what is offered in the name of religion is a factual assertion can there be any possibility of head-on conflict. There can be logical contradiction between two factually significant assertions, such as 'Men were descended from monkeys', 'Men were not descended from monkeys' (and in the case of such disputes we must of course side with the scientist, that is, with the person who has taken the trouble to do systematic investigations); but if what is being offered in the name of 'religion' is the language of parable, there can be no question of straight logical contradiction. By the laws of logic 'In the beginning God created the heaven and the earth' can never be in contradiction with *any* assertion that *any* scientist could ever make; and the same holds in the case of all other Christian parables. To insist that such language is parable and not literal truth is

to ascribe a recognizable and legitimate function to a group of basic religious assertions, and the result is to supply a permanent guarantee that these assertions cannot be refuted by the findings of science.

Although there is no possibility of head-on conflict between the language of parable and the language of factual assertion, in the sense of logical contradiction between the two, it remains true that factual discoveries can influence our choice of parable. There is always the possibility, therefore, that those who are impressed by the advances of a particular science may come to regard a particular religious parable as unnecessary or inappropriate, and that those who are concerned with preserving traditional religious parables may regard the growth of a particular science with suspicion. For example those who take the findings of psycho-analysis seriously may be suspicious of parables in which the notions of guilt, sin, and atonement play a major part, on the grounds that a 'healthy' person does not need such parables. Just how much attention ought to be paid to such notions, however, is a problem not of psychology but of moral decision; and it is by no means clear that parables which concern themselves with sin and guilt should *ipso facto* be discarded. There is always at least a possibility of conflict if those who claim to speak for 'religion' and those who claim to speak for 'science' make different decisions. In such cases, unlike cases where the issue is a straightforward factual one, it does not follow that those who claim to speak for 'science' are necessarily right. The scientist's decisions on choice of parable are fallible like anyone else's. He may perhaps argue that his opponents have not taken all relevant facts into consideration; but, in general, such decision is not a matter on which anyone, whether scientist or philosopher, can claim privileged insights superior to those of the rest of mankind. What is required is that those concerned with religion should be on their guard against clinging to a particular parable if recently acquired factual knowledge appears to make that parable irrelevant or inappropriate. They must be willing to frame their parables in a way that is suitable for the age in which they live, just as any speaker on any other subject must address his audience in terms which they understand, rather than rebuke them for their unfamiliarity with alien modes of thought. If scientists, for their part, do not allow major discoveries to 'go to their heads', so to speak—and normally it is enthusiastic but misguided followers who are the offenders in this respect, not the original pioneer worker—there need not necessarily be any differences in choice of parable. There is nothing inherent in the situation which makes a conflict between science and religion inevitable.

(3) The question whether it is reasonable for a person living in the twentieth century to accept some form of Christian orthodoxy can be answered only if criteria are given for determining what exactly constitutes 'orthodoxy'. If 'orthodoxy' involves acceptance of the central Christian parables, which tell us of man's shortcomings, of the infinite love of God, and of the demands made on us if we are to be followers of Christ, then it can safely be said that orthodoxy is not discredited. If a more stringent criterion of 'orthodoxy' is insisted on, much depends on the degree of stringency. A 'fundamentalist' version of Christianity, in which we are required to believe e.g. in the literal truth of the story of Adam and Eve or in the infallibility of the historical Jesus, must be regarded as mistaken; but only a small minority of Christians, I think, would wish to equate 'orthodoxy' with 'fundamentalism'.

Finally, it may be objected that the refusal to make literal assertions about God and the resultant changes in religious practice are a major departure from orthodoxy. I do not myself think that the departure from orthodoxy is as great as it appears at first sight, but the verdict here must rest with the theologians. All that need be said is this: if we allow that in speaking of God we are using the language of parable, then we are no longer in danger of deceiving ourselves with pseudo-empirical assertions which cannot be given appropriate 'cash-value'. Moreover it becomes established, once for all, that the things which we say about God can never be in conflict with the findings of a scientific investigator.

# INDEX TO AUTHORS

# INDEX TO SUBJECTS

**THE END**